A Life in Music

Daniel Barenboim

A Life in Music

DANIEL
BARENBOIM

Arcade Publishing • New York

FIRST ARCADE EDITION 2003

First published in the United Kingdom by Weidenfeld & Nicolson, 1991, and in the United States by Scribner, 1992. This revised and enlarged edition first published in the United Kingdom by Weidenfeld & Nicolson, 2002.

Edited by Michael Lewin
Revised by Phillip Huscher

Library of Congress Cataloging-in-Publication Data

Barenboim, Daniel, 1942–
    A life in music / Daniel Barenboim ; edited by Michael Lewin ; revised by
Phillip Huscher. —1st Arcade ed.
      p. cm.
    "This revised and enlarged edition first published in the United Kingdom by
Weidenfeld & Nicholson, 2002" —T.p. verso.
    Includes index.
    ISBN 1-55970-674-0
    1. Barenboim, Daniel, 1942– 2. Pianists—Biography. 3. Conductors (Music)—
Biography. I. Lewin, Michael, 1958– II. Huscher, Phillip. III. Title.

    ML417.B2A3 2003
    780'.92—dc21
    [B]   2002043750

Published in the United States by Arcade Publishing, Inc., New York
Distributed by AOL Time Warner Book Group

Visit our Web site at www.arcadepub.com

10   9   8   7   6   5   4   3   2   1

EB

PRINTED IN THE UNITED STATES OF AMERICA

CONTENTS

ILLUSTRATIONS

Between pages 52 and 53

Playing the spinet, Mozart's birthplace, Salzburg, 1952.
With Bruno Bandini and the Radio Orchestra, Argentina, 1951.
With my parents in Salzburg, 1955.
My parents and I with Wilhelm Furtwängler in Salzburg, 1955.
With Markevich, in his conducting class, Salzburg, 1954.
Rehearsing with Joseph Krips for my Royal Festival Hall début, London, 1956.
With Zubin Mehta in Tel Aviv, 1965.
Playing Bartók with the Berlin Philharmonic, 1964.
With Jacqueline at our wedding in Jerusalem, 1967.
At our wedding reception in Tel Aviv with Zubin Mehta and Sir John and Lady
    Barbirolli.
At our wedding reception in Tel Aviv with David Ben Gurion and his wife, Paula.
Jacqueline in the Royal Albert Hall, c. 1969.
Recording with Jacqueline and Pinchas Zukerman, Abbey Road Studios, London,
    1969.
Jacqueline and I with Pablo Casals, Marlboro, USA, in 1969.
Recording the Brahms *Requiem* with Dietrich Fischer-Dieskau in Edinburgh, 1972.
    (Clive Barda)
Rehearsing, on tour with the English Chamber Orchestra, in the late 1960s.
My first concert as conductor with the Chicago Symphony Orchestra, 1970.
CBS supper party for Leonard Bernstein on his 55th birthday, August 1973.
During the recording of the Beethoven piano concertos with Artur Rubinstein,
    London, 1974. (Clive Barda)
With Artur Rubinstein and the Israel Philharmonic in the Royal Albert Hall,
    London. (Clive Barda)
With Zubin Mehta, Olivier Messiaen and his wife in Paris in the late 1970s.
With Boulez in Paris, recording his *Notations,* 1988.
With Wolfgang Wagner before my first Bayreuth rehearsal, 1981.
Bayreuth, 1981: with René Kollo, Wolfgang Wagner and Johanna Meier after the
    première of *Tristan.*
Performing in 1989. (EMI Music)

With Sir Georg Solti, Pierre Boulez and Zubin Mehta after a concert by the
    Orchestre de Paris in London, 1988. (Ian Hunter)
Playing with and conducting the Chicago Symphony Orchestra, Chicago, 1991.
    (Jim Steere)

Between pages 148 and 149

With Rafael Kubelík and Georg Solti in Chicago, 1991. (Rosenthal Archives,
    Chicago Symphony Orchestra)
With Harry Kupfer at the Staatsoper, Berlin, 1992. (Monika Rittershaus)
Rehearsing with Placido Domingo in Berlin, 1994. (Kunio Tsuchiya)
In discussion with Sergiu Celibidache, Munich, 1995. (Werner Neumeister)
With Claudio Abbado. (Marion Schöne)
With Patrice Chéreau in front of the Staatsoper in Berlin, 1994. (Marion Schöne)
At the West-Eastern Divan workshop, 1999. (Maik Schuck)
With Edward Said and Saleem Abboud-Ashkar in Birzeit, January 1999.
With Yo-Yo Ma in Chicago, September 2000. (Dan Rest)
Conducting the Staatskapelle Berlin in 1999. (Monika Rittershaus)
In Madrid, June 2000, with Teresa Berganza.
At a performance of *Parsifal* in Berlin in November 2001: with Christian Franz,
    Andreas Schmidt, Elena Bashkirova (Elena Barenboim), Violeta Urmana and
    John Tomlinson.

(Unless otherwise acknowledged, these photographs belong to the author.)

FOREWORD

When I was a child and an adolescent, I was fascinated by biographies. I devoured one after another – biographies about people I admired, people I disliked, or people I did not know. But, much as I enjoyed reading about other people, I think that an artist's personal life should be private. Obviously there are connections between what is public and what is private. Nonetheless, I feel that these two sides of one's life should be kept apart. Perhaps I have become exaggeratedly conscious of this because of the many difficult years in my private life while my first wife was ill, when I became over-sensitive to intrusions into what I felt was private.

As a result, the autobiographical thread in this book exists only to give a certain continuity to the reflections on music and on the relationship between music and life.

I have often observed that music remains with me even in situations which are neither directly nor indirectly connected with it, and I have never felt the need to put music aside, as it were, to do something else. I have enjoyed doing many other things in life, but somehow music has been my constant companion. This is probably the reason why I feel that I have never been able to express myself in words as fully as I have in music. Yet, even though I have never felt the need nor the wish to write a conventional autobiography, I have felt that maybe the peculiarity of not only having music in my life, but of really living my life in music, was worth capturing in words.

It is obvious from what I have said that I have no intention of referring in this book to private or personal matters, nor do I have the arrogance to think that, even after more than fifty years on the stage, I have definitive things to say about music and musicians. I have simply tried to write what it feels like to be obsessed with music and to have the curiosity to examine this obsession.

I

ARGENTINA

My four grandparents were all Russian Jews. At the beginning of the twentieth century, when there were atrocious pogroms in Russia, and when my maternal grandparents were very young, they went to Argentina. I think they actually met on the boat, when my grandmother was fourteen and my grandfather sixteen. They spent their adult lives in the provinces of Argentina and their six children were born and educated there. My maternal grandmother had been a fervent Zionist from her early youth, and in 1929 she took my mother, who was seventeen, and the rest of her children on a visit to Palestine. It is hard now to imagine what it meant then to travel from Argentina just to see the Holy Land. While they did not settle there, my mother's eldest sister remained in Palestine until she died.

The society my grandparents lived in was politically Jewish-minded. My grandmother's house became a meeting place for Zionists, where people discussed Zionist hopes and aims, where they dreamed of Israel as a state based on Zionist socialism – *Mapai*. That was not socialism in the Soviet, but in the Western sense of the word. I knew my maternal grandparents very well. They moved to Israel almost at the same time as my parents and I did, in 1952. At first we even lived there together in a very small flat, and during my childhood and adolescence we were very close.

I never knew my paternal grandmother, who died before my parents were married. My grandfather, a watchmaker, died when I was four or five, so I have few recollections of him, except that he was in no way active in Jewish affairs. The background of my father's parents was different from that of my mother's, although both families were close-knit. My father, passionately interested in music from an early age, was always torn between making a career as a pianist and maintaining family ties. When he was offered the opportunity of going to the USA in the 1930s to perform, he did not accept because the 'pull' of the family was stronger.

My father was always more interested in intellectual than in political matters. I know that he attended lectures by the philosopher Ortega y Gasset in Buenos Aires. He moved in more intellectual circles than my mother's family. When they met and married, they provided each other with wider horizons. My mother encountered an intellectual curiosity she had not known at home; my father became more involved in Jewish affairs and more aware of his Jewishness through the people with whom he now came into contact.

~

I think the last time Argentina had what could be called a democratic government was in the 1930s. Then came Juan Perón, who planted the seeds of Argentina's chaotic modern history. Argentina was a very rich country – ninety-five per cent self-sufficient – the only thing it lacked was petrol. Perón, a gifted demagogue, tried to change Argentina from a purely agricultural country to an industrial one, encouraging great numbers of country people to move into the cities by subsidising them. Even today, almost a third of Argentina's population lives in Buenos Aires and the surrounding towns.

On international issues, Perón was very clever. He opened the doors to the Jewish victims of the Nazis, as well as to the Nazis themselves. Bariloche, in the south of Argentina, was a Nazi stronghold, and during the last years of the Second World War it was not uncommon to see people greeting each other quite openly with the Nazi salute.

At the same time there was general acceptance of Jewish immigration and of the Jewish community. There must have been about 700,000 Jews in Argentina when I lived there. It was the third largest Jewish community in the world after the Soviet Union and the United States. I remember that the Chief Rabbi of Buenos Aires was in close contact with Perón's regime. Political attitudes were cleverly controlled. It was a very rigid dictatorship, but there was really no anti-Semitism. I never encountered any as a child, and never felt it privately or officially. Jewish community life was well organized and very open. I went to a Jewish school and to a Jewish club – Maccabee, it was called – for gymnastics and sports.

I was born on 15 November 1942. In the 1940s Buenos Aires was a musical centre which, unfortunately, it has since ceased to be. Arturo Toscanini came, and Wilhelm Furtwängler, the young Herbert von Karajan, and Richard Strauss before that. Wilhelm Backhaus, Walter Gieseking, Artur Rubinstein, Erich Kleiber and Claudio Arrau also spent a lot of time there.

As in Europe, there were very few gramophone records available – and then only the 78s – so a great deal of chamber music was played in people's homes. There was a German season and an Italian season at the Teatro Colón and also a great many symphony concerts. One of my first memories of an international celebrity goes back to 1949 and is of Adolf Busch playing the Beethoven Violin Concerto and conducting a chamber orchestra in Handel's Concerti Grossi. I went to many of his rehearsals and also played for him – it was the first time I had met a great international figure.

My father had studied the piano with a great Italian pedagogue called Vicente Scaramuzza, who lived to a very advanced age. He even taught Martha Argerich, who was thirty years my father's junior. My father used to play locally, giving concerts with other instrumentalists, but his real passion was teaching, which is why he did not try to become a professional concert pianist. In fact, both my parents were piano teachers. My mother taught children and beginners, my father taught more advanced students, and when I was a child I knew that every time the doorbell rang it was somebody coming for a piano lesson. I grew up in the belief that everybody played the piano and it took me a long time to realize that some people did not!

When I was about four, my father gave some concerts with a violinist for which they used to rehearse at our flat. I suddenly wanted to play the violin, so that I could play with my father. I was rather small, and by the time my parents started looking for a violin that was the right size, I had seen my father playing duets with somebody on two pianos. Realizing that I, too, could play the piano with my father, I settled for that instead. I was five years old when I started. My mother taught me to read music and gave me my first lessons. I then started to learn with my father, who remained my only piano teacher. I never studied with anybody else in these early years and the fundamental basis of my father's teaching has remained with me ever since.

~

All the musicians in Buenos Aires, and anybody who was on tour in Argentina, went to No.1257 Talcahuano, the house of the Austrian-Jewish family of Ernesto Rosenthal, where chamber music was played on Friday evenings. (Rosenthal himself was an amateur violinist.) I had two encounters there that greatly influenced me. One was with Sergiu Celibidache, for whom I played when I was seven or eight. Later I saw him frequently in Israel, always going to his rehearsals and concerts because there was so much I could learn from him. But then I did not see him again until the end of the 1960s. My late wife, Jacqueline du Pré, played with him in Stockholm, but it was not until he came to Munich that I started to play with him regularly.

The other important encounter I had at Rosenthal's home was with Igor Markevich, the Russian conductor and composer. Later on, I was to have less contact with Markevich than with Celibidache, but when I was nine, Markevich said to my father: 'Your son plays the piano wonderfully but I can tell from the way he plays that he is really a conductor.' My father had taught me to play the piano with the sound of the orchestra in mind.

At first sight, the piano is far less interesting than other instruments. Any weight that comes down on the keys produces sound, no matter if the impact is made by Rubinstein's fingers, an ashtray, or a stone. The pressure on the piano keys does not necessarily produce colourful or interesting sound, yet when you become aware of its neutrality, you realize that it is precisely this which gives the piano so many possibilities of expression. One could compare this to a painter faced by a completely white wall, as opposed to a wall that is blue or green. The wall itself is less attractive but, if you want to paint on it, the whiteness gives you extra scope. This does not apply to the violin or the oboe: they have an individual colour. Great violinists naturally have to have a special sound, and the sound of David Oistrakh is not that of Isaac Stern, or anyone else. But it is always the sound of a violin. With the neutral sound of the piano, the pressure on the keys produces the sound, and therefore the piano is at first both easier to play and less interesting. I believe that the piano can create the illusion of other sounds, unlike any other instrument. The neutral piano became an illusory orchestra to me, and perhaps that was why Markevich thought that I was a born conductor. My father also taught me the importance of rhythm, which is indispensable to a conductor.

It was Adolf Busch who encouraged my parents to let me play in public — contrary to what was said to be his advice to the young Yehudi Menuhin, namely not to play in public but to concentrate on studying first. The only thing I remember — and it is difficult to distinguish between memory and hearsay — is that it seemed perfectly natural to me to step on to a platform and play. I loved playing for people. At the Rosenthals' chamber music evenings I would play for anybody who was willing to listen, and people were always curious to hear what a seven-year-old could do.

In August 1950, still just seven years old, I gave my first official concert in Buenos Aires. I played a variety of pieces, including one by Prokofiev.

I started school in Argentina and later went to school in Israel. Even after I began to play more frequently in public, at the age of thirteen or fourteen, I did not go on long tours, so that I really had a perfectly normal education. If I was away in the middle of term, I made up for it and, looking back now, I cannot say that I missed any of my youth or schooling because of my concerts. The only negative effect of these interruptions in my schooling was a certain difficulty in organizing my work and in adjusting to discipline. I am not a very disciplined person. I used to practise for one and a half to two hours a day, but once a week I was allowed to play whatever I liked, for as long as I wanted. This enabled me to develop my sight-reading, and become acquainted with a vast amount of repertoire.

I gave my first concert with an orchestra in Buenos Aires when I was eight, playing Mozart's Piano Concerto No. 23 in A major (K. 488). Although I have played Mozart from the very beginning of my musical life, Beethoven was at that time the composer who meant most to me. My grandmother, who knew nothing about music, always used to say, 'Beethoven, pfui!', and I remember as a child, when I started to play the piano, she would say, 'Now you are playing Beethoven again!'

When the State of Israel was created in 1948 my parents decided to emigrate there. We did not need to leave Argentina, and the reason for leaving was not anti-Semitism. It was a conscious decision taken for very positive reasons. It was, though, a major upheaval for my father to leave Argentina. Unlike my mother, he had not been an enthusiastic Zionist and his Jewish and Zionist awareness developed relatively late.

~

I studied with my father till I was about seventeen. I believe I was very fortunate in not having to change teachers. Many instrumentalists move from one teacher to another and each time learn a different method of playing. You have to forget what you were told by the previous teacher and adapt yourself to a new method. This may even apply to technical matters – some teachers tell you to play with a high wrist, others with a low wrist, with flat fingers or with curved fingers, and all these changes reduce the directness and spontaneity of your playing.

For me, learning to play the piano was as natural as learning to walk. My father had an obsession about wanting things to be natural. I was brought up on the fundamental principle that there is no division between musical and technical problems. This was an integral part of his philosophy. I was never made to practise scales or arpeggios. What was needed to develop my abilities as a pianist was done exclusively through playing the pieces themselves. A principle that was hammered into me early, and which I still adhere to, is never to play any note mechanically. My father's teaching was based on the belief that there are enough scales in Mozart's concertos.

I often meet musicians who try to solve certain problems in a technical, mechanical way first, and then try to add the 'musicianship', like cream on top of a cake. The two must be linked from the very beginning because the technical means used to overcome certain physical problems will influence the expression.

I always practise the technically difficult passages first – separately and slowly – so that I learn to control and phrase them. One must resist the temptation to try out the right tempo until one has perfect control at the slower tempo. I never play such passages mechanically with the intention of adding the phrasing later. A technically difficult passage needs to be played more slowly until you learn to control it – but with the right musical expression. To separate the technical from the expressive side in music is like separating the body from the soul.

My father also laid great emphasis on polyphony – on the independence of voices – and therefore made me play a lot of Bach in my childhood. The piano should not be played with two units, with two hands. It should either be played with one unit made up of two hands – Liszt used and composed arpeggios and passages that go seamlessly from one hand to the other, thus showing us that the two hands are one unit – or it should be played with ten units, namely the independent fingers. Ideally it should be a combination of the two, but the hands should never be regarded as two separate units. I think we are physically handicapped by having two hands – for piano playing it means absolutely nothing.

The importance of polyphonic listening and playing was instilled in me very early on. My father's preoccupation with everything having to be completely natural derived from a philosophical concept that a healthy mind can only exist in a healthy body. He maintained that the way you sit at the piano signifies your mental state and insisted on a natural position, at a distance that enables you to put the full weight on the keys. The chair must be neither too low nor too high, so that you sit with a straight back. My father wanted me to sit at the piano as naturally as if I were eating at a table, for arms and hands would then drop on the keys in a natural position. The shoulders should not be lifted because that wastes energy needed for playing. If you sit straight at the piano with the power coming from relaxed shoulders, the wrist becomes a natural continuation of your arm, and you get one uninterrupted line from your shoulder to the tip of your finger. All these are principles which I adopted, and later adapted.

The next problem is to control wrist movement and to decide whether to play with flat or with curved fingers. One could perhaps compare the wrist to the bow used on a string instrument, for it should move horizontally, never vertically. This is the most important factor for legato playing. The fingers, not up-and-down movement of the wrist, are responsible for articulation. People tend to think of legato as no more than binding one note to another. But there has to be articulation of each note even within the legato. This is where the significance of flat or curved fingers comes in. To understand the correct position, imagine holding a small apple in your hand – all your fingers appear to be the same length. If you hold your fingers flat, the little finger is much shorter – unless you have a very unusual hand like Rubinstein, whose fingers were all more or less the same length. My little finger is not only much shorter, it also curves inwards, yet when I hold all my fingers slightly curved, their length is almost identical and it is much easier to control the weight and pressure of each.

Piano playing and music are not just part of my life, they constitute its essence. They are part of my upbringing, as important to me as food and drink. And although suffering and passion play a great part in musical expression, I think you need to lead a normal, healthy life and to have a positive attitude in order to express these feelings. If your own emotions are too directly involved, they will get in the way and prevent you from bringing out the expressive qualities of the music itself.

I believe you need to contemplate and recollect at a distance in order to express something in music. The most passionate moment in Wagner's *Tristan und Isolde*, for instance, can only be expressed after a certain degree of contemplation. Contemplation and recollection are as important to a performing musician as passionate involvement. There is a clear difference in English between recollection, and remembrance or memory. In music and musical performance this is an important distinction. A young man remembers and an old man recollects. Memory is something that immediately comes to your aid, whereas recollection can only come through reflection. Recollecting is an art for which you require skill in the use of illusion. To give a simple example: the sensation of feeling homesick although you are at home. This involves recollection and has little to do with memory. This is very important and creates a lot of problems for interpreters today, since we play so much music from memory. Recollection requires individual effort. Everything in musical performance depends on the power of recollection. In other words, even if you have learned *Tristan und Isolde* by heart, and know it by heart, and you can feel the white-heat intensity of the music, you must be able to *recollect* this white heat, not just remember it, and from one performance to another add up the sum of recollections you have.

Conducting by heart really means knowing every single detail, every note, and not relying on the orchestra. It is not enough to remember the notes but also how they should be played. Memory alone, if it lacks the support of recollection, becomes unsafe and mechanical. The ability to recollect is a creative condition.

One obviously has to work, to train. But 'practising' is such an unmusical word. It is a problem of linguistics. In Hebrew, by comparison, the words art, training and faith have the same root (לגלב), and I do not believe it is merely a coincidence.

All individuals have different spans of concentration. I have no strict rule myself, such as playing eight hours a day or no more than forty-five minutes. Both extremes are equally counterproductive. I never play a single note when my concentration is no longer at its height, for to do so would be to fall into the trap of playing mechanically.

A lot of people practise for many hours for non-musical reasons, like boosting their self-confidence. You can only gain confidence by knowing what you are doing and how you are doing it. If you need to build up your self-confidence, playing music is not a suitable way to do so. The great composers – Beethoven, Wagner, Debussy, Boulez or Mozart – did not write down their innermost feelings so that we miserable pianists could gain self-confidence. Self-confidence depends on character and an ability to reason. We can only improve it by greater depth of knowledge or insight, never by mechanical repetition.

Some of that knowledge or insight can come from sight-reading, the technique of which can be learned. I have a horror of taking the easy way out, of saying, 'Ah, this is too difficult, I will not bother with it.' It is not just a question of patience but also of knowing the difficulties involved, and, of course, training. If done regularly, sight-reading can be learned, if your mind, eyes and fingers get used to grasping a whole section in one. Then you can go into the details. If you only see the details, you cannot sight-read. By definition, sight-reading means looking ahead, playing bar one with your eyes while your brain is on bar five.

The lessons learned from my father I later developed for myself although, after playing the piano for more than fifty years, I have neither forgotten nor altered what he taught me, so I cannot claim to be self-taught as a pianist. As a conductor, however, I have developed my own methods, even if the musical education I had from my father and the influence of many great musicians and my observation of great conductors since early childhood have helped me tremendously.

2

EUROPEAN INTERMEZZO

~

We left for Europe in July 1952 on our way to Israel. My family had been wanting to go to Israel for a long time. My parents' main desire was for their son to grow up as a member of a majority population, and not in a Jewish minority somewhere in the Diaspora.

When I met and played for Markevich at the Rosenthals in Buenos Aires, he told my parents that there was a basic sense of rhythm in my piano playing which he would like to develop. He had the feeling that I was born to be a conductor. Markevich had what you might call a *folie de grandeur* in those days. He had his own very individual way of conducting and wanted to set up a school for conductors. He told my parents: 'Bring him to Salzburg and he can take part in the last concert of the conducting class' – which I did, playing the Bach D minor Concerto. And throughout the summer of 1952, I observed his conducting class.

We flew from Buenos Aires to Rome and then travelled to Salzburg by train. Nowadays this would be a perfectly simple journey which would involve fourteen or fifteen hours' flight from Buenos Aires to Rome with maybe, at the most, one or two stopovers, and then one could presumably fly from Rome to Salzburg. In 1952, however, as if the upheaval of leaving Argentina were not enough, the trip itself took fifty-two hours. The plane stopped, if I am not mistaken, in Montevideo, then made two stopovers in Brazil, one in São Paulo and the other in Recife, then on an island called Isla del Sol, which lies between America and Africa. Then we went on to Madrid and finally to Rome.

Once in Rome, we went straight from the airport to the railway station and took the train to Salzburg. I still remember my excitement, in spite of being absolutely exhausted from the trip, at setting foot for the first time not only in a European city, but in *this* city. With its connection to Mozart, Salzburg meant so much to me as a young musician.

We had rooms rented in a private house; we were going to stay in Salzburg for quite a long time and our finances did not permit us to live in a hotel. We left our belongings in the room, just freshening up and changing our clothes, and immediately went to the Festspielhaus. It was late afternoon, and on our way we stopped in the Getreidegasse to look at Mozart's birthplace. Then we watched all the people going to the Festspielhaus. In those days the Großes Festspielhaus did not exist, only the Felsenreitschule and the Kleines Festspielhaus. I do not know if the concert-going public then was as impressive-looking as it is today. I have no memory that it was not as elegant and high-class a public as it is now, but, in any case, it was impressive to see the small street leading up to the Festspielhaus and all the people going in.

My curiosity was naturally tremendous, and I saw that the performance that evening was to be *Die Zauberflöte*, conducted by Karl Böhm. I had never been to the opera, and was terribly excited and wanted to go in. It was, of course, impossible to get tickets, but I said to my mother that I thought I could slip into the public gallery without a ticket – I was a small boy, only nine years old, and nobody would take any notice. But I did not know where to find my parents afterwards, because they were obviously much too law-abiding even to try to get in without tickets, so they looked around and told me that they would wait for me in Café Tomaselli, which is within walking distance of the Festspielhaus. Hiding myself in the middle of the crowd where nobody would notice me, I waited till we all seemed to be in and then opened a door which fortunately led to an empty box. Sitting down very comfortably, and feeling extremely happy and proud of myself for having managed to get in without a ticket, I waited impatiently for the conductor to start the performance. As soon as he did I was overjoyed; there was applause and the overture started. I remember perhaps about ten or twenty bars – I suppose that thereafter total exhaustion from the trip overwhelmed me and the excitement was just too much – for I promptly fell asleep and did not hear a note of either the rest of the overture or the singing or dialogue that followed.

The next thing I remember is waking up and suddenly being terribly frightened. I had no idea where I was, I heard music being played and everybody was sitting down, and for a second I could not remember where my parents were or what I was doing there, so far away from any familiar surroundings. I started crying very loudly, whereupon the usher came and very firmly, if not brutally, took me out of the box where I was disturbing the public, and threw me out of the Festspielhaus. Then, of course, I remembered that my parents were at the Café Tomaselli and went to join them, still crying. But by this time my tears were more because I had been so stupid as to have started crying and lost all sense of direction. I had not had the intelligence to realize where I was and to have stayed and listened to the music – and it was too late to go back. That was my first encounter with a Mozart opera, which obviously did not augur very well for the future!

Many years later, in the 1960s, I played at the Salzburg Festival in the Großes Festspielhaus, performing Brahms's D minor Concerto with the Vienna Philharmonic Orchestra. Once again, Karl Böhm was conducting. I was stupid enough to tell him this story, thinking that he would find it amusing that his was the first opera performance I had attended, even though I could not stay awake because of the trip. I think, though, he was rather offended by my lack of musical taste and I realized then that his sense of humour was to be found more in music than in such situations.

It was in Salzburg that I had my first encounter with the Swiss pianist and conductor Edwin Fischer. I played for him and often attended his classes as a listener. A few years later I heard him with the Danish Royal Orchestra during a tour in Europe, when they performed Mozart's *Haffner* Symphony, the Piano Concertos in C minor (K. 491) and E flat (K. 482) and, as an encore, the Rondo in D major. I was fascinated to see Fischer conduct from the piano – he really did conduct.

He was very kind to me, very gentle, and I was full of enthusiasm for his music making and very attracted by his personality. I told him that it was my dream to conduct Mozart concertos from the piano one day and he told me: 'If you want to conduct the Mozart concertos from the piano, you must first learn to conduct independently. You cannot merely rely on the quality of the orchestra. You must both conduct and play, and only then will you get a homogeneity not easily attained with an independent conductor.'

Fischer had two qualities that stayed fresh in my mind, and which I very much admired: he had the most natural legato I have ever heard in a pianist. He was able to play legato without the pedal, which meant that he could use it for additional expression. A legato played without the pedal has a directness and clarity of articulation that is quite different from a legato which is only achieved by using the pedal. There was also a natural luminosity of sound when he played chords, as, for instance, at the beginning of the slow movement in Schubert's *Wanderer Fantasy*. That was quite wonderful. To me, he played the Mozart concertos exactly as they should be played. He had a liveliness in the fast movements and a simplicity. and richness of expression in the slow movements that I shall always remember. I rarely listen to recordings but, if I wanted to hear a Mozart concerto, I would probably want to listen to a Fischer recording.

The other composer with whom he identified closely, which as a result influenced me very much, was Bach. His recordings of *The Well-Tempered Clavier* and the *Chromatic Fantasy and Fugue* remain incomparable. There was something very uninhibited about his interpretation of Bach, an extraordinary vitality in the fugues. He was able to achieve an almost peasant-like, plebeian element in Bach's rhythmic configurations.

It is a great shame that Fischer was better in performance than in his recordings. Perhaps the studio inhibited him. There are so few recordings of Fischer in general and particularly of Fischer at his best, but I still remember how impressed I was with his recording of Beethoven's *Emperor* Concerto under Furtwängler. (There are a few really wonderful records on which he simply conducts, including Haydn's marvellous Symphony No. 104 with the Vienna Philharmonic Orchestra.)

I heard him at his last recital in Salzburg, when he played the Beethoven Sonatas Op. 28, Op. 53, and Op. 111, and the Fantasy Op. 77 as an encore. He had a wonderful gift of making everything sound improvised; he often gave you the feeling that he was making things up as he played. Fischer may not have been a great virtuoso, nor even pretended to be one, but his playing was quite breathtaking, as in the last movement of Mozart's Piano Concerto in E flat (K. 482). There was a natural brilliance and vitality to his playing. He was a complete musician, and able to make an orchestra play the way he wanted.

~

If you leave a country at the age of nine, you cannot say that you grew up there, yet a lot of my habits of thought, not to mention gastronomical tastes, were established early on. I spoke only Spanish, and a little Yiddish which I had learned from my grandmother. It was only much later that I realized how greatly I had been influenced by the Argentinian mentality and language, and that I had no wish to erase them from my life. My parents were completely formed by and educated in Argentina, and I continued to live with them until I started travelling on my own.

The Argentinian ethos owes a lot to European culture. The Spanish influence, in particular, is very strong, that special gift for enjoying life, which is a very Latin characteristic. With all the admiration and affection I feel for many other ways of life, such as the Anglo-Saxon or the German, I find the Latin quality of attaching importance to very simple things, such as the midday meal, very attractive. I cannot get used to the American habit of having a hamburger for lunch between two rehearsals. In Argentina you enjoy a proper lunch with a good piece of meat. I like to sit in a café in the afternoon with time for a coffee and a cigar. I can accept the need for the occasional *dolce far niente*, even during a heavily booked-up day. And I identify to an extent with that purely Spanish trait of quixotism – not that I, like Don Quixote, want to fight windmills – but I have a certain respect for things that stem from the realm of fantasy and imagination. I can identify with the texts of Verdi operas or Mozart's da Ponte operas, which I think I might not have if I had grown up in Vienna, New York or London. All this became particularly apparent during the fifteen years when I worked in Paris, because there is a certain similarity between the Spanish and the French mind.

One of the difficulties of Argentinian life when I was young, and I do not think it has changed dramatically since, is this: although European culture has been accepted and adopted by many of the Argentinian intellectuals, the Argentinians as a nation have a slight inferiority complex. (Of course, this is an oversimplified generalization.) It is something they share with the Australians who have adopted European culture and European thinking: they feel geographically far removed. The shock of coming to Europe for the first time, coming to Salzburg as a child, was quite an experience. Although I was already a musician and had played in public, to go to Mozart's birthplace, the very centre of things, was a great occasion for me.

I had heard a great deal about European music and its traditions. The Rosenthals, for example, had the kind of house and way of life which I imagine was very common in Berlin and Vienna at the beginning of this century and also during the nineteenth century, when music was played regularly at home, accompanied by a great deal of interesting conversation. Austrian food, for instance, was something I associated with such occasions, in my childish way – there was always *Apfelstrudel* with whipped cream at the Rosenthals. To me that was connected with Mozart, Schubert and Brahms – whatever chamber music happened to be played on any particular evening. Salzburg and its way of life were therefore not entirely unknown territory.

Food is a very good indicator of the way our civilization has developed. In the 1950s when I went to England, there was hardly any international food to be had – there were not, for instance, as many Italian restaurants in London as there are now. It seemed that each country laid great emphasis on its national heritage, national culture and national food. Today, if you happen to have been born in Buenos Aires, or in London, and you go to Italy for the first time at the age of nine, eating spaghetti is no novelty because there are hundreds of Italian restaurants in all great cities.

We stayed in Salzburg until the end of August 1952. Then we went on to Vienna, where my father gave a lecture at the Academy. I played a succession of concerts in Vienna, including one at the American Institute, half of which was devoted to American composers. The conductor I was supposed to play with, Heinrich Hollreiser, was taken ill at the last moment and on the day of the performance a very young, at the time unknown conductor took his place – his name was Michael Gielen.

I found it very strange to see Vienna as an occupied city, with its four allied sectors. I remember certain things were forbidden, like entering the Russian sector, but, as a child, I was unable to analyse the things I saw around me in any way. There was the political difference between the Soviet and the American systems, for instance. I was very much aware of America's contribution, in a material not a political sense – there was Coca-Cola everywhere in Vienna. The Russians were more astute in those days – they did not send Coca-Cola, they sent David Oistrakh! They wanted to use their influence in a cultural way. I was aware of the Soviet Union's wish to set up cultural contacts and influence life in Austria and, I suppose, Germany too. On the other hand, what the American Marshall Plan did for Europe can never be estimated too highly.

We led a very close-knit Jewish family life and, when I was a child, we moved either in Jewish or in musical circles. There were so many Jewish musicians, though, that the two were frequently inseparable. While I had not been aware of any Jewish problem in Argentina, I began to feel it in Austria. I remember being taken by some Jewish Austrian friends to somewhere near Salzburg – I think it was Bad Gastein – where there was a big waterfall and being told that Jews had been thrown down it during the Nazi period. This was my first inkling of such horrors.

As a young Jewish boy in Vienna, I could not help asking myself if I met a non-Jew – what did he do during the War? Did he participate in the extermination of so many Jews actively, or passively merely through acceptance? This problem had not existed in Argentina. Of course, as a child it was impossible for me to understand the full significance of the Holocaust, but I remember very clearly being greatly disturbed by the stories that I heard from people whom I met with my parents in Salzburg and Vienna. It was only later that I came to appreciate the full horror of this chapter in the history of the Jews and of mankind, but even as a young boy it made a great impression. My parents had, of course, talked about the events in Europe, and they explained to me that this was one of their reasons for going to Israel.

From Vienna we went to Rome, where I gave a recital in November or December. In those days, nothing was planned years and years in advance. Even the most successful artists played to the end of the season, in April or May, and then made plans for the next one, which started around October or November (apart from a few festivals like Lucerne, Salzburg and Edinburgh). In Rome I auditioned for many organizations and was engaged to play for the Società Filarmonica Romana, whose General Secretary at the time was Massimo Bogianckino. He later became Director of the Opéra in Paris and Mayor of Florence. Such experiences, however, were accidental. We went to Rome because we had plane tickets to travel from there to Israel – it was as simple as that!

3
ISRAEL

The foundations of the State of Israel and its very nature were created, above all, by David Ben-Gurion. In Israel a Jew was not necessarily someone from the Diaspora who was a member of the professions or an artist: suddenly there were Jewish agricultural workers. In other words, a broadening of the Jewish profile took place when Jews became integrated in a state where they were no longer a minority. This transition was accomplished by the population of the time in a remarkable manner, despite the great differences between Jews who came from Europe, the Arab countries, South and North America, and despite the atrocities that had decimated Jewish populations during the Second World War. This evolutionary process continued uninterrupted until 1967.

We were all very conscious that, for the first time in two thousand years, the Jewish people were living in a state of their own again. The age-old preoccupation with how the Gentiles would react to this or that had gone, the need to assimilate non-Jewish customs had disappeared completely. There was, however, a strong element of European culture and I did not come into much contact with Sephardic culture.

The large-scale immigration of non-European Jews, which took place during the time I lived in Israel, also brought in rather poorly educated people. There was a large influx of Jews from Yemen while I was there, which was known as the 'Magic Carpet' because El Al planes flew to Yemen and brought back Jews from there or from Iraq. The question of how they could be integrated was much discussed. I remember, for instance, a boy at school who had just arrived from Yemen and did not know how to use a fork. These people were just not used to what we considered the most elementary social skills.

At this time anything superfluous to the essentials of life was frowned upon. When we started to join youth movements, we found there was a very strong feeling against anything which suggested superficiality. A boy who started growing a moustache, for instance, was considered bourgeois; a girl who used lipstick was looked down upon. It was the first time that I had seen a society founded on idealism. This had a very strong influence on my life, it affected my way of thinking and later my way of making music. I came from a very different tradition, from a Latin country where appearances were all-important − Argentinian people set great store by their dress. Social graces were essential in Argentina, whereas in Israel there was a passionate rejection of such superficial matters. This went so far that even elementary traits, such as politeness to each other, were scorned. This was the less agreeable, less attractive side of living in Israel. But it was not just an attitude of *je m'en fou* (couldn't care less); it derived from a healthy preoccupation with idealism and positive thinking.

People outside Israel still tended to look upon the Jews as they were remembered from the Diaspora. But so much was new − a pioneer feeling, a great sense of activity and purpose. I had a feeling of achievement, complemented by the education I received at home, which was based on self-observation, self-analysis. This was very important to me as a musician, someone who is automatically in the public eye. There is always the fear: will they or will they not like what I do? This positive side of − not Jewish but Israeli − thinking in the 1950s only confirmed this independence of thought that infiltrated my family life. Home and country became one unit and there was a feeling of emotional security which stayed with me for a very long time. It was not until much later, when I had to cope with the personal problems which arose from Jacqueline's illness, that this emotional stability was attacked by forces outside.

This sense of emotional security and the constant preoccupation with building up − oneself, one's society, one's life and country − often conveyed to the outside world an impression of arrogance. This was sometimes justified, because − to put it mildly − Israeli behaviour very often bordered on a kind of arrogance that came from a total disregard of social graces. But I hope that only the healthy side of it has remained with me since.

~

When we went to Israel, I had to cope with the major shock of a new language. It was one thing to spend a few summer weeks or months in Salzburg and Vienna, quite another to arrive in Israel in the middle of the school year, in December. I had already missed half a school year because summer in Europe coincided with winter in Argentina, and in 1952 I had started the school year in Argentina in March or April and then left in July. To start school in Israel immediately, in the middle of the school year, with a language of which I did not understand a word, not to mention a different alphabet, was not all that easy, to say the least!

None of my family could speak Hebrew, which shows that our move to Israel was decided relatively quickly, probably prompted by Markevich's invitation to Salzburg. I am sure that I would have been made to study Hebrew, and would not have joined the school halfway through the year. I felt at ease and got on well with the other children, but the language was a considerable problem. Of course, there were many immigrants in Israel from many different countries, but the extensive influx from Europe had taken place earlier, around 1948. I cannot remember if there were other Spanish-speaking children at my school.

Once the initial shock was over, the adaptation to new conditions happened rather quickly, as is usual with children. I was neither particularly inhibited nor particularly shy, and I made friends easily. Because of the climate, children spent most of their free time outside. I learned to play football in the streets of Tel Aviv – something which would be unthinkable today, but at that time Tel Aviv was just a small town and, with the exception of the time I spent practising the piano or at school, I played in the streets most of the day. Later on I joined some youth movements, but in those days a young child's social life really went on in the streets. There were none of the problems of today, with drugs and crime. Israel was the centre of Jewish idealism. We believed that certain things could not happen to Jews as long as they lived in a Jewish state. Even the notion of having Jewish policemen was strange. In the Diaspora, Jews were usually members of the liberal professions: doctors, lawyers, artists, writers or bankers, but the idea of a Jewish policeman, a Jewish soldier, or a Jewish thief

– all these signs of normality were new in Israel. In those days, nobody ever locked their houses. Doors and windows were open; people called out to one another from one house to the next. The streets were relatively narrow, so that was how people communicated.

Everyone was intent on building a new life, a new country, a new society – this mixture of the Zionist and socialist ideals was in evidence twenty-four hours a day and everyone had a very positive attitude to life. I remember a few years later learning at school about Auguste Comte and positive thinking, which was really an intellectual verification of the way we then thought and lived. We were confronted daily with the fact that the country had been a desert and that we were trying to irrigate it to make parks and build houses. Such creative challenges were the driving force of Israeli society at that time.

I did not leave Israel at all between December 1952 and the summer of 1954, when my entire family – my parents, my grandparents – lived together in one flat. It was a real home, and there was nothing outside that home to disturb my sense of security. I think this is a most important point, because nowadays it is almost impossible to find such harmony anywhere in the world. At the same time, I reacted totally against both Argentina and anything that came from the Diaspora. To me that was the past, and I did not want to hear about it or even to speak Spanish. It was, of course, a childish reaction, but I had the feeling now that this was our country, our society and our home.

I was very fortunate in having an excellent headmaster at the primary school I first attended. He was a teacher who complemented the education I received at home – not only by helping me to learn the language, but also in maintaining the same values I learned at home. I started to learn English – it is still the second language in Israeli schools today – but, and this was of paramount importance, I began to develop a Jewish consciousness. It was a very different one from that experienced by Jews in the Diaspora, which is based on being 'different' and on being perceived as such by non-Jews. Jewish consciousness is quite different in Israel. It is an historical consciousness. Israel was a very secular state at the beginning, though there were always the extreme religious elements. The Bible was studied as part of our history – our heritage, something closely related to our daily life. Holidays like Passover, in fact all Jewish holidays, are really celebrations of historical rather than religious events. The Jewish past – the distant past of many centuries ago – was taught at school as something which was vividly alive. This was very different from the way history is taught even now in France, for instance, where you learn about Charlemagne, or in the USA where you learn about the American Revolution as things that happened long ago and have little or no bearing on events in our time. I believe that subjects at school should be taught as having a relation to our lives today. Our instinct for deduction should be encouraged, and we should apply what we learn in one subject to other subjects too.

This sense of the importance of history was very strong in Israel. I was reminded of it when I began to study opera, where what you show on the stage should relate in some way to life today. This connection between history and daily life is something I tried quite consciously to apply to operatic performances, but also to abstract music – symphonic music, piano music, or chamber music – this awareness that something that was written two hundred years ago has great relevance today. This sense of Jewish history playing an active part in contemporary life helped me to realize that every great piece of music has two facets – one relating to its own period and another to eternity. And it is from this second aspect that our interest in music that was composed two or three centuries ago comes.

During my teens I became interested in philosophy. I read quite a bit of Spinoza and Kierkegaard. As a very young man in Israel I came under the influence of two philosophers who impressed me greatly – one was Martin Buber and the other Max Brod. Martin Buber made me realize that things are never what they seem to be but how one thinks about them. At school in Israel, we did not study the Bible in a religious sense, but as part of the Jewish tradition. The different books of the Bible were discussed from a philosophical angle. Very early on I was filled with a great respect for thought and for its importance in everyday life. A great deal of human anxiety and anguish is caused by an inability to think, and even those people willing and able to think regard philosophy and philosophizing as all very well for music, politics or history, but feel, in the ups and downs of daily life, one can manage without them.

My father continued to be my music teacher, but I also studied composition for a while with an Israeli composer, Paul Ben-Haim, who had come from Munich and whose name was originally Paul Frankenburger. He was quite a good composer and taught me harmony, but he was not strict enough. You might call it a Hindemith simplification of musical education, with short cuts in the more laboured aspects of traditional methods. It was not until 1955, in Paris, that Nadia Boulanger really put me through the mill, as they say. From her I received an ascetic, strict musical education.

I gave some recitals in Israel and also played chamber music in public. In the summer of 1953 I gave my first concert with the Israel Philharmonic Orchestra. The conductor was Milton Katims, a very fine musician who had been solo viola player under Toscanini with the NBC Orchestra, and later became a conductor in Seattle. I had a rather mixed reception from the players and the audience. On the one hand they felt that I was a rising talent, a young boy of great promise, and on the other hand there was the typically Jewish reaction – Ah well, we have seen too many child prodigies.

The Israel Philharmonic Orchestra was only seventeen years old when I first played with them. Bronislaw Hubermann had founded it in 1936, and most of its first members, mainly German and Polish, were still there when I made my début. It was very much a central European orchestra. Events came full circle for me, and for the audience, when I went to Israel with the Berlin Philharmonic in April 1990 and brought with this orchestra the sound to which older people in Israel were accustomed, the sound I grew up with. This was not just in the strings but also in the woodwind. The Israeli players had a way of phrasing that you meet in the best central European orchestras.

In the 1960s the Israel Philharmonic underwent a transformation, not only because the original members were replaced by younger players, but also because of the arrival of Jewish musicians from the Soviet Union. In its first 'life', its first phase, it had been a German-Jewish and Polish-Jewish orchestra. Today there are American woodwind players, Russian string players, and a new generation of Israeli string players. There is an Argentinian oboist – the orchestra has become an amalgamation of styles. But in its early stages it had a warmth and intensity of feeling, a certain richness of expression which we have become familiar with and associate in particular with

ISRAEL

so many great Jewish violinists – Bronislaw Hubermann, David Oistrakh or Isaac Stern. There is still, however, an extraordinarily well-organized musical life in Israel. The Israel Philharmonic has over thirty thousand subscribers, yet Tel Aviv and Jerusalem have not many more than a million inhabitants between them.

There was no question of trade unions, of commercialization in those early days. The members of the orchestra did not feel they were just providing a service or doing a job. Music making was an organic part of their lives.

There was then a very fine conductor of Czech origin called George Singer. He was a man of great experience and the first person I met who knew anything about opera. The first time I saw a Wagner score was when he showed me *Siegfried*. I could not read it, of course, and it was the first time I had seen all these 'odd' instruments like Wagner tubas. I was far too young and also totally uninterested. But later, when I started to take an interest in Wagner and to study him, I realized that it had been George Singer who had first shown me the complexity of Wagner's orchestral instrumentation. When Rubinstein came to Israel, he always wanted Singer to accompany him because he was such a thorough musician with boundless knowledge. I, too, played with him, in Haifa and in Jerusalem.

4

EUROPEAN INTERMEZZO II

In the summer of 1954 my parents decided that I should go to Salzburg to begin to study conducting with Markevich. I spent many hours learning and preparing scores so as to be able to attend his classes. There were long arguments between my father and Markevich, because the latter wanted me to stop playing the piano and continue my musical career as a conductor only. My father felt that I should also continue to develop as a pianist and build up a repertoire while studying conducting too. He saw no need to make such a drastic decision of choosing one or the other when I was only eleven years old, and he was right. Later I, too, had to fight hard to continue with both activities.

I was the youngest member of the conducting class, for all the others were well over twenty years old. I remember that many of my so-called colleagues, who were conductors already, were not particularly friendly – I was, after all, a mere child. There was one exception, Herbert Blomstedt. He was very sweet to me and always took the trouble to explain things when I had language problems – I spoke very poor English and the only German I knew had been picked up in Vienna and Salzburg as a nine-year-old.

Markevich's assistant for the class was Wolfgang Sawallisch. On the list of works I was expected to prepare before coming to Salzburg, I remember Mendelssohn's *Italian* Symphony, Beethoven's Fourth Symphony and Brahms's *Haydn Variations*, which I conducted at the end of the course. I had prepared these but obviously had no practical experience of conducting and playing them. As to transposing, I was handicapped by the fact that in my theoretical studies in Israel, Ben-Haim had simplified things too much. He made me do all the four-part exercises in the bass and the treble clefs only, and not in different keys. It was only when I studied with Nadia Boulanger in the winter of 1955 that I was taught to operate with four or five keys at the same time.

I believe that there are short cuts which can save time, and not just in music, but it is dangerous to take them without having some idea of the long way round. Often essential elements are lost in a short cut. This is a principle I always apply to piano playing. A difficult passage in a Beethoven sonata may be easier if you divide the notes between the two hands because they are easier to control, but part of the expression, the need to struggle with the difficulty, then gets lost. For instance, at the beginning of the *Hammerklavier* Sonata the jump from the low B flat to the chord in the left hand is very precarious. It is easy to play wrong notes in the chord, but if you divide them between the two hands and play the low note with the left hand and the chord with the right, which is easy, the sense of the enormous geographical distance between the bass note and the chord is lost, together with a lot of the expression.

Markevich insisted on rhythmical precision and balance, and he was very keen on clarity of sound, clarity of rhythm and clarity of gesture. The main aspect of conducting that he taught was to get rid of unnecessary motions, to do away with gesticulations which only distract. I sometimes felt that he oversimplified things, but he was certainly a healthy influence. He laid great emphasis on posture – how to stand, how to position one's arm, how to hold the baton in a certain way. He was firmly convinced that the right hand was not only there to beat time but also to indicate what the conductor expected from the orchestra dynamically. He had invented the concept of a horizontal figure of eight, which was the way one should beat legato. In other words, you must not beat in an angular manner but with rounded movements of the arm, indicative of an unbroken musical line. He also had some very simplified gestures for the left hand to indicate loud or soft volume.

The Salzburg course had the enormous advantage that an orchestra was available for five or six hours a day, every day of the week, so that the students could gain tremendous practical experience.

In the summer of 1954 I met Wilhelm Furtwängler in Salzburg. I was introduced to him, played for him, and he was impressed by my playing. He wrote a letter which, I have to admit, opened many doors for me. He said: 'The eleven-year-old Barenboim is a phenomenon ...' This was to be my letter of introduction for the next twenty years! He also invited me to play with him and the Berlin Philharmonic Orchestra. This was the greatest honour he could bestow on me, but my father declined. I think he felt that after all the atrocities that had taken place it was too soon for a Jewish family to travel from Israel to Germany. (It has always puzzled me that in those days there were no diplomatic relations between Israel and Germany, yet they existed between Israel and Austria. Somehow the Austrians managed to convince the world that they were victims of the Nazis and Hitler. The Austrians really are the shrewdest people in the world: they have managed to turn Beethoven into an Austrian and Hitler into a German!)

Furtwängler also let me attend his rehearsals. He was rehearsing *Don Giovanni*, which was to be filmed. I remember I sat near the harpsichord. I was also at one of his concerts, an all-Beethoven programme when the Vienna Philharmonic played the Eighth Symphony, the *Große Fuge* and the Seventh Symphony.

In November of that year, 1954, Furtwängler died. As a conductor, his methods were almost exactly the opposite of what we were being taught in class every day. We had been told not to make any superfluous movement, whereas Furtwängler's way of conducting was very intuitive as far as gesture was concerned – an instinctive 'repertory of movement' as the Germans might call it! I remember being greatly impressed by the intensity emanating from the orchestra. When he was rehearsing the Seventh Symphony, he only rehearsed the transitions – at least that is how I remember it. I cannot remember that he ever played a piece right through, just the moves from, for example, the introduction to the Allegro. However slight the transition, he took great pains to rehearse every last detail. That applied not only to the phrasing, or the balance in the actual phrase, but to the bars leading up to it. I had a strong impression of this meticulous preparation on hearing Furtwängler live, and I was fascinated by the man himself. Everything else I learned about and from Furtwängler came later, through recordings and talking to people who had played with him, and studying his scores at his home in Switzerland after his death.

If you observe his dynamic and tempo indications, they give you an insight into what made Furtwängler's conducting so very special. He had his own terminology which was necessary for his way of making music. It was not just a matter of finding the C in the word 'crescendo' with a magnifying glass, but the whole psychological preparation, and the architectonic, almost topographic place in the structure of the beginning of the crescendo. The problem with Furtwängler's posthumous influence is that it is relatively easy to imitate the external manifestations of what he did, and they can be exaggerated.

It always fascinates me that musicians, whenever they feel the need for a slight modification of dynamic, will, nine times out of ten, slow down to obtain greater expression. Many musicians have no hesitation in getting slower but would never dream of going faster. It is important to understand that the terminology employed in music – which stems mainly from Italian or German – really means something: the words have a definite significance, which can be analysed. Rubato, for instance, means 'stolen', and when you have stolen something, you have to give it back! Musically speaking, this means that if you take your time over something to make it more expressive, you must 'return' that time at some point. Modification, flexibility and fluctuation of tempo must be related to metrical strictness. In an ideal situation, when a rubato takes place over three or four bars, then over eight bars or sixteen bars, or whatever the metric pattern is, the loss of tempo should be compensated for, so that if you put on the metronome at the beginning of the sixteen bars and play around it freely, you should, at the end of the sixteen bars, be back level with it. This applies to the rubato as it is known in Mozart and Chopin. The melody is somewhat free but the metrical accompaniment remains strict.

Furtwängler's use of rubato was never wilful or capricious, or used only to underline the beauty or drama of the moment. It was an additional means of underlining the structure. He was able to concentrate both rationally and emotionally, and to transmit all the necessary intensity to the orchestra. I do not know to this day just how much he thought out rationally and how much was felt. Sometimes the two are so interrelated you get the impression that he achieved that ideal state – of thinking with the heart and feeling with the brain.

After his death, I went to his house in Switzerland and his wife very graciously let me look at his scores. Some of these were marked in the most interesting and careful manner. Most of the markings had to do with balance and the relative strengths of the dynamics. It is no coincidence that most of his tempo indications in German are expressed in the negative, like 'nicht zu geschwind, nicht zu schnell, nicht zu langsam', whereas in Italian it is 'allegro, più vivace'. Furtwängler was constantly preoccupied with the relativity of dynamics – this is seen in the short film excerpts of his conducting Schubert's *Unfinished* Symphony – and with the legato. One often has the feeling that it was all intuitive, and when you talk to people who worked with him or observed him regularly, like Celibidache or Fischer-Dieskau, they will tell you how often he would stop and say something like, 'It's not beautiful enough' or 'It doesn't sound right,' and that he sometimes achieved what he wanted with rather awkward movements of his hands. When you read his writings, you realize how much of what he wanted and achieved was, in fact, thought out.

There was never any manipulation or utilization of sound for its own sake. Sometimes it is incredibly beautiful and touching, but it is always related to the expression Furtwängler wanted to achieve. He had the ability to make the orchestra play with almost terrifying intensity, as in the climax of the first movement of Beethoven's Ninth, or in the return of the Passacaglia in Brahms's Fourth, when the high A at the entrance of the strings is almost physically painful. It is dangerous to speak of music in poetic terms because music can mean different things, but I have never heard the expression of desperation so clearly from any other conductor. His Haydn symphonies, and some of his Schubert interpretations, I find beautifully light. When you hear the Berlin Philharmonic today, after so many generations, you feel – or at least I do – that many of the things you associate with Furtwängler are still there.

I think the musical relationship between Furtwängler and the Berlin Philharmonic was so fruitful and positive because, ultimately, you cannot tell what he gave to them and what they gave to him. The more time I spend with the orchestra and the more I listen to Furtwängler's recordings, or reread his writings, the more I feel there was an osmosis between him and the orchestra. He could achieve only with them the interpretation he wanted, but at the same time, he gave them something which continues to be transmitted from one generation to the next.

I think Furtwängler was very much aware of the parallels between music and nature, with flowing rivers and tempests – and no matter how much a work was rehearsed, preserved in alcohol as it were, there was a kind of eruptive quality on the night which has remained unmatched since his time. He is always referred to as the last Romantic. What does 'Romantic' really mean? If you do not play strictly in time and adopt a certain freedom with dynamics, people think you are a Romantic. If you play expressively, but in tempo, you are a classical conductor!

Jean Cocteau defined imitation as the highest form of flattery. Maybe one flatters Furtwängler by imitating him, but imitation can only recreate the surface, the outside. A Furtwängler accelerando or a Furtwängler ritardando or a Furtwängler agogic accentuation derived from an inner necessity and, if you are unaware of this inner compulsion, the outward manifestation becomes a caricature. In the late 1960s, many younger musicians said that Furtwängler was their idol, that he had the urge of freedom, which was very fashionable. But Furtwängler's freedom had a link to structure which many of his imitators lacked.

There is a wonderful recording of Furtwängler playing the piano in Bach's Fifth *Brandenburg* Concerto, where the cadenza is quite breathtaking. I do not know how far one should tolerate the impurity of style, but the breadth of it and the colour make you think that an organ is being played. I find it fascinating. In Mozart's Symphony in G minor (K. 550), the first and last movement are really 'allegro molto alla breve', without that over-elegiac character one so often hears. I have never heard a more convincing performance.

~

When I was not giving concerts, I was at school in Israel, but I went abroad on several occasions. I played in Zürich some time in 1954 or 1955, and also in Amsterdam. I remember playing in Bournemouth; it was my first concert in England. I had to learn a concertino for piano and orchestra by Walter Piston, the American composer.

In the winter of 1955–6 I went to Paris, where I stayed for a year and a half, studying with Nadia Boulanger. I think the contact with Nadia Boulanger was established through Markevich because he was a close friend of hers. My parents accompanied me to Paris and we led a normal family life there, although every now and then my father had pupils. My parents felt that the closeness of the family was necessary. I had a scholarship from the America-Israel Cultural Foundation, and that helped with the costs of our stay.

It was almost a game with Nadia Boulanger when I went for a lesson. She always had the music of Bach's *Well-Tempered Clavier* on the piano and she would turn the pages and say: 'Play this one in E flat minor' – in other words, transpose it. I found this extremely difficult at the beginning. She was very strict in teaching counterpoint but very tolerant regarding my compositions. She was never scholastic in her approach to what I wrote, and there was nothing rigid about her methods. I had private lessons with her once or twice a week, and every now and then, on Wednesdays, I went to a group class. She made me aware of the fact that musical structure is not a dry subject but an integral part of music – that it can be perceived emotionally, and not just rationally.

In January 1956 I played in London for the first time, with Josef Krips conducting. I remember having to travel from Salzburg to St Moritz during the conducting course in the summer of 1955. Krips was there on holiday and I went to play for him. He had heard a lot about me but did not want to engage me without an audition. He was very insistent on always producing a beautiful singing tone when playing the classical composers, especially Mozart and Schubert, and he rejected the slightest roughness. At the same time he paid great attention to strictness of tempo and rhythm and would not yield to the temptation of slowing down for purposes of expression. He always used to say that music was aristocratic and not democratic – certainly a correct assumption as far as tempo and rhythm are concerned.

At that time I made my first recordings, for Philips. The fact that you can start and stop as often as you like in a recording studio should in a way make you play more spontaneously, more recklessly. But, in fact, very often the opposite is the case. In studio recordings there is a tendency to bring out all the elements one has thought about and prepared in advance. It becomes a very conscious effort.

Although in a concert you also try to bring out everything you have thought, studied and felt about a piece, time does not and cannot stop, and this adds the necessary element of urgency.

I do not share Glenn Gould's philosophy that, today, recording is the only way to produce music. To me, music runs parallel to nature, and in relation to what has been and what comes afterwards. The passionate wish to make the clock stand still is just not possible in life – it keeps ticking away. This naturalistic idea of music is the very antithesis of recording, and recording can at best be only the historical record of a given moment.

Glenn Gould was absolutely right when he wrote in a polemical article that I would normally not allow a producer to make more than two takes of a movement, and that I would be satisfied with those results. I do not believe that, were I to spend a couple of weeks in the studio recording a piano sonata, the result would be that much better, because I would have given away naturalness in return for sterility. Today, I like live recordings most of all. They are evidence of a musical opinion at a given moment, records of a certain performance, and they possess the spontaneity and intensity of a public performance which you will never achieve in the studio.

Although I have worked on Bach's *Goldberg Variations* for almost half my life, I did not play them in public till 1989, in a concert in Buenos Aires in the Teatro Colón on the occasion of the fortieth anniversary of my musical début. This was released as a live recording and I am sure that a studio recording would not have brought a better result. Who knows, moreover, how I might interpret that work two, five or ten years later? Glenn Gould replaced his first recorded version of the *Goldberg Variations* years later with a very different version, and nobody can tell if this would have been his final version if it had been his lot to live to do a third one.

In April 1956, I took part in a piano competition in Naples. I was sent there by Carlo Zecchi – I got a diploma after observing his piano classes at the Accademia Santa Cecilia in Rome. In the summer of 1956 I joined his conducting class in Siena. I had met Zecchi in Salzburg, where I had played for him. He was particularly pleasant to me and encouraged me to continue my studies in conducting. His lessons marked the beginning of my friendship with two fellow students, Claudio Abbado and Zubin Mehta, who were in the same class. There is a poster in the musicians' room of the Berlin Philharmonic which I gave the orchestra as a present. I had found it in my parents' old house – a poster of the last concert that summer of 1956, with the three of us conducting! Claudio is ten years older and Zubin six years older than I, but there was a real camaraderie between us, and we played all kinds of silly games.

~

Although my friendship with Claudio has continued until today, a special bond existed from the beginning between Zubin and me which made us even closer friends. And we are as close now as we were in 1956. The difference of six years in age was, of course, much more noticeable when he was twenty and I was fourteen than it is now, and I grew to look upon him as an elder brother who was much more experienced and adult, more experienced not only as far as conducting was concerned but also as regards life generally. He was already on the verge of getting married, and I was only a beginner in the art of looking at girls.

Very soon, in 1962, Zubin became Music Director of the Montreal Symphony Orchestra, and a few months later Music Director of the Los Angeles Philharmonic as well; he has, in fact, directed two orchestras simultaneously throughout his adult life, first in Montreal and Los Angeles, later on in Los Angeles and Israel, and then in Israel and in New York, with the New York Philharmonic. From the very beginning I was fascinated by his facility in learning music and in translating musical ideas into gestures, and in dealing with people in general and orchestral musicians in particular.

He is probably the only person who became a soulmate of mine very early on and has remained one since. So many events have brought us very close together, especially events related to Israel. It was not only very touching but also very admirable that, in 1967, when the Six Day War broke out, he cancelled all his engagements and flew to Israel simply because of his desire to be there with his friends, which meant not only Jacqueline and me, but his friends in the orchestra. His feelings for the State of Israel have remained a constant leitmotif, both in his life and in the life of the Israel Philharmonic.

For me, Zubin Mehta is also the first and most important example

34

of someone who has 'internationalized' music, in the best sense of the word. Up to and including the Second World War, it was generally accepted that German musicians played German music, French musicians played French music, and Italians dedicated themselves to Verdi and Puccini. This is, of course, a very oversimplified way of putting it and there were many examples that proved the contrary, but it was generally believed to be so. I remember reading a fascinating book by Wilhelm Furtwängler's composition teacher, Walter Riezler, an almost philosophical exercise in trying to prove that one has to be German in order to understand Beethoven. Suddenly, here is an Indian of Parsee origin who happened to study in Vienna and who not only has achieved a total sense of identification with Western music, but is also one of the most eclectic conductors today, equally at home with Wagner and Strauss as with Puccini and Verdi in opera, not to mention his vast symphonic repertoire.

In this sense Zubin Mehta became an example, I think, not only for me, but for many younger conductors in later generations. It was especially touching to hear him in the early 1960s with the Vienna Philharmonic Orchestra, conducting Bruckner symphonies with a naturalness which could have led you to think that he had been born in the suburb of Linz. I remember there was a review in one of the Austrian newspapers after his performance of Bruckner's Ninth Symphony, with the headline, 'From Bombay to Linz it is not so far'. It was through Zubin that I became interested in a great deal of music that I did not know, especially opera and also Strauss and Bruckner.

In 1968 the Israel Philharmonic Orchestra named Mehta Music Director. Later they made him Music Director for life. He was the first person to hold this title: the musicians had until then taken great pride in the fact that they had been able to govern themselves both artistically and administratively without a music director, but in his case there was not only a strong reciprocal musical attachment but also great admiration and a feeling of gratitude for his involvement with Israel. His first visit to Israel in 1961 had immediately created a very close bond between him and the orchestra. They played a programme consisting of Dvořák's Seventh Symphony, Stravinsky's Symphony in Three Movements and Kodály's *Dances of Galánta*.

His sense of attachment to Israel is in some ways difficult to explain. As I have already said, Zubin comes from a Parsee family. The Parsees are a small minority group – there are only one hundred thousand of them throughout the world – and they are members of the Zoroastrian religion. It is thought that they are descendants of Cyrus, the Persian King who gave back independence and freedom to the Jews in Israel after the Babylonian invasion, but I do not think that this is what brings him so close to Israel. He is very cosmopolitan and fits in well in any society, whether it is in Vienna, Los Angeles or Florence, where he is also very active. But I believe that in the depths of his heart there is no real sense of belonging to any of these societies. Israel, however, maybe through the coincidence of his attachment to the orchestra but also because of the way of life, has something that must remind him of Bombay. I think there are certainly more similarities between Tel Aviv and Bombay than between Vienna and Bombay, which make him feel very much at home. The generosity with which he has acted through all these years towards the Israel Philharmonic has meant that it has become a pillar of cultural life there.

In 1991, during the Gulf War, we were in Israel together for the third time in war conditions: the first had been in 1967, the second, 1973. In 1991 we gave concerts as soon as the orchestra was allowed to play again – for security reasons, they could not for a number of weeks. In the middle of February Isaac Stern came and the world was made aware of what music meant not only to the players of the orchestra but also to the audience. In the middle of a concert in Jerusalem with Stern, Mehta and the Philharmonic, the sirens sounded and the orchestra had to stop playing, the whole audience had to put on their gas masks, and Isaac came back on stage to play Bach unaccompanied on the violin. My young colleague Yefim Bronfman also played, and I performed in the very last days of the war with the orchestra and with Zubin.

This experience during the Gulf War in Israel and another, in certain ways very different one, which took place in Berlin in November 1989 with the dismantling of the Wall, have made me reflect on the falseness of the argument that culture is something that one can devote oneself to or afford only when 'real problems' have been solved. It is an argument very often used by politicians who, when there is a need to save money, look first at culture. These two different experiences have made it very clear to me that music can and should mean something other than what this argument presumes the attitude of the public to be. In Israel in February 1991, when the sirens sounded because of the missile attacks coming from Iraq, people had to get up twice a night, put on their gas masks, go into sealed rooms and wait for five minutes to see whether they were to survive. This put tremendous psychological pressure on the population of Israel. And yet, as soon as it was safe to do so, the Israel Philharmonic started playing two concerts a day, at twelve o'clock midday and at three o'clock in the afternoon, because it was not safe enough in the evening. Only five hundred people at a time were allowed into the auditorium, and they had to bring their gas masks. There was a real need for music to be played, for the musicians to be able to play and for the audience to listen. For some, it was a way of forgetting the tension of the night before, for others it was a moment to hope, of not thinking of the next night with the inevitable alarms sounding. In every case, it was anything but a superficial form of entertainment.

In Berlin in November 1989, when the Wall came down, it was the musicians of the Berlin Philharmonic Orchestra who wanted, spontaneously, to play for the people of East Germany, who had not been able to come and hear the orchestra during the years when the Wall divided the city. The concert that I was privileged to conduct on 12 November 1989 was an expression not only of the joy that the musicians felt at being able to play for their countrymen from East Germany, and the joy of the audience on hearing the Berlin Philharmonic, but also of the need that people feel to make and hear music at a time of intense emotion.

~

I went back to Israel when I had finished Carlo Zecchi's conducting class in Siena. October 1956 saw the start of the Sinai Campaign, which outside Israel is known as the Suez War. The Israelis, in conjunction with the French and the British, went into Egypt. Although I was not actively involved in it, this is my first memory of war. There was a blackout in Tel Aviv, mainly as a precautionary measure. It was amazing how we continued to play concerts every evening with the Israel Philharmonic Orchestra in spite of the war. The public seemed to need music even more passionately at this difficult time. The conductor was Francesco Molinari-Pradelli, who won everybody's affection with the courage he displayed by staying in Israel. Another non-Jewish musician who refused to leave was Zino Francescatti.

Israel was at war and surrounded by enemies who wanted to 'throw the Jews into the sea'. If you look at the country's geographical situation, you will see how easily this could have been done. It is well known that Israel managed to survive thanks to its determination to defend itself, and to its strong army.

There was a feeling of claustrophobia in Israel: if you wanted to get away, for holidays or anything else, you were forced to go to another continent. In a minor way you could compare our situation with that of West Berlin – with the difference that it was not the declared intention of the people in East Germany to throw the inhabitants of West Berlin into the sea. For us it was not a question of travelling by train from Switzerland to Italy in a couple of hours – we had to fly or go by boat.

In December 1956 I went on my first trip to North America and gave my first concerts there, thanks to an invaluable introduction from Artur Rubinstein. My first concert in New York in January 1957 was what might be described as a fair success: it was not a failure, but no sensation either. I think that my agent, Sol Hurok, had to work hard to secure me further engagements. I was no longer a child, and yet not grown-up – a difficult age, not only for me, but also as regards public acceptance. However, Sol Hurok was constantly encouraged by Rubinstein not to lose faith in me – and he never did.

~

When I was a child in Buenos Aires, Rubinstein often played there. It was always a great occasion – he was one of the most popular musicians, and people queued all night, and sometimes even longer, in order to get a ticket – they were mad about him. I remember the feeling of pride when I was thought grown-up enough to be allowed to stand in the queue for two hours. Each member of the family would take it in turns to go and queue, and I was allowed to go from ten o'clock in the morning to buy tickets for the recital in the Teatro Colón.

There were two pieces he played of which I have particularly clear memories – one was Schumann's *Carnaval*, and the other Beethoven's *Appassionata* Sonata. I remember vividly my sheer fascination at his playing, at the sound he made, and even at the way he sat at the piano, erect and simple, without all those distortions that I saw later on in other pianists. He really was a legend. My parents had a photograph of him with a personal dedication to my father. When I met him later on, he told me that he already knew my parents when my mother was pregnant with me.

Among the people I met in Paris in 1955 was the Polish composer Alexandre Tansman, a friend of Stravinsky. He seemed quite taken with me, and thought I should play for Rubinstein. My father did not want to approach Rubinstein himself, feeling that he might think, 'Here is this acquaintance from Argentina wanting to push his talented son on me.' But, if Tansman could arrange it, it would of course be wonderful! So it was arranged that I should play for Rubinstein. Accompanied by Tansman, I went to Paris, where Rubinstein lived in the Place de l'Avenue Foch. Rubinstein was terribly late, and equally upset to have kept us waiting. We sat down and I played for him. I was twelve or thirteen at the time, and what impressed him most was Prokofiev's Second Sonata. I remember this because he often mentioned it in later years. I played everything I could think of, and then, an hour or so later, my parents came to pick me up. One can imagine Rubinstein's surprise, for he had no idea whose son I was.

He was extremely kind and generous. He suggested that I should play in America and said that he would introduce me to his manager. At that time, New York was really the centre of the musical world. Europe was still in the process of being rebuilt. Germany, in addition, had its own problems: there were many artists who did not want to appear there – Rubinstein, Vladimir Horowitz, Jascha Heifetz, Isaac Stern, and others.

One day Mrs Rubinstein phoned to ask whether I could come to their house that evening. There were a great many people, including Sol Hurok and Ernesto de Quesada – the latter had been Rubinstein's manager in Spain and Latin America since the First World War. I played for them and Rubinstein told Hurok that he felt I should play in America but that I should not be exploited, and that he should see to it that my parents could accompany me as I was so young. He also told Hurok that he would not make any money out of me for a number of years, but that he felt sure I was heading for a great career. Rubinstein practically negotiated my first contract for me!

I have never forgotten his generosity. And he always kept in touch. Two or three years later he came to Israel, when I naturally went to all his concerts. He always asked me to come and play for him; he was anxious to see how I was developing, and kept a close eye on me.

I remember quite an amusing incident in Israel. Rubinstein was staying at a hotel outside Tel Aviv, and one morning, when I attended his rehearsal with the Israel Philharmonic, he invited me to come to see him the following afternoon. I must have been fifteen or sixteen at the time. When I arrived at the hotel, the porter told me that Mr Rubinstein had gone on an excursion to Galilee with his family. I said this was very odd, as he was expecting me at five o'clock. I was ill and had a high temperature, but the last thing I wanted was to cancel the appointment. So I sat in the hotel lounge and waited for at least two hours. At last Rubinstein arrived, and I could read the consternation in his face – he had forgotten our appointment, and he saw that I was not well. But I was so happy to see him, so pleased to be there, that he was quite touched. We went to his room, and I played a Schubert Impromptu in F minor, Brahms's *Handel Variations* and the Liszt Sonata. He gave me some advice, particularly about the Liszt Sonata, which he saw as having a kind of Faust theme, and he explained his ideas about the relationships between the tempi and about sound. When I was ready to go, he said, 'No, no, you must stay and have dinner with us,' which was an extraordinary thing for a young boy like myself. It was the first time I drank vodka, and he gave me a cigar. You can imagine my mother's face when I got home about two o'clock in the morning. My parents had no idea where I had been and I had quite a lot of explaining to do!

Rubinstein was famous for the unique sound he produced on the piano. It was truly noble and full – he disliked what you might call a disembodied sound (which can be quite useful for playing French music). To him, sound had to have a centre and a natural and expressive quality. He frequently warned me – especially with regard to the Liszt Sonata – about the pianissimo becoming so ephemeral that there was no body left in the sound. Even when Rubinstein played very loudly, however, the sound was never hard. He had a way of almost leaning on the keyboard – sometimes he even got up from his chair with his fingers still on the chord – to make the contact clear. He insisted that, at the most dramatic moments of a piece, one must never hurry but let the phrase sing at the top of the melody, at the top of the climax. He also had a unique sense of rhythm, of correct rhythm; there was something almost physical about his rhythmical stability. He claimed that when he was younger he had played many things too fast, but his wonderful sense of rhythm added a sense of great pride to some of his playing, especially the typically Polish pieces like Chopin's polonaises and mazurkas. He made me aware of the relationship between rhythm and the feeling of pride. He taught me the connection between very short staccato figures and a certain comic effect, especially when played by the bassoons in an orchestra. A similar association can be created in a Haydn symphony: when there is an unexpected pause and an empty bar, it can also produce a comic kind of effect. When you think of music that has pride in it, there is always a concrete rhythm. It does not need to be military, but it should have a strong sense of rhythm. And Rubinstein had that to the end of his life. It was one of his most valuable assets, just as the sound he produced was personal and unique. His sense of rhythm gave his playing an inimitable vitality. The Chopin F sharp minor Polonaise sounded like an orchestra when played by Rubinstein.

When I started conducting, Rubinstein was one of the few people who did not say: 'Be careful because your piano playing will suffer.' He was interested in other music besides the piano. He knew *Salome* by heart, he loved *Die Meistersinger*, he went to the opera, he knew symphonic literature. He was an all-round musician, with an all-round musical awareness, and he encouraged me greatly when I started conducting.

In 1966 I was in Prague at the same time as Rubinstein and his wife. He was playing with the Czech Philharmonic and I was conducting the English Chamber Orchestra. It was one of my first trips with this orchestra and Rubinstein was very interested in this new stage of my career. The only thing he felt unsure about was whether playing and conducting at the same time was a good idea, and it was not until later, when he came to one of my concerts and saw and heard me do both together, that he was convinced. He attended my concerts whenever he could – in New York, and in Paris in the early 1960s – and he always invited me to his house afterwards.

In 1966, he bought a house in Marbella and invited me there. I had to refuse because at the end of August and the beginning of September I was at the Edinburgh Festival, and after that I was ill with glandular fever. This is how I met Jacqueline du Pré: she, too, had the illness very badly and we started talking on the phone, comparing notes. A few months later, Rubinstein was in Portugal, where he heard Jacqueline's first recordings and was very taken by her playing. Then he invited us both – we were married by that time – to his house in Spain. He always made us play for him – he loved hearing Jacqueline – and there were innumerable occasions when we played until the early hours of the morning.

In January 1967 I conducted what was, I suppose, my first major concert in Europe, apart from those with the English Chamber Orchestra. It was in London with the Philharmonia Orchestra, known as the New Philharmonia Orchestra in those days, and we played Mozart's Requiem. It was a much publicized affair because I had taken over the concert at a few days' notice from a conductor who had fallen ill and people did not expect very much from me. After all, I was better known as a pianist. I think I was asked only because they could get no one else to conduct the concert. Anyway, it was a success and opened up a large number of opportunities for me in many places. A few months later, it must have been the spring of 1967, when I was in Paris and invited to a meal at the Rubinsteins, he told me: 'The manager of the Israel Philharmonic was here just now. I am supposed to play there in September – would you like to come and conduct that concert?' It was a concert to celebrate the tenth anniversary of the opening of the new concert hall in Tel Aviv. This is how Rubinstein became my first soloist! It was a wonderful sign of his confidence in me. After that, I often played with him, until his final retirement. I recorded the Beethoven concertos with him, and Jacqueline and I felt almost like members of the family. When I was appointed Music Director of the Orchestre de Paris I visited him regularly – his house was always open to me – and we performed in Paris together every year until he stopped playing altogether.

Rubinstein wanted to record the Beethoven concertos again, but not the first and second because he had not played those so often. At a concert in London in March 1975 he was due to play the fourth and fifth on the same evening. The concert was on a Sunday, and Rubinstein arrived on the Saturday. We had a short rehearsal and then dined together, staying quite late. In those days I was quite good at doing imitations – I imitated all sorts of people, other pianists and so on, but not him, of course. My imitation of Rubinstein was reserved for the other members of his family. I never quite dared to do it in front of him – out of respect as well as fear that he might not laugh! The next morning we went to the rehearsal – he was then eighty-eight, but quite happy to play both concertos again from beginning to end. Of all the great artists I have worked with during my life, soloists or conductors, Rubinstein was by far the most direct and least pretentious. He used to say: 'You are the conductor, you are responsible for the concert, what time do I have to be there?' He could have laid down his own conditions, but he had exemplary professionalism.

We gave the concert that evening, the next day we recorded the two concertos in two sessions, and then did the third concerto the day after. He was quite excited because everything had gone so well and said that he also wanted to do the other two but would need about a week to freshen them up. Two or three weeks later we recorded them.

So much has been written about Rubinstein – that he was a bon vivant, that he liked good cigars. Of course all this was true, but I do not think the written word can ever do justice to the man or to the richness of his character. There was something so alive, so charming, so vital, so intelligent, so cultured about him. He was a marvellous raconteur, and some of this was caught on television, but there was also a very serious side to him, especially as a musician. He retained his great interest in and curiosity about things to the end of his life. Even when he could no longer play himself, he spent most of his time listening to all kinds of chamber music that he had not had time to hear or study before. I remember how fascinated he was when he discovered the Mozart Piano and Wind Quintet.

He used to play in America from November until February or March, and in Europe in the spring. We played together in Paris in 1974 at the Champs Élysée Theatre and were supposed to play again in 1975. But he did not want to make up his mind about playing until he had come back from America, because he was beginning to feel his age a little and had difficulties with his eyes. He took great pride in the fact that, throughout his life, he had never, or hardly ever, had to cancel a concert, and he did not want to commit himself now when he was unsure whether he could keep the promise. When he got back from America in March, he told me that he felt all right and that he wanted to play. By this time the very large Palais des Congrès had been built in Paris, but it was available for only one evening, all the others having been booked.

People felt it was a pity that he would be giving only one concert. There were so many people who wished to hear Rubinstein play, but it was impossible to find another date when both the hall and orchestra would be free. When I explained this to him he said, well, all we can do is to play twice on the same day, as in the cinema, once in the afternoon and once in the evening. He played Beethoven's *Emperor* Concerto. The first concert was at six-thirty or seven, and the second at nine or nine-thirty, and there was absolutely no sign that he was physically exhausted.

Orchestras all over the world have certain rules – one of them says that they must not do more than two sessions a day, which is right, as it would otherwise be easy to overwork them. But this meant we were faced with a difficult situation – if we wanted to do the concert, we also had to rehearse with him in the morning. This eighty-eight-year-old man was willing to do three sessions in one day! The orchestra committee had been asked to make an exception in this case, and they did, for Rubinstein – I think it was the only time such a thing has happened. This was the last time I played with him. I saw him for the last time about three weeks before he died. He was already quite ill, but happy to see me because he knew I was going to have a child. I told him that if it was a boy, he would be named after him ... My elder son's name is David Arthur.

In retrospect, one of the most interesting things about my conducting with Rubinstein was that we played most of the works I had played myself, with the exception of the Chopin F minor

Concerto. He had a unique flair for convincing one that the way he played a piece was the only possible way of playing it. He was also very open and alert to what was happening in the orchestra – he knew how to play chamber music with a symphony orchestra. He did not play a phrase in a certain way because that was how he had always played it, but was always aware during the concert of how the orchestral introduction was leading up to the entry of the piano. He was the most chivalrous accompanist when there was a big solo in the orchestra, the clarinet, for instance, in the first movement of the Schumann Concerto, and he took great pleasure in following it. There was none of the attitude of 'I am the great Rubinstein, and I play at this tempo and everybody else had better fit in.' He had great respect for his fellow musicians, especially those in the orchestra.

5

FROM CHILD TO ADULT

I had another meeting in Paris, when I was studying with Nadia Boulanger, which was very important in my development – I played for Leopold Stokowski, also at Alexandre Tansman's house. I had heard a lot about Stokowski; he had achieved greater fame than most musicians through his work in Hollywood, particularly on Walt Disney's *Fantasia*. Later I was astounded to find how much he had accomplished with the Philadelphia Orchestra and how interested he was in contemporary music. He conducted Arnold Schoenberg's *Gurrelieder* in Philadelphia at a very early date, which was the first American performance.

He, too, was extremely kind to me. I played various pieces in different styles and his comment was: 'This is very good, would you like to play in New York?' What a question! I said, yes, of course I would, and he asked: 'What would you like to play?' I told him, Beethoven's Third Piano Concerto. 'Very good,' he replied, 'you shall play Prokofiev's Concerto No. 1.' Even today, Prokofiev's First Piano Concerto is played very rarely, and in those days it was totally unknown. Naturally, I had no choice – I wanted to play in New York – and playing with Stokowski was a unique opportunity. So I sat down and learned Prokofiev's First Piano Concerto, and played it at my début. Considering that I had played mainly the German classics and Romantics like Beethoven, Mozart, and Brahms, it was strange that my first concert in New York should have been the Prokofiev concerto.

The programme of my first concert as a pianist with the Berlin Philharmonic was another unusual choice: Bartók's First Piano Concerto, which I also had to learn specially for the occasion. I think it is very good to be forced to learn certain things at an early age.

Later one can make one's own selection, but Bartók's First Piano Concerto has remained in my repertoire. I have played it innumerable times all over America, in Europe, and in Israel, and I still have the highest regard for it – I always feel a sense of adventure when playing it. But the Prokofiev concerto I have not played again since that first time in January 1957.

I shall always thank my father that, as a child and adolescent, I was made to learn such a broad spectrum of the repertoire. I played everything imaginable – for instance, Prokofiev's Ninth Sonata, his last, in Paris in 1955, only two years after his death. I think that was its first performance in the West. The only area in my musical education that may have been neglected is the second Viennese school. I came to Schoenberg and Alban Berg considerably later, mostly through my contact with Pierre Boulez. In the early 1960s, my interest in twentieth-century music came from my education at home, and later also from Nadia Boulanger who was, however, totally uninterested in the works of Schoenberg and Berg.

There is no doubt that Stokowski was a great showman, but he also had very detailed technical knowledge of the orchestra, and his preoccupation with sound and colour was not just showmanship. One might call him a manipulator of sound. Towards the end of the 1960s in England, there was a television broadcast of Beethoven's Fifth Symphony, which he conducted. I did not see it myself but to my amazement Otto Klemperer had seen it and was very impressed, and he recognized Stokowski as a great conductor.

Stokowski had anything but an orthodox career, unlike Arturo Toscanini, for instance, who stayed in New York with the Philharmonic, and for whom the NBC Orchestra was later created. Stokowski, however, was interested in young musicians and young orchestras. The All-American Youth Orchestra was one of them – they even came to Argentina in the 1940s. Today there is the wonderful European Union Youth Orchestra, but in the late 1950s people were not all that interested in youth orchestras. Stokowski conducted the Symphony of the Air Orchestra, which was the successor to the NBC Orchestra after Toscanini's death, and he also conducted the American Symphony Orchestra. One could say that after his reaching a peak with the Philadelphia Orchestra, he was still active for many years, if in a less conventional way. He spent most of the last years of his life in Europe, where he conducted a number of concerts in England and elsewhere.

But the Stokowski legend is linked to his Hollywood period, which probably has something to do with a tendency to typecast people. Among composers, Mozart is often regarded as a rococo cavalier, Beethoven as a Titan, Chopin as a tubercular melancholic, Liszt as a Don Juan with a religious aura in his later years. The same applies to performers, and it rarely does them justice. I often heard wonderful performances of works that were quite different from what I had been led to expect. I remember the Franck Symphony in D minor beautifully conducted by Furtwängler, a marvellous performance of Berlioz's *Symphonie fantastique* conducted by Klemperer. Probably the most satisfying interpretation of Debussy I have ever heard live was by Claudio Arrau.

From 1957 on, I started giving regular recitals every year at the Wigmore Hall in London. The Queen Elizabeth Hall was not built until 1967 and the Wigmore Hall was really the only hall available for such recitals, except for artists like Rubinstein, who played at the large Royal Festival Hall. The cycle of recitals at the Wigmore Hall, under the title The London Pianoforte Series, took place on Sunday afternoons, and I played there regularly for about eight or ten years.

Success came only gradually. When I played there for the first time, there may have been only fifty to eighty people in the audience but, little by little, and with a lot of perseverance, I built up a name for myself by these regular appearances. But it was not until ten years later, in the 1960s, that I gave my first recital at the Festival Hall.

Between 1957 and 1959 I regularly gave five or six concerts a year in the USA. On one occasion, in 1957, I played with Dimitri Mitropoulos and members of the New York Philharmonic Orchestra. He had the most phenomenal memory of anyone I have ever met. I remember attending his rehearsal of Berg's *Wozzeck* in Salzburg in 1955, with the Vienna Philharmonic. He always rehearsed from memory and knew every note by heart, as well as the text. It was absolutely staggering. The story is told that when he was Music Director in Minneapolis and was supposed to conduct the world première of a new American piece, the orchestral parts did not arrive until the day before the first rehearsal, and the conductor's score never arrived at all. So he took the orchestra parts home and spread them out on the floor in the way the orchestra sits. He then memorized the piece overnight and the next morning rehearsed it from memory.

He was a very pure musician of great intensity and integrity. When I played with him in New York, the programme was Mendelssohn's G minor Concerto. It was a benefit concert for the America-Israel Cultural Foundation in New York, which had given me a scholarship to go to Paris. Having been a pupil of Busoni he was also a fine pianist. I had a piano rehearsal with him before the orchestra rehearsed, and he played the orchestral part, from memory, with great agility. He was very self-effacing, and probably one of the most altruistic people I ever met.

In 1958, in addition to concerts in North America and Europe, I went to Australia for the first time. This was a far more complicated procedure in those days than it is now. There were no direct flights, and many stops en route. You could only tour Australia if you stayed a relatively long time and my first tour took four months. In Australia, as in South America, the months in which seasons fall are the opposite of those in Europe, so the trip coincided with my school holidays. July and August were the main months for giving concerts there. I played over forty concerts, and for the first time performed with Rafael Kubelík. I remember my first encounter with him with great pleasure. He impressed me tremendously with his combination of seriousness and great vivacity. I had met very vivacious people before, but they were often superficial; I had met serious people before, but they lacked Kubelík's vivacity. I played Beethoven's Third and Fourth Concertos with him in Melbourne. I remember one phrase in the Third Concerto where I played an unforgivable crescendo in the middle of a passage that was marked piano and Kubelík told me, 'Of course, what you are doing is wonderfully effective, even beautiful, but you must sometimes sacrifice the beauty of the moment for the beauty of a long line and structure.' The concept was not new to me because I had grown up with it, but Kubelík's articulation was so clear, and linked to such a very precise case in point, that I have always remembered it.

I had the greatest admiration for him as a musician and as a human being. He was one of the few examples of a really independent musician – he had adopted a line without any artistic compromise, the line of most and not of least resistance.

The reception for my concerts in Australia was good but not overwhelming – there was always mixed criticism. I played at every little town during my travels, with an extensive repertoire of pieces – a Brahms concerto, Tchaikovsky's Concerto No. 2 and, of course, Beethoven's concertos.

The head of the Australian Broadcasting Commission at that time was Charles Moses – a most impressive and authoritative personality, with a great sense of humour. He took a special liking to me, and invited me back to Australia in 1962. In those days, Australia was the only place where one planned three or four years in advance. I had already conducted a few concerts with the Haifa Orchestra in Israel – a small orchestra in those days – and I really wanted to do more conducting. So I told him that I would also want to conduct next time I came. He agreed and booked me, for 1962, to give one concert with the Melbourne Symphony Orchestra and another with the Sydney Symphony Orchestra. It was really from the time of this second Australian trip that conducting became a regular part of my life.

After my first Australian tour I went back to school in Israel. In 1959–60 I was seventeen, and life was not too easy from the career point of view. I was neither a child nor an adult, so there was no longer any interest in the 'child prodigy', nor as yet an interest in my adult development. I had no concerts in the USA, very little to do, and went through the usual adolescent crisis. I remember being very upset, unhappy about my life and wondering what I was going to do. There was a small auditorium in Tel Aviv, in the so-called Journalists' House (*Beit sokolow*), and the man who organized concerts there asked whether I would like to give a few recitals. With the reckless-ness of adolescence I said, yes, I would like to play all the Beethoven sonatas – and I did! It was spring 1960, I was seventeen, my last year at school, and every Saturday I gave a recital. It was a therapy for all my unhappiness. I had started something where I had to work hard and constantly. I learned all the Beethoven sonatas and played them in eight consecutive concerts.

~

One of the dangers of playing in public is to be too conscious of the audience. In other words, you must not go on stage thinking you are going to impress them, nor with a strong wish to project this or that.

I think the best communication between artist and audience occurs if the artist becomes unaware of the public as soon as he or she starts playing. The audience receives the strongest projection of a musical performance when the performer is concentrating solely on the music. But this, of course, is not always easy to do. I remember Rubinstein saying that he could never really work or practise if anybody was present. He told me the charming story that, even when he was in his hotel room and the waiter brought in the breakfast, he immediately and automatically started to play for the waiter. It was just not the same as playing alone!

The fact that the piano is such a neutral, uninteresting instrument is precisely what enables you to create far more colours on it. The basic fact is simple – you cannot produce a single beautiful sound on the piano. By combining a wonderful Stradivarius and a great violinist, a single beautiful note can be produced by varying the colour, the intensity and the volume of the note. With the piano, the concept of beauty starts with two notes. As soon as one note is softer or louder or shorter, and you are able to articulate the difference between two notes, you can begin to create an expressive sound on the piano. If you take this to its logical, almost ridiculous conclusion, you see that one of the most important qualities required for playing the piano is an ability to create what painters call a perspective. When you look at a painting, you can see that some elements appear nearer to you and others further away. The piano works in a similar way. It creates an illusion. You can create the illusion of legato. In order to make a portamento sound like a singer, you have to go from one note to the next without breaking it. All the great pianists of the past like Busoni or Eugen d'Albert – I can only judge this from recordings – had this ability in one form or another.

The notes played on the piano are balanced in such a way that some seem closer to the ear. It means, as I have said before, that the two hands do not represent two units, but one unit, or ten. The independence of the fingers is all-important, and I can only recommend, with great emphasis, that pianists should constantly work at the fugues from Bach's *Well-Tempered Clavier*.

No matter what instrument you play, or whether you conduct or sing, you will only produce the sound you want if you can hear it in your head a fraction of a second beforehand. This is the part of music which is impossible to teach. I could teach people how to put down their hands, how to balance the two Ds, the three Gs and the three Bs in the opening chord of Beethoven's G major Concerto, that there is a register where the note has a tendency to be louder, and that the thumb has more weight than the little finger. But if a student is unable to imagine the sound before he starts to play – even if it differs from what I am trying to explain to him – he will never produce the sound he wants. This ability to hear the sound and the phrasing you want in the inner ear is one of the most essential qualities.

The other quality that cannot be taught is the intensity of feeling towards the music, the relationship between musician and music. There are many elements in music that can be explained, elements that are not only intuitive. What you cannot explain is the degree of intensity. The greatness of a musician is measured by the degree of fanaticism he brings to his playing. If you want to play a sforzando, for instance, but do not want it to sound harsh, you lean on the note. If you are unable to produce that at a given moment, it should cause you almost physical pain. If you are able to say, 'Well, so the accent was a little more harsh than I intended,' that is not good enough. The degree of intensity between musician and music is projected to and understood by the audience.

The physical characteristics of the hands can have their advantages and disadvantages. There are some passages in Chopin or Liszt where you need a very wide span, which is more difficult for me than, perhaps, for other pianists. There are some pieces I cannot play, like Bartók's Second Concerto, which is one of my favourite pieces of twentieth-century music, simply because I cannot stretch my hand far enough. But I have seen pianists with much larger hands who can manage all that, but who have difficulty in reducing the size of the hand when playing certain passages which require precise finger control. There are certain pieces, like Brahms's First Piano Concerto, where the actual physical strain of playing is part of the music. There is a story about Schumann wanting to make his hand bigger. He disfigured it, using a mechanical device designed to stretch its span.

Playing music well is a matter of balancing the technical and the musical sides. You cannot separate the two – every technical solution has an influence on the musical expression. For instance, in the last movement of Beethoven's *Appassionata* Sonata it is difficult enough for a pianist to play the notes at the required speed but not as difficult as playing the sonata with full expression, as far as musical line, phrasing and intensity are concerned. The Greek word *tekhne* (τεχνή) means 'art' but the term 'technical' is now used exclusively to signify the mechanical aspect of an artistic performance. When the technical problems of finger dexterity have been solved, it is too late to add musicality, phrasing and musical expression. That is why I never practise mechanically. One must maintain a certain unity from the start. If we work mechanically, we run the risk of changing the very nature of music. If we define 'art' as the application of skill to the work of creative imagination, we use 'technique' as it is misunderstood today, namely as meaning something mechanical. Something purely mechanical cannot be considered as skill.

Another term that often leads to confusion is 'musicality'. It is not used as often in English as in German and French. 'Musicality' is a somewhat ambiguous description of a sensitivity to musical expression. It is a much-abused term, often coupled with another frequently misunderstood term, 'inspiration'. Inspiration is not a divine gift for which we can passively wait. You cannot train mechanically and hope that, during the actual performance, some divine inspiration will descend upon you. We should not be amazed by the beauty of music, but we should endeavour to fathom the cause of its beauty, to understand its laws and its ingredients. Only then can a divine spark illuminate what was perceived by reason. Shakespeare actually defined skill as reason. Inspiration can only constitute the next step after reason has been applied. It will certainly not come about while waiting for a miracle, like the advent of the Messiah.

Music involves a number of simple rules: no mechanical training, no passive waiting for inspiration, but rather a conscious search for a link between the expression and the means of attaining the desired effect. Seemingly opposing elements form a unit: the rational, the emotional, the technical, and the musical elements are really indivisible. Making music must be a conscious process. Inspiration and intuition come more easily if the groundwork has been done.

I cannot see music as a profession but rather as a way of life. Immersion, complete concentration, is a condition *sine qua non* for the interpreter and performer, because the conscious projection of music for the pleasure of the listener instantly changes the character of a performance. We must not permit our thoughts to wander: the best way to communicate with the listener is to communicate with ourselves, and with the music we are performing.

Our going on stage to perform a piece of music is almost an act of egocentricity, because we assume that what we are about to do is worth the instant and full attention of two or three thousand people in the audience. As soon as the performance is over, this egocentricity must be eliminated, otherwise it will make our life, and those of others, unbearable. Purified of outward show, the ego can become the centre of creation and imagination. It is as negative to build on the quality of the ego as it is to disregard it.

As far as the thinking, rational aspect of recreating music is concerned, there comes a moment when you have to make a synthesis, when you cannot produce all the different interpretations at the same time. The two concepts go together – the analytic goes from effect to cause, and the synthetic from cause to effect. The knowledge of an effect depends on, and involves, the knowledge of the cause. Different composers may have concentrated on different expressive elements – the development of certain instruments may have added further possibilities – but all these belong to the temporary and changeable means of expression, and not to the expression itself. So even in a philosophical sense it can be said that to rely on anything that is mechanical or not thought out properly means arriving at a misinterpretation.

If we try to understand music as philosophy, we find that it includes three disciplines – physics, metaphysics and psychology: physics because a musical composition only exists as physical sound, and is subject to the physical laws of acoustics and overtones; metaphysics, for what it is capable of expressing beyond the physical – a poetic way of expressing this would be to say that music can make a silence audible; and psychology, because the different elements in a musical composition relate to each other, certain elements being more or less dominant, with tension between harmonies, rhythms, or patterns that are reminiscent of psychological situations.

Every performance must retain a natural quality and not reveal the analytical work which preceded it. During a performance the

Playing the spinet, Mozart's birthplace, Salzburg, 1952.

With Bruno Bandini and the Radio Orchestra, Argentina, 1951.

With my parents in Salzburg, 1955.

My parents and I with Wilhelm Furtwängler in Salzburg, 1955.

With Markevich, in his conducting class, Salzburg, 1954.

Rehearsing with Joseph Krips for my Royal Festival Hall début, London, 1956.

Left: With Zubin Mehta
in Tel Aviv, 1965.

Playing Bartók with the
Berlin Philharmonic,
1964.

With Jacqueline at our wedding in Jerusalem, 1967.

Left: At our wedding reception in Tel Aviv with Zubin Mehta and Sir John and Lady Barbirolli.

Right: At our wedding reception in Tel Aviv with David Ben Gurion and his wife, Paula.

Jacqueline in the Royal Albert Hall, c. 1969.

Recording with Jacqueline and Pinchas Zukerman,
Abbey Road Studios, London, 1969.

Jacqueline and I with Pablo Casals, Marlboro, USA, in 1969.

Recording the Brahms *Requiem* with Dietrich Fischer-Dieskau in Edinburgh, 1972.

Rehearsing, on tour with the English Chamber Orchestra, in the late 1960s.

My first concert as conductor with the Chicago Symphony Orchestra, 1970.

CBS supper party for Leonard Bernstein on his 55th birthday, August 1973. *Front row:* Janet Osborn, Felicia and Leonard Bernstein, Pierre Boulez, Jacqueline and I.

uring the recording of the Beethoven piano concertos with Artur Rubinstein, London, 1974.

With Artur Rubinstein and the Israel Philharmonic in the Royal Albert Hall, London.

With Zubin Mehta, Olivier Messiaen and his wife in Paris in the late 1970s.

With Boulez in Paris, recording his *Notations*, 1988.

With Wolfgang Wagner before my first Bayreuth rehearsal, 1981.

Below: Bayreuth, 1981: with René Kollo, Wolfgang Wagner and Johanna Meier after the première of *Tristan.*

Opposite above: Performing in 1989.

Opposite below: With Sir Georg Solti, Pierre Boulez and Zubin Mehta after a concert by the Orchestre de Paris in London, 1988.

Playing with and conducting the Chicago Symphony Orchestra, Chicago, 1991.

conscious and the subconscious, the rational and the intuitive become one – you should feel that you can think with your emotions and feel with your thoughts.

The problems of human existence have not been answered by the progress we witness in technology and other sciences. The human being has always had to live with himself. He has to establish his position within his family and within society. This may be what Spinoza means by the need to discover the union between mind and nature. This is what music is about, and this is what renders it so unalterable. We may be able to change Beethoven's orchestration, or use a modern piano with far greater possibilities than the instruments Beethoven was familiar with, but his music, the expression of his place in the universe, remains unchanged.

Every work of art has 'two faces', one directed towards eternity and the other towards its own time. There are conventions or fashions typical of a certain epoch, and some compositions express an epoch. This aspect of a composition may age and be of little interest to future generations. The part that remains is the spirit of the work, its essence. Music is therefore completely independent; it needs neither confirmation of its values, nor the help of science or other arts in order to exist and to be understood. A musical composition should be seen as existing by itself and for itself, and not as having been created for a purpose, however positive or beneficial. It can be used for a profitable end, material or spiritual, but the music itself has no such characteristics. Music is not only descriptive of other things. It is neither benevolent nor malevolent. Superficially we know that music can imitate sounds – a bird, or the waves of the sea – but that is a minor detail. A certain musical atmosphere may remind us of a love scene, another of a majestic procession, but these evocations are representative of us and not of the music. I often experience totally different feelings about the same piece of music at different times. It may be an oversimplification to say that if one feels sad, a piece of music may enhance this feeling, and if one is happy, one may find the same piece of music joyful. There has, of course, never been an occasion to think of the funeral march in the *Eroica* Symphony as happy music, but this is the exception rather than the rule.

We can perceive the infinite in music only by searching for this quality in ourselves. As human beings we do not possess infinite qualities, but as musicians I believe we can extend our finite power to a point where we can create an illusion of infinity. It is only by knowing ourselves that we come to know the things outside ourselves. When working with music, we must know if a certain passage gives rise to a difficulty in physical control, or to an excitement that throws our reason and understanding aside. I think it is dangerous to emulate great musicians who were less attractive as human beings. Wagner is an obvious example. His negative qualities did not make him the great composer he was: he was a great composer *in spite of* these negative qualities.

This may sound pretentious but, if artists are honest with themselves, they will admit that they have a tendency to feel that they are a law unto themselves. The transition from music making to everyday life is very difficult. Qualities that are necessary for the one may not necessarily be positive for the other. This may be the reason why so many artists have difficulties in their personal lives. I always feel like advising young musicians that they should be very clear about these two aspects – to retain all the determination and fire and authority in their unique art but to remember that there is nothing unique in their outside lives. We are all very much of a muchness!

In 1960, when I played the complete cycle of Beethoven sonatas for the first time, I met a musician with whom I was to become very close in later years, and whom I greatly respected – Sir Clifford Curzon. He was playing with the Israel Philharmonic Orchestra, and was sufficiently interested in me to come and hear one of my Beethoven recitals on his evening off. There was a generosity and appealing warmth in the way he treated me. Later I came to know him quite well, and often conducted concerts for him. He came from a very different background – that of an English gentleman of an earlier generation. He was a nervous type who rarely found things simple or easy. I was totally different – young, a product of the very positive Israeli philosophy of education, and to me so many of the things that worried Curzon seemed to have been made unnecessarily difficult and negative. But I had great admiration for him as a musician and as a pianist. Some of the most satisfying performances, particularly of the Mozart concertos, I owe to him. I once heard him play something not closely associated with him, the Grieg Piano Concerto, where he produced quite extraordinary colours on the piano, and a performance of Liszt's A major Concerto which I conducted with the Cleveland Orchestra remains in my memory as one of the most convincing interpretations of the piece.

Curzon had a very personal sense of sound – especially with Mozart and Schubert. He produced a bell-like quality on the piano. He had an almost fastidious sense of rhythm which was developed in his work with Wanda Landowska, who used to encourage a great amount of freedom within a classical framework. Curzon suffered tremendously under nervous strain during concerts, and there was a certain *élan* about his playing at home which he found difficult to achieve in public. Curzon came from the Schnabel school, where he had been a pupil of Artur Schnabel himself and Wanda Landowska, and he told me a lot about their teaching, which I found fascinating.

There were basically three distinct camps for piano music: the admirers of the virtuoso school, who had no time for either Fischer or Schnabel; the so-called intellectuals, who were fascinated by Schnabel's analytical capacities, as manifested in his edition of the Beethoven sonatas, and who regarded Edwin Fischer as a sensitive and vivacious but purely intuitive, improvising type of pianist. The third camp, the Fischer camp, looked of course upon the Schnabel adherents as being far too intellectual and rational. It was through my friendship with Sir Clifford Curzon that I became aware that a musician could combine great flair and intuition with deep thought and analysis, and that this was the essence of Schnabel. Schnabel was criticized by the purists for being too emotional, and by admirers of the intuitive approach for being too cerebral. In actual fact there is no contradiction between these two qualities.

One did have the feeling that a slight lack of intellectualism in Fischer was interpreted almost as a lack of intelligence. I do not agree with this at all. There was a certain naivety, a preoccupation with naturalness. Everything had to sound as natural as possible. He always looked for naivety in musical expression, in the positive sense, for freshness and purity, the very opposite of manipulation. At the start there should be a naive encounter with a work of art. The next, more complicated stage concerns the way one works and what one can learn from analysis and observation. This should ideally lead to the third stage, to an increased knowledge about a work of art, a kind of conscious naivety. This type of music is often found in Mozart, in Beethoven's op. 27, no. 1, in the introduction to the slow movement of Dvořák's Cello Concerto – something almost childlike. One has to be very clear, though, about certain philosophical concepts. Child-like does not mean childish, just as sentiment is not sentimentality. The childlike element in art and musical expression is very important. It is a development few great artists achieve, and Fischer was an outstanding example.

There have been different piano schools. There was the so-called German school, which stemmed to a great degree from Theodor Leschetizky in Vienna. Under its various guises, one could count such a variety of pianists as Artur Schnabel, Edwin Fischer, Wilhelm Backhaus, Walter Gieseking and Wilhelm Kempff. And there was the very famous Russian school, which was well known throughout the world through the great Soviet virtuosi such as Emil Gilels and Sviatoslav Richter and, earlier on, through Rachmaninov and Vladimir Horowitz and others. And before both of these there was a French school, which was more limited, but which gave us Alfred Cortot and Yves Nat – to my mind a great pianist but much underestimated outside France; and the great Italian school that went from Busoni to Arturo Benedetti Michelangeli and Maurizio Pollini. Each of these schools had, in a certain sense, a connection to Liszt. None would have been possible without this grandfatherly person. To my mind, the Hungarian-Slavic side of Liszt was developed by the Russians; the elegance of Liszt's playing went to the French school, and the slightly more intellectual side to the German and the Italian schools. When you analyse these piano schools you can almost see the different stages of Liszt's life: Budapest with the connection to the East, Rome in later years, Weimar and, of course, Paris.

The German branch, which came to us through Busoni and Arrau in more recent days, was probably influenced by the side of Liszt that was interested in Wagner and in the transcriptions of the Beethoven symphonies and the songs, most of which were by Schubert. The Russian branch was more concerned with virtuosity; the pure, pianistic side of Liszt was developed there with a much greater sense of freedom in rubato, a great ability to bring out hidden voices in the chords of the piano – the prime example of this was the Polish pianist Josef Hofmann – and a great capacity to develop the sense of perspective in piano playing. In this school you feel a much greater dynamic range between the melody and the accompaniment. You very often hear the melody being played in a good healthy mezzo forte or forte and the accompaniment pianissimo, whereas the German school balances the accompaniment and the melody within a very narrow area. This is only one of the Russian school's characteristics, which was then carried over into the modern Soviet school.

The Soviet Union produced a number of great pianistic talents. As it closed its doors to exchanges with the West, a certain purity in this so-called Romantic style of piano playing remained intact for much longer in the Soviet Union than elsewhere. The first time I went there in 1965 I felt very strongly the contradiction between the very free, imaginative way of playing the piano and the very grey and dreary daily life. It was as if musicians were able to pour into the instrument all their frustration over the lack of anything ornamental or pleasurable in life. There was a very matter-of-fact kind of life and a very imaginative world of sound. It is not surprising that in the last twenty or so years, when there have been so many more exchanges and when so many of these musicians have come into much closer contact with the West and the modern way of making music, they have lost some of this, for me, very appealing and old-fashioned way of playing music. It is as if they have been drawn to the less attractive side of the West. I was very interested in the changes which led to the reunification of Germany in 1989, which is when the process really started. It is important for the West not only to impose its more liberal way of life on the East, but also to take from the East a certain sense of values which are not necessarily eastern but which are a combination of the character of the people and the system which existed for so many years – years when there was so little opportunity for entertainment and pleasure that there was a much greater emphasis on human and cultural values. The fact that I saw so many people reading Dostoevsky and Chekhov in the underground in Moscow may be a result of restrictions imposed on them in the past, but this does not mean that we have to reject everything because it is associated with a political system which we despised. It is my hope that they will share their cultural values with the West. I am sure that they are prepared to do so, provided that the West is open to this kind of influence. Otherwise the so-called liberation of East Germany is only a modern version of colonialism.

~

In the spring of 1960 I finished school and took my leaving certificate. Then I went on my first tour to South America. My father came with me to Buenos Aires – it was our first visit since we had left eight years before. I went to Peru by myself, and to Brazil, Venezuela and Mexico. I played all the Beethoven sonatas – my earlier Beethoven recitals in Tel Aviv came in very useful – in Medellin in Colombia, which has since become a drug capital, but which in those days was a South American cultural centre. Then I returned to the same difficult situation as before – there was not much work waiting for me. The following year I played my first complete cycle of the Mozart sonatas in Tel Aviv and in Jerusalem and gave recitals elsewhere in Israel. I played in Elath for the first time – in fact, during this period, I spent most of my time in Israel.

It was only after my second Australian tour in 1962, when I played and conducted, that life became easier. I conducted the Melbourne Symphony Orchestra, when we performed Mozart's Symphony No. 40, the Clarinet Concerto and Beethoven's Fourth Symphony. We played almost the same programme with the Sydney Symphony Orchestra, but with the Concerto for Flute in G major instead of the Clarinet Concerto.

I returned to the USA in the autumn of 1962 and played in New York again. I started performing regularly with William Steinberg, a really marvellous conductor. In the late 1950s and early 1960s he was Music Director both of the Pittsburgh Symphony Orchestra and of the London Philharmonic. I played with him in both cities: in London there was a particularly satisfying performance of Beethoven's Fourth Piano Concerto, and I performed in Pittsburgh almost yearly. He then also became adviser to the New York Philharmonic and I appeared with him very often there, too. I remember especially playing Mozart concertos, a number of Beethoven concertos and the Brahms First Piano Concerto.

Steinberg was an extremely cultured musician, had been a very

fine pianist himself and had played the piano part in *Pierrot Lunaire*
by Schoenberg under Otto Klemperer in Cologne. Steinberg was the
person who really trained the Israel Philharmonic, which had been
founded by Hubermann as recently as 1936.

The first person to conduct the Israel Philharmonic in concert was
none other than Arturo Toscanini. Of course, a new orchestra with
members from different countries needed to be trained and prepared
for Toscanini's arrival, and it was Steinberg who was chosen to do the
groundwork. He was a very fine conductor, with an unusually high
degree of control over the orchestra and a very large and eclectic
repertoire. He was not only at home in the German repertoire –
Bruckner and Mahler, not to mention Beethoven and Brahms – but
was also a great champion of two composers not normally associated
with German-trained musicians and not played that often in the
USA, especially in the 1950s and 1960s – Berlioz and Elgar.

He always had very interesting and pertinent suggestions to make
about every piece that I played with him. One of the details I
remember was in the transition from the second to the third movement of Beethoven's *Emperor* Concerto. The second movement ends
in B major; the music comes to a grinding halt and there is a magic
moment when the B remains totally without harmony and descends
a semitone to a B flat, the dominant of E flat, the key of the last
movement. And then comes a slow premonition of the theme of the
movement, played by the piano, accompanied only by the sustained
horn and pizzicato chords in the strings as if the theme of the last
movement is presented in embryo, very tentatively. There is then a
pause on what is the upbeat to the last movement – all pianissimo –
and then all hell breaks loose and the piano presents the theme of the
last movement fortissimo. That upbeat is, of course, very difficult
because the sound has a tendency simply to die away and it is hard
to fill the gap between the last B flat in the piano and the beginning
of the last movement. Steinberg told me that he remembered hearing
Eugen d'Albert, who had been a great Beethoven interpreter, and
said d'Albert created the illusion of a huge crescendo on this last note
of the transition, thereby making the explosive nature of the
beginning of the last movement appear inevitable. Very often I have
thought of that when playing this piece and it is absolutely true, and
I have always been amazed at how this illusion is projected to the

orchestra, and I assume and hope also to the audience. This is only one of many examples I could cite of Steinberg's great knowledge and imagination.

It is one of those odd coincidences in life that one of the cities that always stayed faithful to me, and engaged me whenever I went to the USA, was Chicago. My connection with Chicago dates back to 1958 and Sol Hurok, an old-time impresario. You had the feeling that he only needed to see somebody walk on to the stage to know whether he – or she – would be a success. He made no pretensions to musical culture, but he had an impresario's instinct. He was a self-made man, a typical example of the Jewish-European emigrant. He came to the USA without a dime, and worked his way up to considerable success.

There was also a man in Chicago called Harry Zelzer, who had a kind of absolute power over recitals given there and whose 'Allied Arts' included a piano series. He always used to book me, and it is ironic that I have now gone back to this city in another capacity, as Music Director of the Chicago Symphony Orchestra.

From 1962 onwards I started to spend more time in England. During that period I played with Sir John Barbirolli for the first time. Apart from being a great musician and a great conductor, Barbirolli had a very individual way of conducting and of learning and preparing scores. He was intuitive rather than rational, and had great vivacity and imagination. Despite having a French mother and an Italian father, he was a real Londoner – he spoke perfect Cockney.

Surprisingly, perhaps, Barbirolli had a special affinity with Mahler. He was the man who brought Mahler to the Berlin Philharmonic Orchestra, playing several of the symphonies with them. He was also an excellent cellist – he played the cello in the orchestra at the world première of Edward Elgar's Cello Concerto. He also played the cello in what I believe was the first performance in England of Arnold Schoenberg's Chamber Symphony No. 1 in 1925. He was, without doubt, a very progressive musician, very eclectic, equally at home with Mahler, Haydn, Puccini or Brahms. Some of the finest per-formances of French music I ever heard were conducted by him – Debussy's *La mer*, and some Ravel. And then there was always Elgar, for whom I think he felt a particular affinity. I must add that during his lifetime, people in England often criticized his musical personality in general, and his Elgar in particular. They considered him too emotional and thought he took too many liberties. But I felt that he brought a dimension to Elgar's music which is so often lacking, a kind of nervous quality which he had in common with Mahler. It is probably no coincidence that Mahler conducted Elgar's *Enigma Variations* at one of his last concerts in New York. There is almost a certain over-sensitivity in some of Elgar's greater works, which is sometimes sacrificed for the conventional idea of Elgar as the perfect English gentleman, the Victorian composer. It reminds me of the simplistic idea of 'Papa Haydn'.

Elgar had a fate similar to that of Berlioz, who was accepted in Germany before being accepted in his own country. Elgar had one of his first great successes in Düsseldorf in 1904 with *The Dream of Gerontius*, and his most enthusiastic admirer was Richard Strauss. It was Strauss who 'promoted' Elgar at a time when he was not at all popular in England. Things have changed since then, and he has become a national hero.

Barbirolli also had a great affinity with other English music, especially that of Vaughan Williams, and he had, too, a strong affection for Haydn. He conducted some very special performances of Haydn symphonies with the Berlin Philharmonic. There was something very natural about his music making – what in German is called a *Musikant*. What is less well known, but which is just as interesting and has proved very beneficial to me, is the precision and care with which he used to prepare his rehearsals. It was not just the way he studied the scores but the fact that he personally bowed every string part of almost every piece. His great knowledge enabled him to propose bowings to the string section which automatically made them produce the sound and articulation he wanted. He could produce the 'Barbirolli sound' with almost any orchestra he conducted.

Barbirolli was a very warm-hearted person, loved by most of the musicians with whom he came in contact. His insecurity was probably the result of an unhappy time he had as Toscanini's successor with the New York Philharmonic Orchestra. I used to play with Barbirolli fairly regularly in Manchester with his Hallé Orchestra, at a time when he was beginning to do the Mahler symphonies. He often engaged me to play a Mozart concerto before a Mahler symphony.

~

Between 1962 and 1966, I played mostly in England but also in Montreal in December 1962, where I performed Richard Strauss's *Burleske* for the first time with Zubin Mehta conducting, and soon afterwards I gave a concert with János Ferencsik in Los Angeles.

In 1963 I started going to Germany. My début there was in Munich, with Fritz Rieger and the Munich Philharmonic, and shortly after that I played in Berlin with the RIAS Symphony Orchestra in a series called 'RIAS stellt vor' (RIAS presents). It was during 1963 that Wolfgang Stresemann, Intendant of the Berlin Philharmonic, heard me and invited me to play with the orchestra the following year. He booked me for two concerts, one in June and the other in September 1964.

For the June concert he had already engaged Pierre Boulez to conduct the orchestra in one of the concerts belonging to a series dedicated to twentieth-century music, and Boulez had, in fact, already decided the programme, which was to include Bartók's First Piano Concerto. Therefore I had the choice either to learn the Bartók Concerto, which I had never played nor heard at the time, or skip the chance to play with the Berlin Philharmonic that season. Of course, I chose the former.

That was the beginning of a long and very fruitful friendship with Boulez. Stresemann then told me that for the second concert in September I could make suggestions as to what I wanted to play. It being the tenth anniversary of Furtwängler's death, I thought it would be appropriate to play his Piano Concerto. I have never forgotten the surprise in Stresemann's eyes when I suggested the idea. I am sure he expected me to come up with one of the Beethoven or Brahms concertos, or maybe Mozart – the Furtwängler Concerto was the last thing on his mind. But he said that if I really wanted to do it, it would be very natural for the Berlin Philharmonic to play a composition by their former chief conductor. It was played in September 1964 with Zubin Mehta conducting.

For more than thirty years Wolfgang Stresemann was not only a friend but a guiding spirit for me in Berlin. He was a conductor himself, a great admirer of Bruno Walter, and an extraordinarily cultured person. There was not one concert that I played in Berlin at which he was present where, afterwards, he did not have something very pertinent to say about the performance. Very often he made illuminating points about tempo or balance in the orchestra. I always greatly appreciated not only his friendliness and admiration, but also his total honesty and courage in telling me what he thought – which was not always complimentary.

Furtwängler's Piano Concerto was a labour of love. It is very long – it lasts over seventy-five minutes – and very difficult, but not uninteresting. The piano concerto literature is very poor in post-Romantic works. There is a concerto by Reger but nothing comparable to Mahler, Bruckner or Richard Strauss (except for the delightful *Burleske*), so Furtwängler's concerto really fills a gap. You can feel the influence of Brahms, Tchaikovsky, Wagner, and even César Franck, but it is extremely well written and orchestrated, and I think it deserved a place in the repertoire. Before playing it in Berlin, I had played it for a radio broadcast in Zurich. I also played it in Los Angeles once, and would play it again. I conducted the Scherzo from his Second Symphony with the Berlin Philharmonic Orchestra on the occasion of its hundredth Anniversary, and then in 2002 I did the entire work with the Chicago Symphony.

With Zubin Mehta I did not play solely in North America, for he also invited me to Paris in 1963 or 1964 for concerts with the Société des Concerts du Conservatoire. My friend had become my guiding angel! There were always a few people who believed in me. Sol Hurok fostered my interests in the USA, and Ian Hunter did so in England. They continued to give me chances at a time when there was no financial benefit in it for them. The Chilean pianist, Claudio Arrau, who also started his career at an early age, said that 'the longer one's trousers became, the smaller one's success'.

Since my childhood, Claudio Arrau has been the ideal musician. First of all he was someone with an uncanny control of his instrument, with probably the widest repertoire of any pianist, past or present, and with a tremendous interest in areas outside his instrument. You could meet him every free day when he was on tour in the opera house, in the bookshops and at every possible exhibition. Arrau was one of the best examples of the fusion of the Latin and German mentality. He came as a very young boy to Berlin and had all his education there as a pupil of Martin Krause, who had been a pupil of Liszt.

Arrau opened my eyes to many important musical points. It was known and accepted that he was a great exponent of the Beethoven sonatas and concertos and, of course, the Brahms concertos, but he was the first musician to make me aware, when I was still a child, that Liszt was not only the virtuoso that people knew him to be, but also a very important and expressive musician who had uniquely fused the Hungarian temperament with elements of French education and literature (and not only through Marie d'Agoult), while at the same time maintaining a very close contact with all that was interesting and important in German musical life. Liszt's importance, historically, should not be underestimated. Wagner would not have written the way he did without having come into contact with Liszt. This is something which is well known and accepted today, but in 1950 it certainly was not. That Arrau, with the reputation of a great, serious musician who played Beethoven, not only had the pianistic control but the interest to devote so much of his time and energy to the works of Liszt, was an inspiration to me and many others.

Arrau also had a very characteristic way of playing the piano. There was nothing stiff about the way he put either his hands or his arms on the keys – indeed, he fought against the stiffness of certain schools of piano playing. One must not forget that even well into the twentieth century there were many piano teachers who taught their pupils to put a coin on the upper side of the hand, and no matter how fast the fingers moved or how they jumped from one end of the keyboard to the other, the coin was not allowed to fall off. There was admiration in some circles for stiffness in playing the piano, which was very unmusical and against which Arrau fought. He developed a much warmer, softer and richer sound on the piano than one could hear elsewhere. I heard him very often in the 1950s and the 1960s and performed with him regularly as a conductor. He was greatly revered for his uncompromising nature.

He had the courage to play only according to his convictions and his ideas, not in any way yielding either to easy success or to cheap effects simply to win an audience. This applied to his choice of tempi and to the expression that he distilled from the music. It applied as much to Liszt and Debussy as to Schubert and Mozart, where he allowed himself the luxury to see in the music a degree of intensity and depth that was not normally associated with these composers. This refusal to compromise stemmed also, of course, from his tremendous honesty and sincerity. He often came to my concerts as a pianist even when I was very young and never showered me with empty compliments. He always had something critical to say and said it in the most positive way. I never felt discouraged by what he had to say to me, but he was never non-committally polite and always gave me food for thought.

~

There is a law in Argentina that if you are born there you remain an Argentinian citizen for the rest of your life. This law saved the lives of many German and Polish Jews who had emigrated to Argentina in the 1920s. Many returned to their original countries later with children who had been born in Argentina. When Hitler came to power, he could not touch them, or at least he had greater difficulty in getting hold of them if they had Argentinian passports. When I was nineteen or twenty I was called up for military service in Argentina. At that time, selection for military service was run by lottery, which meant that not everyone was called. The lower numbers were exempt from military service, the middle numbers had to do military service for one year and the higher numbers were detailed to the navy, where they served for two years. I drew a high number, but managed to get a postponement for a couple of years on the grounds of my studies in Europe, and because I had been giving concerts in Europe and America. But then the point came when the authorities said that two postponements were enough. But I did not go back to Argentina, arguing that I was an Israeli citizen with an Israeli passport, which was perfectly legal. This did mean that I could not now go to Argentina on my Israeli passport. I could go anywhere in the world on my Argentinian passport, except to Israel, and anywhere in the world with my Israeli passport, except to Argentina! I was supposed to return to Buenos Aires in 1963 to give a concert, and it was then that my passport was confiscated and the tour cancelled.

I had been staying in Berlin for several months when this happened and it was a difficult situation, because at that time there were no diplomatic relations between Israel and Germany and the Berlin Wall had already been erected. Berlin was practically an enclosed island. I was left in Berlin without an Argentinian passport and without a German visa in my Israeli passport!

During this time I became friendly with some people who worked at the Komische Oper in East Berlin, and regularly attended Walter Felsenstein's rehearsals. In fact, it was the first time I had ever attended opera rehearsals. I saw performances of Puccini's *Tosca*, and Benjamin Britten's *A Midsummer Night's Dream*. One of the people I got to know was a wonderful black American soprano called Ella Lea. We used to play chamber music together, mostly Lieder. I often played Lieder because there were many singers around and I was reasonably good at sight-reading, so I was always at the piano to accompany them. In 1963 I also went to Bayreuth for the first time, and played two concerts at Haus Wahnfried, one on my own and the other with Ella Lea. At the solo recital, I played a Beethoven sonata, the Liszt Sonata, of course, but also insisted on playing Brahms – in Bayreuth! Count Gravina, who had up till then been very pleasant to me, left the room in protest.

6

ENGLAND

One year, about 1964, Ian Hunter told me: 'The next time you come
to Manchester the Hallé Orchestra will unfortunately be on tour, but
a visiting orchestra will play at their subscription concerts and you
will perform with them.' And this is how I first came to appear with
the English Chamber Orchestra in Manchester with John Pritchard
conducting. I had an immediate and excellent rapport with the
orchestra, with the musicians, and with the lady who managed the
orchestra, Ursula Strebi. She is the widow of the excellent trumpet
player Philip Jones, who was a member of the Philharmonia
Orchestra at that time. She knew of my ambition to play and
conduct: we talked about Edwin Fischer, who was a fellow Swiss, and
I told her how impressed I had been when he played and at the same
time conducted the Mozart concertos.

It was in Moscow, on my first trip to the Soviet Union in 1965,
that I received a telegram asking me if I would play and conduct two
concerts with the English Chamber Orchestra, one in Reading, and
the other in Cambridge – and that is how my association with them
all started. After those two concerts we did a number of studio
recordings for the BBC, some concerts in London and went on our
first tour in 1966, to the Prague Spring Festival, where I met
Rubinstein, who gave an unforgettable performance of Brahms's
Second Piano Concerto. Afterwards, the orchestra and I went to
Greece and to the Lucerne Festival. And then, gradually, a situation
evolved where the main work of the orchestra was divided into three
parts. There was Benjamin Britten, who worked with the orchestra
primarily, though not exclusively, on his own pieces and very often
composed for the orchestra at his Aldeburgh Festival; there was
Raymond Leppard, who specialized in early music at that time –

Handel, Bach, and so on; and myself. The English Chamber Orchestra had three musicians working with them, with complementary repertoires and styles of music. I used to spend about three months of the year with them. We played in London a great deal and went on many tours together. We also made a number of recordings – all the Mozart piano concertos, the Requiem, several symphonies, the divertimenti, the serenades, some twentieth-century music, including Bartók's *Music for Strings, Percussion and Celesta*. We went on tour at least once but sometimes two or three times a year – to Germany frequently, to Spain and Italy, to Paris and to Scandinavia. Then, in 1968, we travelled to the USA for the first of several visits. In 1969 we went on a world tour, covering the USA, Australia, New Zealand, Italy and Israel.

In 1973 we also went on a long tour to India and Japan. The Indian interlude was particularly touching because of our visit to Bombay, where I found the most enthusiastic and knowledgeable audience, people who knew everything about musical life in Europe in the most intimate detail, mostly through their contacts in England. They had gramophone records and listened to broadcasts by the BBC. I was very concerned about the programmes that we were to play in Bombay because we made no concessions, as it were, to popular taste. Among other things we played Schoenberg's *Verklärte Nacht*. I consulted my friend Zubin Mehta before going as to whether he felt that we could play a fairly esoteric repertoire, or if we should limit ourselves to the well-known masterpieces. He told me that we could play anything we wanted. I trusted him, although I could not help suspecting that there was a slight degree of chauvinism in his advice. I was very surprised by the Bombay audience's enthusiasm and their degree of knowledge. Incidentally, the greatest part of the audience were Parsees; they are the part of the population most interested in classical music.

The English Chamber Orchestra was 'owned' and run by Quintin Ballardie, who had been with the Philharmonia under Furtwängler and Klemperer, and was then principal viola player of the London Philharmonic Orchestra. In some ways he was rather autocratic. I do not mean this in the negative sense, but simply that he knew that to maintain high standards it was sometimes necessary to be tough. I think that his model for running an orchestra was Walter Legge, who owned and ruled the Philharmonia with a rod of iron. You have to remember that even today, many players in the London orchestras, with the exception of the two opera orchestras and the BBC orchestras, do not have full-time contracts like the subsidized orchestras of Paris, Amsterdam and Berlin. They often work from day to day, from engagement to engagement. And they get paid per session – so much per rehearsal, so much per concert. It makes one admire British players, because they have a far harder life than their colleagues on the continent. They are sometimes forced to play far too many sessions simply to earn a living. I do not know how things are at present, but at that time each of the four London orchestras had thirty concerts a year at the Festival Hall. There were, on average, three rehearsals per concert, per programme, so it took two days to do a concert – one for the first two rehearsals, and one for the general rehearsal and the concert. That meant sixty or so working days. And for this they used to get a very meagre fee, so they had to look for additional work through their manager or their board for the rest of the year. In the long run this had an adverse effect on programming in London. With such small subsidies came a greater dependence on box-office takings, and therefore a greater number of very standardized programmes, aimed at attracting the average audience. Either that or the programmes were linked to financially lucrative recording projects.

In the 1960s, London was the recording centre of the world. The Orchestre de Paris was to be created only in 1967 and the other French orchestras were very much ad hoc. The Berlin and Vienna Philharmonic Orchestras did a certain amount of recording; the Berlin Philharmonic at that time recorded almost exclusively with their principal conductor. The American orchestras were too expensive. London had the advantage of very high quality facilities and recordings could be made swiftly – English musicians are famous for their speed and their ability to read anything at sight. The whole process was, therefore, less expensive. I think one can say that their standard of playing never went below a very professional level but also that it rarely rose above it! It was a very high-middle level. This is not meant as criticism of the musicians. The conditions under which they had to work meant that there was no continuity of employment, no place where the orchestras were at home. You rehearsed somewhere different every day. If you had more than three rehearsals, you rehearsed in two or three different halls, and then played the actual concert at the Festival Hall. An orchestra usually had only its general rehearsal in the hall where the concert was to be played. There were all sorts of halls in and around London which were used for rehearsals. Since then they have built the Henry Wood Hall, but it is not ideal as its acoustic is very different from that of the Festival Hall.

The differences between London's four symphony orchestras were minimal. The string players, especially, went from one orchestra to the other whenever they had two days off and could fit in another session. It was not unusual for a musician to have two rehearsals on Monday, one on Tuesday and a concert on Tuesday evening with the London Philharmonic, and rehearsals with the London Symphony or the Philharmonia on Monday evening and Tuesday afternoon. Musically speaking, it was a chaotic arrangement. I was full of admiration for the professionalism of British musicians.

There were also quite a number of chamber orchestras, although then the English Chamber Orchestra was probably the only permanent one. The players were mostly people who played in quartets and other ensembles but had the English Chamber Orchestra as their base. The leader of the orchestra at the time was Emanuel Hurwitz, who was a well-known chamber musician. The first viola was Cecil Aronowitz, known from his recordings – he often played quintets with the Amadeus Quartet. The orchestra was not exclusively, but largely, influenced by people who had emigrated to England from Europe or elsewhere, and they had the same profile as the players of the Amadeus Quartet. Of course, there were a lot of English players too, but the style of the orchestra came from a central European chamber music background, with all that is positive, and sometimes perhaps a little negative about it. There was a strong commitment to music – and a great sense of enjoyment in making music – a sort of *Hausmusik* on an enlarged scale. In other words, the motivation was not merely professional, and certainly not financial. In fact, they were a very unusual group of people. The orchestra was not dissimilar in sound and character to what I had grown up with in the Israel Philharmonic ten or fifteen years earlier. The strings, in particular, had a warmth unequalled in other English orchestras, and many of the wind players were great soloists.

Musical life in England was changing quite considerably, partly through the building of the Queen Elizabeth Hall, which is the right size for a chamber orchestra since it seats eleven or twelve hundred people, and then, later, the building of the Barbican Centre. Good though it is to have such facilities at home, the work done on tour is invaluable, for the simple reason that, at home, each member of the orchestra plays at rehearsals and concerts as part of his daily routine. He also has his family life and other professional activities. On tour, rehearsals and concerts become the centre of his activities, and the effect that touring has on the fusion and homogeneity of an orchestra cannot be overestimated. I found the same thing when touring with the Orchestre de Paris in the fifteen years I was with them. It was the recording work and touring that brought both the orchestra itself, and the orchestra and me, closer together, in the musical sense.

The English Chamber Orchestra went through a process of change and a new generation took over, including a very fine leader, José Luis Garcia, whom I had known since our first trip to Madrid. He started at the last desk of the second violins and very quickly made his way to the first desk of the first violins. He eventually became not just the leader of the orchestra but also a fine soloist. After we finished the cycles of the Mozart concertos, I tried to keep in touch with the orchestra because it had given me so much, and my own development was so very closely linked to it. The only reason I have done so little with it since then is lack of time.

I think the basis of all music making comes through listening to each other. When you have only one person playing – the pianist, for example – each hand or each finger has to listen to the others and not play independently. As soon as you have two players – a violin and piano duet, or a Lieder singer and an accompanist, or just two wind players, the basis of musical expression comes from listening to each other. Listening is a far more active process than hearing; it is difficult enough not just to keep playing your line but to listen to your partner at the same time. You can imagine how difficult it is to play in a sextet or an octet, or when you reach the size of a chamber orchestra. In the English Chamber Orchestra we used to play with six or eight first violins. At the Festival Hall we occasionally played with ten. This means that each player's contribution is far more individual than in a symphony orchestra with sixteen first violins. In the violin section, which usually plays a primary role in chamber orchestra repertoire, when you have six or eight first violins, one player with a slightly harsher, more acid sound than his colleagues will stick out like a sore thumb. Playing in a chamber orchestra is different and more difficult because the personal contribution is so much more important. Moreover, the role of the conductor evolved from what was, in the eighteenth century, the equivalent of the chamber orchestra today. It was very often led by the violin, which is why in Britain one still speaks of a 'leader of the orchestra', and not a 'concert master'. In the old days an orchestra the size of the English Chamber Orchestra playing Mozart would have done so without a conductor.

My work with the English Chamber Orchestra taught me, amongst many other things, that the impulse, the impetus has to come from the musicians. Musically speaking, the conductor inevitably has to organize an orchestra, and also impose on it his musical thinking and personality. But a chamber orchestra cannot play with a civil-servant mentality. There has to be active participation on the part of the musicians, which is something I have since tried to develop with symphony orchestras. In the English Chamber Orchestra, the musicians had their own very clear sense of articulation and phrasing, and I tried to make it larger and broader in expression and sustaining power. When I did the Mozart opera recordings with the Berlin Philharmonic, I almost had to do the opposite. I already had this wonderful sustaining sound, for which the Berlin Philharmonic is rightly famous, so I concentrated primarily on articulation and phrasing. A good player in a chamber orchestra usually has a more precise sense of phrasing and articulation, simply because his individual contribution is more important.

Although most of my time was dedicated to the English Chamber Orchestra I started conducting other orchestras more regularly. This marked the start of the second phase of my career in 1965.

~

Jacqueline du Pré and I were engaged to play a concert together in April 1967 with the English Chamber Orchestra, but we first met in

December 1966, at the house of Fou Ts'ong, the Chinese pianist who was married at the time to Menuhin's daughter. We were all to spend the evening playing chamber music together. Jacqueline and I were drawn immediately to each other, both in a personal and a musical sense. About two or three months later we decided to marry. She was already by then studying Judaism, because she intended to convert to my religion. I did not influence her at all; she wanted to do it, partly for me, but also because at that time we hoped to have children. It may also have been because so many of the great musicians she knew were Jewish, and she wanted to share this experience.

David Ben-Gurion attended our wedding in June 1967, and he was photographed with Jacqueline and myself. Though he did not really care about music, he was a great admirer of hers. There was also the special significance of an English girl, and a Gentile at that, who had come to Israel in 1967 when the country was at war. She became a sort of a symbol in Israel, and Ben-Gurion was very aware of that.

A few weeks after we had met I remember playing a recording to Jacqueline of the Prelude and 'Liebestod' from *Tristan und Isolde*. She had never heard a note of Wagner before but, when she listened to something for the first time, it immediately became part of her. Whatever I showed her, or whatever she heard, seemed to bring out something that was already in her. She had a horror of anything that was fake, or insincere, of anything artificial. She had a gift very few performers have, the gift of making you feel that she was actually composing the music as she was playing. She did not know what it was to have technical difficulties, nor what it meant to play safe. There was a sensation of pure abandon when she played and it was that quality that endeared her to her colleagues and to her audience. There was something in her playing that was so completely and inevitably *right* – as far as tempo and dynamics were concerned. She played with a great deal of rubato, with great freedom, but it was so convincing that you felt like a mere mortal faced with somebody who possessed some kind of ethereal dimension.

Musically speaking, she was something of a rebel – she had her own brand of obstinacy. There was something deep inside her that revolted against the obvious, the accustomed or the conventional. Yet, it was not just her personality or her charisma, but the intensity of her feeling that made you wonder if there could be, after all, some valid reason for changing the printed score! With other musicians one would have felt that such a reaction was wilful or capricious, but there was nothing wilful or capricious about Jacqueline's music making.

She was an extremely kind person who could be quite hard in her judgement of other musicians when it concerned lack of commitment or intensity, or what was considered lack of honesty. Anyone who was not willing to give all of himself was a dishonest person. Even as a young girl of fifteen or sixteen, when attending Pablo Casals's master classes in Zermatt, she was already quite a rebel. Then she went to Moscow for a few months to study with Mstislav Rostropovich, and was quite a bit of a rebel there too. She also studied with Paul Tortelier for a few months. She did not accept authority automatically – it had to be proved to her that there was a reason for it. She was a rebel but also naive in the sense that she had a directness, and instinctive, almost physical contact with music. Those are the traits that remain in my memories of her as a musician.

In those days it was much simpler to make recordings, and there was only one other cellist of Jacqueline's calibre – Tortelier. The other cellist who caught the public's imagination was, of course, Rostropovich, but he was in the Soviet Union and only sporadically came to the West. There was certainly no other cellist of her generation and she therefore had practically no competition.

The first recording we made together was in 1967, when she played the Haydn C major and Boccherini cello concertos. In 1970 she wanted to record the Dvořák Concerto with me and we thought of doing it in Chicago because it had such a wonderful orchestra and because she had played with them before. She also made a record of the Chopin and César Franck sonatas, and another of the Tchaikovsky Trio, live from Tel Aviv, but by then there were already periods when she was unable to play. She had such a very short time.

Jacqueline's way of playing did not really change from the time she was a teenager – you can hear that on some of her very early recordings, which were released after her death. Even then, she played with incredible intensity and vivacity. Obviously she continued to develop, but the basic personality and character of her cello playing was established at a very early age. Of all the great musicians I have met in my life, I have never encountered anyone for whom music was such a natural form of expression as it was for Jacqueline. With most musicians you feel that they are human beings who happen to play music. With her, you had the feeling that here was a musician who also happened to be a human being. Of course, one had to eat and drink and sleep and have friends. But with her the proportions were different – music was the centre of her existence.

Until her illness began to cripple her, she was able to do whatever she wanted on the cello, and needed very little practice. She had a capacity to imagine sound such as I never met in any other musician. She was really a child of nature – a musician of nature with an unerring instinct.

~

In March 1967 I was engaged to play the Mozart Concerto No. 25 with Otto Klemperer and the Philharmonia Orchestra. After the concert, we recorded it. A rapport was established between us immediately. I had already heard Klemperer in London a few times. He was a very direct person and of the thousands of people I have met in my life I have rarely encountered anyone less interested in outward appearances. (His daughter said that she had never once seen him look at himself in a mirror, not even to comb his hair.) He was totally uninterested in anything decorative – with the exception of women ... Perhaps he did not regard them as exclusively decorative! The strength he conveyed to the orchestra was due to the fact that he approached the essence of what he wanted directly and without hesitation. He was too great a musician not to be interested in sound, but his main preoccupation was with the correctness of execution as far as tempo, dynamics, and balance were concerned. He took great pains to balance carefully the different instruments of the orchestra, and then he concentrated on intensity. I do not think he really used sound as a main ingredient in music making.

Although I was so much younger than him, we became very close personally, if one can say this about anybody as awe-inspiring, and he also made friends with Jacqueline, whom he admired greatly. After hearing us play the Brahms F major Sonata, he paid her the memorable compliment of saying that he had never imagined Brahms could compose such passionate music. He was really taken by her musical personality, and her total devotion and commitment to music.

Klemperer was the most uncompromising musician and human being. From this point of view, he was and should remain a moral example to all musicians. Moreover, these qualities were somehow communicated to the orchestra and there was never any doubt about the inner strength that emanated from him. He was very sensitive to anything that was false in music making or, indeed, in other people. Then he could become terribly cynical and hard, traits which gave rise to many of the Klemperer stories that sometimes make him seem almost cruel.

But during the years I knew him, from 1967 until his death, he never once showed me any unattractive sides of his nature. After we had played and recorded the Mozart concerto, he suggested recording the Beethoven concertos. He had recorded everything else by Beethoven – the symphonies, the *Missa solemnis*, *Fidelio*, and the Violin Concerto – but never the set of piano concertos. People were very keen that he should do them, and he wanted to do them with me, which was, of course, very flattering. He also derived great fun from testing my abilities and my endurance. For instance, when we recorded the Beethoven concertos, he would never tell me in what order we were recording them. He just said, 'You are a good enough musician, a good enough pianist, you can do anything,' and he greatly enjoyed that.

He was very warm and very understanding if he felt people were honest. Honesty was probably the quality he respected most, both in others and in himself. One of the people he was most interested in, and for whom he had great respect, was Boulez. For Klemperer, Boulez not only represented the future, he was somebody who worked with the same uncompromising honesty as himself.

Klemperer was incredibly curious, right to the end. Remembering his curiosity, one can imagine what his days at the Kroll Opera must have been like. He was not a great believer in convention and would never accept things just because they had always been done that way. When I played Berg's Chamber Concerto with Boulez in London, in March 1967, at a time when it was relatively unknown both to musicians and to the public, Klemperer was so interested that he came to every rehearsal and listened very attentively.

Klemperer started recording Strauss's *Don Quixote* with Jacqueline in 1968 or 1969, and I was supposed to play with him in the same concert. The programme consisted of Beethoven's Choral Fantasia and Fourth Piano Concerto, and *Don Quixote*. Klemperer had the habit of recording first and performing in concert afterwards; but as he felt unwell, the recording had to be interrupted and the concert was conducted by Sir Adrian Boult.

I saw Klemperer whenever we both happened to be in London. He accepted me as a conductor. In fact, he came to several of my concerts in 1967. Then I was invited to Rome to conduct a concert performance of Mozart's *Così fan tutte* for the radio. I asked Klemperer if I could talk to him about the opera and take his advice. He very generously went through the entire score with me – which took a long time. He was very positive about my conducting, and greatly encouraged me, though he felt – and he was absolutely right – that at the beginning of my conducting career I had a tendency to take pieces too fast.

Once he invited me to visit him at his hotel. When I arrived, he asked me to play excerpts of his opera on the piano. Afterwards he asked me: 'How do you like my music?' When I hesitated he turned to his daughter and said, 'Barenboim is a very nice fellow, it is just too bad that he has such a bad taste in music.'

The last time I saw him was in Jerusalem. It must have been at the end of 1972 or the beginning of 1973. He had converted from Judaism to Christianity in his youth – he told me that at that time he had naively thought one had to be a Christian to conduct the great Christian pieces like Bach's *St Matthew Passion* or *St John Passion*. Later he reconverted to Judaism, and even had an Israeli passport. He was the most famous Israeli conductor who never conducted the Israel Philharmonic!

7

ON CONDUCTING
AND CHAMBER MUSIC

If you were to ask a first-class orchestral player, he would say that few conductors have any influence on the orchestra. They play the tempi indicated by the conductor, adding the nuances or the balance he wants, and that is the end of it. But with a good conductor, musical contact can be so strong that the musicians react to the slightest movement of his hand, his finger, his eye or his body. If the orchestra is at one with the conductor, they play differently if he stands up straight, or bends forward, or sideways or backwards. They are influenced by every movement. The conductor's up-beat, moreover, has an influence on the first sound. If his up-beat has no authority, the sound is dead, unless the musicians ignore him totally. If they cannot or do not want to play for him, feeling that he has nothing to impart, they will just play the Beethoven symphony the way they have played it a thousand times before. But if they respect him, they will be with him from the up-beat, which has a direct influence on the first note, whether it should sound hard or soft, on the way it is sustained and to what extent it should vibrate.

A good conductor will do away with beating every bar or beat, and the orchestra and the audience should be made to forget that there are beats or bars at all. That is to say that, while a phrase consists of a certain number of bars, if the conductor beats every one, or every beat within the bar, he brings the music back to its most basic level.

Moreover, a good conductor must beat time in such a way that what he wants is quite clear. Beating time means conducting in a way that the orchestra knows how to play. The actual beat, the manual movement, must be capable of showing the musicians not only where to play but also how to fill the space in between notes. When I conduct the two orchestras I know best, in Chicago and Berlin, I can sometimes leave out three or four beats altogether because I know the musicians can fill them in themselves. I can leave the responsibility to the musicians until the next point where I want a certain pronunciation, and then I come down again with a hand movement.

You cannot conduct in such a way that every movement is calculated beforehand: that would merely constrict you. Every movement should be a sign to the whole orchestra or to part of it. Although you can play an instrument or sing intuitively, you cannot conduct only intuitively. The conductor's influence on and communication with the orchestra must have a rational basis. They must know that a phrase has four bars here, and eight bars there, and where the climax is. As a solo instrumentalist or singer you can use intuition on a greater scale, though it is not ideal to rely on it exclusively. That is why a prodigy like Yehudi Menuhin could, at the age of eleven, play Bach, Beethoven and Brahms concertos with the Berlin Philharmonic. But a child of eleven, however gifted, cannot stand in front of an orchestra and conduct a Beethoven or Brahms symphony. This would be impossible, because the communication with an orchestra must have a rational basis.

I usually work in three steps. The first step is to study the score at home; the second step is the rehearsal, and the third step the performance. Studying the score is the opposite process to that of composing. The composer has an idea, it may only be a fragment, on which he builds. Whether it is inspiration, knowledge or intuition, he can build on it and, after a certain time, he will produce a complete piece. This does not have to be a Bruckner symphony. The principle is the same with the smallest piece by Mozart, Chopin, or Webern. When a conductor sees a piece for the first time, he does not notice the details. He must re-compose with the whole work in mind and then search for the details. You could compare the conductor's work with that of a car mechanic who can take a car to pieces and put it together again. A conductor must, for instance, bring out every detail in the first movement of Beethoven's *Eroica*: the harmonic connections, the rhythmical connections, the dynamic connections, and even the geographic distance between the notes. Beethoven often moved from large intervals to smaller ones, thus reducing the geographical distance between the notes but augmenting the tension. If the *Eroica* were written up to the first great fortissimo without chromatic intervals, there would be no tension at all.

When Sergiu Celibidache said that none, or very few of his colleagues could read scores, a lot of people got cross. But they were taking what he said at face value. What he meant was that many conductors cannot hear the sound, the dynamic or balance of the orchestra during their reading. When you look at a score and at a certain point it says crescendo, then the whole orchestra plays crescendo from pianissimo to fortissimo. Now, if the second flute, which is not unimportant, and the kettle drum, the trumpets and the trombones, all start the crescendo at the same time, as is pointed out in the score, you can hear this. But for that you need knowledge and the ability to read. In order to realize a crescendo in an orchestra, the instruments cannot all start at the same time. The crescendo must be organized in such a way that everything can be heard, the full capabilities of every instrument have to come through. A conductor must be able to think acoustically, and that is very difficult. For instance, take the beginning of Wagner's *Die Walküre*. The cellos and the double basses play five semiquavers and a crotchet all marked forte, and after that the second beat is subito piano. You cannot just play forte, and then the subito piano. The forte must rise so that you get the effect of a precipice before the subito piano. This is all part of the reading: the first two crotchets are forte, and the third piano. Everything can be learned in detail except the intensity. The intensity of a forte or a piano, the strength with which you play a forte before getting through to the subito piano is something that cannot be learned.

Take, first, the dynamics, the relation between piano and forte. Piano is not something you can measure scientifically, so-and-so many decibels makes a piano, and then so many more and it becomes mezzo forte. Nor is tempo absolute. It is right when all other ingredients are right: balance, dynamic, vibrato. When a violinist plays a very fast tempo, he plays with a certain type of vibrato. When the conductor asks for a tempo modification, he must know what other changes are necessary in articulation or sound quality. That starts with the bowing; the speed of the bow is more important than its direction. (A good violinist can do a crescendo with a down-bow, which is really against nature, because there is more weight at the frog than at the point of the bow, and he can just as well do a diminuendo with an up-bow.) The modifications come when the tempo is altered and, if the musician cannot do this by himself, the conductor must know it. What Furtwängler said is still true – the correct tempo is that which, at the moment of playing, cannot be imagined any other way. This is now becoming far more difficult since people compare live music with records.

Chronologically speaking, you first study the score before you begin to rehearse. Your first problem, therefore, is that you have only experimented theoretically, in the abstract. If you play an instrument, you can try out various kinds of phrasing and articulation to hear how they sound. But when you stand in front of an orchestra it is far more complicated. Your time is limited and you are not alone. The musicians start to play and it is suddenly difficult to tell them how you have experimented, even down to the number of crescendos or sforzandos you want. A rehearsal lasts from ten a.m. to twelve-thirty or one o'clock, and you have to fit in your experimentation as well as the preparation for the concert. You know that the people playing these instruments are thinking about everything you are suggesting to or asking from them, as well as concentrating on their own (physical) problems with their instrument, and you must give them as much help as possible. For instance, if something is difficult, a young inexperienced conductor might very well say only: here comes the great sforzando, or, here we want more diminuendo. If it does not work exactly the way he wants it, he may imagine the players are not trying. Of course, there are difficult people in every orchestra because it is, after all, made up of people who are pleasant or not so pleasant, intelligent or less intelligent. The orchestra musician may have twenty or twenty-five years' experience; the conductor may only have been conducting for a few years. The ideal balance between the musician's experience and the authority of the young conductor can be very difficult to achieve.

The problem changes with the conductor's age and experience. You reach a point when you are not that young any more yourself and gradually get to a point where the orchestra is younger than you. The problem of experience versus inexperience is then reversed. A young oboist or flautist may have a beautiful idea, and then you should not be so stuck in your ways that you cannot listen to and work with them.

I think it is very important for the conductor to be spontaneous, to know his score, and to have absolute command on the technical side. You have to understand that the people in the orchestra have their own problems and musical difficulties. It is vital to be able to admit your own mistakes. Nobody is infallible. If you have a wonderful orchestra, and something goes wrong, it may well be the fault of the conductor. If you strike the wrong beat, if you show three instead of four, or the other way round, it is pointless to grumble. You must be able to say: 'That was my fault.' If you can say that, the matter is finished and you win the orchestra's respect. (In addition, if you admit your mistake, you are in a far stronger position to correct someone else's on the next occasion!) A young conductor should avoid wanting to be popular. The most you can hope to achieve is respect. Love comes quite naturally, or not at all.

I have always been prepared to rehearse whenever the orchestra or I felt it necessary. I have always had the interest, the curiosity and the readiness to work. Curiosity means wanting to discover new things. If this curiosity is lacking, if a musician says, 'I have played this Beethoven symphony for forty years, there is nothing new in it for me,' it cannot be helped. A really great orchestra is made up of both experience and curiosity. Musically speaking, when the hard work has been done, you should be confident and at ease, and feel goodwill and respect and love.

One of the most important things during rehearsals is to know what is important and in need of emphasis and what is not. The equivalent in writing would be to know what to underline. If you write a sentence, and underline every other word, there is no point in underlining. It is the same with playing music and phrasing. The first thing is to have a clear conception or idea, and then to rehearse until the musicians know exactly where you want an emphasis. If you are at one with the orchestra, and know that they do not just follow you blindly but join you, then each concert can be emphasized differently. The principle, and the place of intonation are fixed, but not the manner of playing, and this gives the concert a feeling of spontaneity.

Absolute pitch is a help in correcting false intonation. Intonation does not exist in a vacuum, since it is often influenced by correct or incorrect balance. A note may be too high or too low, or a chord may sound unclean because it is wrong from the point of view of balance. Or the overtones may suddenly be too weak or too loud in the chord, or the sound is not homogeneous. In a woodwind chord an instrument like the oboe can sometimes be very penetrating and harder than the others, and that automatically sounds wrong and unclean. You may then get the impression that the oboe is too high, but in fact it is only too hard. With orchestras you know really well, you can correct these things during the normal rehearsal time. They present no problems to me in Chicago or Berlin.

It is often said that orchestra musicians dislike rehearsing, but it must be said in their defence that some conductors waste a great deal of time. The conductor has to be able to play a piece through, to remember everything, and to correct things immediately because he might otherwise forget them. The more consciously you have analysed and worked during the study of the score, or at rehearsal, the more freely you can improvise on the night. It is almost like walking in a wood for the first time. You do not know where the path leads but, if you have studied the map, you can feel relaxed. Some musicians think that if you analyse or rationalize musical problems too much, the freshness will be lost, but the freshness can be far greater if rational work has gone before.

I also believe that you cannot conduct or bring out the full significance of what you, as a musician, can see in a Beethoven symphony unless you know the piano sonatas, the string quartets, and a few other key pieces as well. Certain cycles represent the essence of a composer's creation. In the case of Beethoven I think it is the piano sonatas and the string quartets, with Mozart the piano concertos and operas. How could you conduct the *Jupiter* Symphony without knowing *Die Entführung aus dem Serail*, the first act of *Don Giovanni*, or the C Major Piano Concerto (K. 467)? I do not think you can conduct Berlioz's *Symphonie fantastique* if you do not know *Roméo et Juliette* or *La Damnation de Faust*. How can you consider conducting the *Unfinished* Symphony, if that is the only Schubert you know? You cannot conduct *La mer* unless you know the Debussy preludes and études. You need as broad a knowledge as possible of the composer's output. The difference between the *Eroica* and the

Pastoral Symphony can be far greater than the difference between two composers whose works are similar. Beethoven was able to, or felt a need to adopt or create a new musical idiom for almost every piece he wrote. You need to know these pieces so as to apply your knowledge to the interpretation of the one you are actually performing.

Every young conductor is faced with the problem of consciously or unconsciously imitating the gestures of other conductors. This is natural enough, if he sees that the result he wants was achieved in this manner or that. Eventually, however, he will have to find his own code of gesture and movement.

This whole question has something to do with that much-abused word 'charisma', which is so often applied to conductors. If you try to imitate someone endowed with this gift, you will only produce a caricature, a travesty. You can only – and this is relatively easy to do – imitate the outward appearance.

In Furtwängler's case it would have meant imitating either his gesticulations or trembling hands, which are known from his films, or his fluctuations of tempo, without trying to understand the reasons behind them. Or, it would mean imitating Celibidache only as far as his slow tempi are concerned, without taking into consideration that he may have chosen a slow tempo because he needed time to make clear every last detail in the music and the relationship between them.

There is a limit to what one can play or conduct but it is important to remain curious. Klemperer had that curiosity – he came to rehearsals of pieces he did not know. Claudio Arrau, who had a vast repertoire, also knew an enormous amount of music he did not play himself. I think this kind of insatiable curiosity is the only guarantee that we will continue to develop.

~

The highlight of my collaboration with the English Chamber Orchestra was working on the complete cycle of the Mozart piano concertos, which we did in the course of ten years and played several times in Paris, London and New York.

The whole problem of simultaneously conducting and playing the piano is related to the nature of the works one is performing. It is not just a question of what can be done without a separate conductor. Nowadays one could even play a Chopin concerto with a fine orchestra, and conduct at the same time, but there would be little point in doing so.

With Mozart we have a real dialogue, a dualism. Sometimes it is piano and orchestra, sometimes piano against orchestra. A unity of articulation and phrasing can be achieved by playing and conducting in a way that is impossible with a separate conductor. The same goes for the early Beethoven concertos. There are, too, some lighter pieces that can be played with a great sense of fun and enjoyment in the virtuoso manner. I would put the Ravel Concerto in this category. Mitropoulos used to play and conduct Prokofiev's Third Concerto. I would have loved to have heard that. He played it in the 1920s with the Berlin Philharmonic. But the main interest in conducting from the keyboard applies really to the Mozart concertos.

The point of playing and conducting at the same time is to achieve a unity. Even in a situation of dialogue, and sometimes juxtaposition of piano and orchestra, there is a great advantage in having one source of musical direction throughout. The orchestra listens to the solo instrument more attentively when there is no separate conductor, not just to know precisely when to play, but also how to play.

The difficulties, however, are obvious: you must be able to split your concentration between what you are playing and what you are conducting. There are physical problems in playing difficult, elaborate passages while at the same time using the left hand, or a facial expression, to tell the orchestra what you want from them. The piano often finishes a phrase quietly while the orchestra comes in forte. One must be able to control these things mentally and physically. The pianist must be in charge of both his instrument and the orchestra.

My experience with playing and conducting – I did this for the first time in the late 1950s, so it is over forty years now – taught me that it is essential to be a professional conductor. Just consider the complexity of the opening tutti of a Mozart concerto. Perhaps one does not have to be able to conduct Stravinsky's *Rite of Spring* or similar complicated works, but one must be able to conduct a Mozart symphony. Good orchestras can more or less play by themselves, but that is not the purpose of the exercise.

I think it is against the nature of music and professionalism to play without a conductor. The terminology 'to follow' the soloist is already a misconception. In order to follow somebody you have to be behind him! There is a great difference between playing and conducting a Mozart piano concerto at the same time, and playing a Mozart concerto without a conductor. I think the reason that this happens so often is not a musical one. It is done for the sake of convenience, for showmanship, or, to be cynical, to save the cost of a separate conductor. And it is an insult to the orchestra. The Berlin Philharmonic is perfectly able to play a Mozart symphony without a conductor, and they could also play a Mozart concerto without a conductor. The added musical dimension can only come from a soloist who also conducts.

~

I played with Pierre Boulez for the first time in Berlin in 1964. Shortly afterwards, in 1965 or 1966, I performed with him in Paris in a series of concerts dedicated mainly to contemporary music and called 'Le domaine musical'. We performed Alban Berg's Chamber Concerto and I also played Schoenberg's piano pieces op. 11 and op. 19. We have had an ongoing professional and personal relationship since then, and have often worked together. I not only played the Chamber Concerto with him in London in 1967 but also some classical works: Beethoven's *Emperor* Concerto in Paris, and the Fourth Concerto in London. I also played with him quite frequently when he was Chief Conductor of the BBC, and later in New York. Our pièce de résistance, or *cheval de bataille*, remained Bartók's First Piano Concerto, which was rarely performed in those days. We played it in London with the BBC, in Paris, in Cleveland, and in Chicago, and made a recording of it. He left France in the 1960s, before I was nominated Music Director of the Orchestre de Paris in 1975, and wanted nothing further to do with Paris or the French government. He would not even allow the Orchestre de Paris to play his compositions. I considered it one of my happiest moments when I succeeded in persuading him to let us perform his works in Paris, and he even agreed to conduct the orchestra.

The exact date of this great event was 5 January 1976, and the programme was Beethoven's *Emperor* Concerto and the complete *Firebird* by Stravinsky. There was great excitement at the return of the prodigal son to Paris, and Boulez started what was to become a regular relationship with the Orchestre de Paris. It was Georges Pompidou who fulfilled all his conditions for the creation of IRCAM, the institute for research and acoustical and musical co-ordination, which was established as a part of the Centre Pompidou in 1977, under Boulez's directorship, for experimentation and research into modern compositional techniques. During the fifteen years I was with the Orchestre de Paris he remained a helpful supporter and a pillar of the orchestra's programmes and of musical life in Paris generally.

For his concerts, Boulez rehearses in great detail, taking not only the score but also the orchestra apart. He rehearses individual groups and makes everybody aware of the structure, of the skeleton of the music, as it were. He has a very particular way of rehearsing. The starting point is his infallible ear. He can hear details in the playing at the loudest and most complex moment, and is able to correct perfectly the slightest fault in intonation. I learned a great deal from him as a result. Having grown up playing the piano, I was, as most pianists are, not particularly sensitive to the problems of intonation, because the question of intonation on the piano is really the domain of the piano tuner. If the piano is out of tune there is nothing the pianist can do about it, whereas on string and wind instruments and with the voice each performer must produce the note himself, which means that any note can be perfectly in tune, too flat or too sharp. It is difficult to hear whether a note is flat or sharp, and very difficult for the performer to control. It requires a great deal of training and must be treated without any emotion both on the part of the player or singer and on the part of the conductor. Very often singers in particular are unable to correct intonation problems which they are made aware of by the conductor because they lose the sense of self-assurance which is necessary, and it becomes an emotional or psychological issue. It is terribly important for all concerned to treat this as a purely musical, technical or artistic problem.

Boulez is known to be very uncompromising in all his musical ideas and wishes and the same is true of him as a person. The way he thinks and behaves is totally devoid of any arrogance, and he expects, therefore, the same total commitment and sincerity from his colleagues and fellow musicians. It would be unthinkable for him to restrain himself from saying something he thought necessary simply because there was a risk of making a mistake, and this directness and his uncompromising nature have made him a musician to be greatly admired and, for me, also a person with a very high degree of integrity. It is the same integrity which has allowed him to fight so many battles against preconceived ideas in music making, and in music administration. It led him to very explosive statements in the early years, such as 'Schoenberg is dead!' 'Opera houses must be burned!' etc. It is this independence of thought that has given him the courage to deal with problems, whether in composing or as Music Director of the New York Philharmonic and the BBC Symphony Orchestra or, later on, in his activities at IRCAM.

As a composer, he is a very interesting mixture. His whole training and early works were strongly influenced by Olivier Messiaen, who was his teacher. His contact with the Second Viennese School and then his activities in Bayreuth, where he conducted *Parsifal* and the *Ring*, have broadened his horizon to such an extent that, as far as I am concerned, his is one of the most versatile musical minds working today. His orchestration is particularly imaginative. There are works such as *Rituel* (*in memoriam Bruno Maderna*), which divides the orchestra into different, independent groups; there are other works, such as *Notations*, where the orchestra is used on the one hand as the huge apparatus it is, but on the other hand also creates individual parts in the strings with a tremendous degree of individuality. One has the feeling that the orchestra is not treated as four groups: strings, woodwind, brass and percussion. One feels rather that it is treated either as one unity, made out of all these elements, or as seventy or eighty units, because even the string writing in *Notations* is so divided that very often every player plays music different from that of the person next to him. I could draw a parallel between that and the problem of having two hands when playing the piano, namely that one either plays with one unit or with ten units. It is the same thing with Boulez's orchestra – it is one unit or eighty units, never three or four.

Notations was meant to be a series of twelve orchestra pieces of which there had been a kind of embryo version, very miniature piano pieces which Boulez wrote when he was very young. He wrote the first four pieces for the Orchestre de Paris, and he has continued the series for the Chicago Symphony Orchestra.

Boulez has also convinced me that the problem of acceptance of contemporary music is due, on the one hand, to the poor level of performance at the première and, on the other hand, to the fact that contemporary works are often played once or twice and then left forgotten in a library. *Notations* I–IV (I conducted the world première in 1981) I did very often with the Orchestre de Paris both on tour and in Paris on at least three different occasions. It was amazing and a great joy for me to see how the musicians not only learned the pieces, but felt that they were part of our regular repertoire, and whenever we took them up again there was a sort of immediate recollection of all the work that had been done on previous occasions. It was therefore possible to play them with the same kind of familiarity and understanding that one brings to the more standard repertoire.

~

Playing some of the best contemporary music is certainly much more difficult than it used to be. This is due to the fact that we idolize the notion of the first performance. Certain works become easier to understand and to remember through repetition, and this repetition of contemporary music is an aspect that has been grossly neglected by performers and musical institutions alike. Certain works remain difficult because they have only been played once or twice, and not repeated for many years by the same musicians or for the same audience.

When I regularly conduct a contemporary work, it becomes part of my repertoire which I re-study the same way as I would a Ravel or Debussy score, not to mention Mozart or Beethoven. If you said, 'There is a world première tomorrow of a composition by Boulez,' everybody would turn up and listen with interest. If, a year later, you were to say, 'We shall now have the second performance of this work by Boulez,' nobody would be interested. I agree fully with Boulez for the need not only to provide a musical education that includes all the systems of music – tonal, atonal, serial – but also to ensure that works one considers important are performed regularly. When listening to Beethoven's Fifth Symphony, you will remember what you know about it, even after a very mediocre performance. But I do not imagine that Beethoven's later string quartets are all that easy to read or play. We tend to think of these works as more accessible simply because the style has had time to settle – just as a good wine needs time to settle and mature. But I am sure that those string quartets were just as difficult for the players and the listeners of Beethoven's time as the Bartók string quartets were in the twentieth century.

In addition, the quality of performances of contemporary music often leaves a lot to be desired. I have battled in Paris and in Chicago, not just for playing first performances, not just for taking care that important new works are given second, third, fourth and fifth performances, but for rehearsals of the more complex scores to take place far enough in advance and not just two days before the concert. If you are dealing with a totally new work, the musicians and the conductor need time to digest the music to achieve a degree of familiarity with it.

To give a concrete example: I played the first four *Notations* with the Paris Orchestra in 1981. The music is very complex and difficult to play, difficult for the listener to perceive and difficult to conduct. It was difficult for us in every way, technically as well as musically, and we rehearsed it very thoroughly. I worked with each section separately, strings, wind, brass, percussion. Then we had rehearsals before giving the first performance. Two or three years later, we wanted to perform *Notations* again. The work was then, of course, slightly easier. Some people in the orchestra had played it already. Some years later we took it up for the third time. I began to realize that this was the first time in my experience that a contemporary piece of music had become a repertoire piece – for the orchestra, if not for the listeners. The players began to develop the same reflexes towards this music as they had towards the repertoire they had played all their lives, such as Beethoven, Brahms, or Debussy. They knew what to expect.

~

Western European classical music, as we know it, is the youngest among the arts. The paintings we know date back two thousand years, the literature we read goes back three or four thousand years, but the music we live with only dates primarily from the end of the seventeenth century. Three hundred years is a very short time.

There are certain elements in tonal music which give me the feeling that they are more than man-made. I do not know whether this is so, or whether, as Boulez says, it is a question of habit: the fact that we have grown up with this music and this system, and therefore tend to see in it a more-than-human dimension which does not really exist. I believe that something happens when the tones in music, the sounds, are set in motion, something that gives them a certain independence. That applies to *Götterdämmerung* as much as it does to the smallest minuet composed by the young Mozart. It is not important to know whether Wagner's chromaticism led to Schoenberg's twelve-tone system evolutionarily, or whether Schoenberg's formula was a break with tonality. The fact remains that it happened. There was a struggle for equality which started with the French Revolution, and was taken to its extreme in the works of Marx, Engels and later Lenin. I see a parallel in the development of music, and, if my theory is right, we are now in a difficult situation, because music has been in an 'impasse', at a dead end, for a long time.

I do not believe there has ever been a situation similar to the one we are experiencing. The majority of today's audiences who attend concerts regularly and with great interest still think of the music of Stravinsky, Schoenberg and Bartók as modern or contemporary. But many of these works were written between 1910 and 1920. The people who saw the world première of *Der Ring des Nibelungen* in Bayreuth in 1876 would certainly not have regarded the late Haydn symphonies or Beethoven's middle period as modern or contemporary music.

There has never been as much interest in music as there is today. There have never before been so many people able to listen to music. But I am not so sure about the quality of the audiences. Beethoven's later works must have been just as difficult to listen to in the 1820s as some of the work of Boulez, Messiaen, or Lutosławski is today. But Beethoven's audiences had something that came from an active

93

musical education: many of the listeners at those first performances had a knowledge of music that today's audiences lack.

~

In September 1966 I went on my first trip to Japan. I am fortunate to have spent a lot of time in many different countries, and am therefore quite fluent in several languages – English, Hebrew, German, French, Italian and Spanish. Since, therefore, I am able to feel at home in most countries I go to, I found it extremely irritating to arrive in Japan and not be able even to read a sign, not know if they were selling bicycles or salt in a shop. It is terribly annoying to have to rely always on interpreters. I had had the same feeling during my first trip to the Soviet Union in 1965.

In Japan the interest in classical music was already so strong then that it was hard to believe that Western music was such a recent phenomenon. I think Beethoven's Ninth Symphony was first performed in Japan during the First World War. Yet today there is probably more music performed in Tokyo than in any capital in Europe or America. I think the most fascinating aspect of giving concerts in Japan is not the fact that there is such an interest in going to concerts, in buying records and in developing the technology that we have all profited from as far as recordings are concerned: what has become more and more obvious to me as I keep going back to Japan is that a Japanese audience's approach to music is very different from what we are used to in Europe or America. There is not the slightest feeling that music is some form of entertainment; there is a palpable feeling of concentration in the audience, which is very inspiring to the musician on stage. Maybe it is due to a certain sense of distance they feel, I don't know, but whatever the reason, there is a seriousness and an awe for culture that we would do well to imitate. It is a quality that I have grown to admire and love increasingly. I have only once conducted a Japanese orchestra, the NHK Symphony in 1973, and it was a memorable experience. In 1990, I played Brahms's piano concertos with the Tokyo Philharmonic under Antonio Pappano and was struck then, too, by the extreme seriousness and respect that the musicians feel for the music.

I am sure that in time the Japanese will also come to feel the same degree of freedom that one encounters in Europe – freedom within the music and towards the music. The awe and respect they feel for music and the seriousness with which they approach it augur extremely well for the development in future generations of a sense of belonging, belonging to the music and the music's belonging to them. Sometimes I feel like telling the Japanese that, although this is Western music and although this is the product of another civilization, there is something universal about music which is much more interesting and much more important than the fact that it comes from France or from Germany.

~

In 1967 I not only played with the New Philharmonia Orchestra as a soloist under Klemperer but also conducted the orchestra for the first time in a performance of the Mozart Requiem.

I had done quite a lot of choral music before I started conducting symphony orchestras in the 1960s – the Mozart and Brahms Requiems, some Bruckner masses, and, naturally, Beethoven's Ninth Symphony. I learned a lot from Wilhelm Pitz, who was a rare musician and a wonderful choral conductor. When I worked with the New Philharmonia Orchestra in the late 1960s, my first experiences of choral conducting were with Pitz, since he was the director of the chorus. I was very taken by his ability to achieve a huge range of expression through very detailed differentiation between legato and marcato singing, and a combination of the two. I remember especially in the Bruckner Te Deum, where the choruses burst in with massive explosions of sound, how much inner tension they possessed thanks to Pitz's preparation. He really roused my appetite for more choral work, and from there it was natural that I should also want to do more opera.

The chorus is often used for big tuttis, and it can sound relatively expressionless if it is just a massive, uncontrolled, inarticulate sound. And yet, after Pitz had dealt with individual voices and the full dynamic range of the chorus, he achieved an extra dimension. I remember particularly how he rehearsed the unison movement in Bruckner's Te Deum, 'Aeterna fac cum Sanctis tuis'. It is sung seven times, and is marked fortissimo from the beginning. Pitz managed to get the chorus to save energy, volume and intensity, so as to achieve an even greater fortissimo at the climax.

In 1968 I went to New York for the first time with the London Symphony Orchestra. István Kertész, who was then Principal Conductor of the orchestra, was taken ill and I replaced him at the last moment. In 1969 I conducted the Berlin Philharmonic for the first time, and later the New York Philharmonic. At that time I was not certain whether I should give up the piano in favour of conducting, or vice versa, and many people I worked with could not see how I could combine the two. Some felt I should give up the piano – a lot of them thought that I was more gifted as a conductor than as a pianist, and that there were many very fine pianists coming up, but not so many conductors. I fought against this rather blinkered way of thinking – I wanted to keep my options open. I had started playing with Dietrich Fischer-Dieskau regularly, and it was hard even for my friends to accept that I could be a fully-fledged pianist on the one hand and an accompanist on the other. And then, of course, I also played chamber music, especially with Jacqueline du Pré and Pinchas Zukerman at that time, and later also with Itzhak Perlman. I was the conductor of a chamber orchestra – with which I both played and conducted, and I conducted symphony orchestras. And when, in 1973, I conducted my first opera, I think people just gave up and stopped talking to me about it. To my mind, they are all victims of compartmentalized thinking; they wish to see each of these different manifestations of music making as separate professions. I must admit that I had never imagined that I could be active in all those spheres. In fact, I have an absolute horror of spreading myself too thinly.

~

I have always wanted to find out how the nature of an instrument, played by a great artist, influences his phrasing and his articulation. I learned a tremendous amount this way and, of course, you can only learn this from chamber music. Most of the chamber music I played with strings was with Jacqueline. Some of my neglect of chamber music in recent years stems from the fact that I never found anybody who could take her place.

The principle of chamber music is one of dialogue, which means that there are times when each instrument speaks independently, and others when one instrument merges with another. The idea of chamber music as the essence of music making is gradually disappearing for a variety of reasons. First of all, it was very much linked to playing music in private homes – not only by amateurs, but by professionals, too. Now people have less time, and a greater interest in passive musical appreciation and listening. Today there are so many more millions of people listening to music, but far fewer playing chamber music just for the pleasure of it. It is a tradition that has been lost. So much music is now available for listening purposes – radio, television, and, of course, records. But I think that the diminishing interest in playing chamber music is part of the whole twentieth-century process of thought.

When a piece of music is performed, it is put in motion, and it evolves differently each time, according to the individual playing, the acoustic conditions, and so on. A composer can have an idea of how a piece should sound only as it is in his head. While it is there, he can make what he will of it. It is purely a creation of his being. As soon as the composer writes it down, though, the piece of music becomes subject to other laws. As a conductor, one must be aware of this. There has to be a perfect equilibrium between the conception – the preconceived idea of how the music should sound and the actual realization, and the realization can never be exactly the same twice.

Originally chamber music was intended for rooms far smaller than the modern concert hall, which seats between two and three thousand people. Paradoxically, television, although seen by millions, retains this intimacy, because the camera can get close to the players. Filming a large symphony orchestra, let alone a big symphony orchestra with chorus and soloists, is very difficult, whereas filming chamber music – a trio, quartet, or an octet – is not only easier, but also far more interesting. Television allows you to get closer to the faces, to the expression of a musician's body. I find it far more satisfying to watch three or four or eight people on a television screen than a hundred and twenty. This has to do with the eye of course, but it is becoming more difficult to separate the eye from the ear. We are subject to terrible noise most of the time, and people do not realise that the ear has a memory. If you come out of a hotel room on the thirty-fifth floor and go down in the lift where some sort of music is being played all the time, and you get into a taxi, where the radio is playing some other kind of music, and you then arrive at the concert hall and hear the first bar of a Beethoven sonata, or a Beethoven string quartet, the ear subconsciously and automatically associates this with all the music you have heard during the last hour. This is why, ideally, I avoid listening to music before a concert, whether I am playing or listening. This is comparable with the pianist or violinist who goes on practising until the moment he goes on stage. This may sometimes be necessary but, if you can avoid it, you will discover the freshness of the first touch, the first contact with the keyboard, which will otherwise be lacking.

I grew up in an environment where it was usual to play chamber music at home once a week. Even as late as the early 1960s we were playing regularly for our own pleasure in our London home. I remember playing as soloist with the Cleveland Orchestra in the early 1960s. At that time the assistant concert master was Arnold Steinhardt. There was a wonderful solo viola player called Abraham Skernik, and the solo cellist was Jules Eskin. I did not even know these people – but during rehearsal we struck up a professional and personal rapport and went to Abraham Skernik's house afterwards, had something to eat, and then played chamber music all night. I did not return to the hotel and when we finished playing the next morning, we had breakfast and went to the next rehearsal.

~

One great musician with whom I had very limited contact but whose influence on music making in general and on string players in particular was of paramount importance was Pablo Casals. I met him for the first time in Puerto Rico, subsequently going several times as a pianist and a conductor to the festival which he organized. I played Brahms's piano concertos and I also once conducted Elgar's Cello Concerto with Jacqueline. Casals is of great historical importance because he was probably the first cellist who had an almost fanatical need to play well in tune. Until Casals came along I think people accepted the fact that the cello was such an impossibly difficult instrument that, when the music went into its higher register, cellists often played out of tune.

Casals' whole concept of intonation and articulation was not only of great importance to string players but influenced me tremendously both about playing the piano and about music. He was of great importance in what we call expressive intonation, namely not simply well-tempered intonation. The piano does not have the flexibility of tuning that a string instrument has, therefore the enharmonics do not exist in the piano: a D sharp and an E flat are exactly the same note. With string instruments you can change the intonation very slightly to make a change of colour and alter the expressive intensity of the note. If an F sharp is a leading note to G in a G major scale, it is considerably higher than a G flat in the key of F major. In other words, as an F sharp going up to G it has a higher pitch than as a G flat going down to F.

The whole point of Bach's *Well-Tempered Clavier* was, basically, to clean up a lot of the problems of intonation. Casals made me very conscious of the geographical position of the notes, that there are certain notes that give a feeling of pulling in a certain direction, going down, and that others have a pushing feeling, going up. This is something which on the piano, of course, you cannot do, but if your ear is made aware of the expressive intonation as opposed to the well-tempered intonation, you balance your hands and the chords that you play on the piano to compensate with intensity for what you cannot change in flexibility of pitch. This is a lesson that Casals taught musicians in his time, and it is a lesson that is very important in all tonal music.

The other aspect which cannot be overestimated, because it is so important, is Casals' preoccupation with the articulation of the shorter notes in any musical phrase. In legato phrases, especially, there is a tendency for the shorter notes to be swallowed up. Casals had a virtual mania for articulating the smaller notes. He had an almost onomatopoeic way of describing this to the orchestra: he said 'la la lai', not only a collection of vowels – aeiou – but vowels preceded by consonants to clearly articulate the notes. You can hear in Bach's C major Suite, in the recording of the rehearsal with the Marlboro Orchestra, what importance he attached to the smaller notes, to the semiquavers.

Those were his two chief innovations in the history of interpretation. As he grew older he became more and more obsessed by these two points, with the result that younger musicians who came under his influence often tended to imitate them to the point of exaggeration, even of caricature.

For me, Casals' ideas were particularly interesting because I was a pianist. I tried to play the piano as a stringed instrument with the kind of legato that only the bow can produce, whereas he tried to play a stringed instrument as a piano. Even in the most beautifully controlled legato there still has to be a kind of natural articulation which the piano, since it has a different key for each note, produces.

Around Casals there were quite a number of musicians who played chamber music with him and came very much under his musical and personal spell. The most extraordinary of these was Isaac Stern, who had begun his musical life as a great virtuoso but soon became passionately interested in chamber music and developed highly original ideas about the capabilities of the violin. Even when playing the most obviously virtuosic works on the violin, such as Wieniawski's Second Concerto, he was never satisfied with producing a conventional, beautiful violin tone, but tried always to go beyond the character of the instrument. Obviously all great violinists try to extend the capabilities of their instrument, but I had the feeling that Stern was more concerned with the ideas of the music than the potential of the instrument itself. This is why, in a very long career, he was able to produce colours on the violin which were not normally attributed to it. Such colours came through a much more varied use of vibrato. He allowed himself the luxury, or the asceticism, of playing with very little, sometimes with none at all, to get a special colour. He also had a highly refined sense of co-ordination between the left hand and the bowing arm. Of all the great violinists, Stern more than others made me aware of the importance of the use of the bow and showed me that there is absolutely not only no reason to play with the full bow every time you start on one end of it, but that it is even, from the point of view of musical expression, counterproductive to do so. One can get a much greater variety of articulation, and therefore of expressiveness, by sometimes playing with a small amount of bow and a very concentrated sound and at the next moment playing with the full bow, where the sound has much more air around it.

Stern's great influence as a musician is felt predominantly among the younger generation of violinists, especially among those who came from Israel, a country to which he contributed so much of his energies outside violin playing. I am thinking, of course, of

Pinchas Zukerman and Itzhak Perlman.

I met both of them very briefly in Israel when we were all children. Pinchas came to the concert of the Budapest String Quartet when they played the Beethoven quartets in Israel and when Casals was there, but I met him in 1968 in New York when he was nineteen years old and already had a reputation as a child prodigy who knew all the chamber music literature by heart. It was said that he was able to play either the violin part or the viola part in any chamber music piece that one could think of. We met after a concert I had given with the Philadelphia Orchestra, conducted by Eugene Ormandy. The next day we played chamber music for our pleasure in the hotel where Jacqueline and I were staying. There was immediately a sense of affinity, a musical affinity, between the three of us, but also such a close affinity between the two string players that we decided on the spot that we wanted to play trios regularly. And we did.

Pinchas also played with me very often as violin soloist; it was with me that he gave his first concerts in England and, together with the English Chamber Orchestra, we played in New York in 1969. For the short time that Jacqueline was still able to play, he became an integral part of our musical life, with the trio evenings becoming a high point. There was an understanding between him and Jacqueline as string players, in the way they matched the vibrato and the attacks, which I have seldom encountered in ensembles made up of great soloists.

Itzhak Perlman in those days was more the pure violinist. He was also interested in chamber music, but chamber music was less an integral part of his life. With, on the one hand, his unique talent and, on the other, the strength of character and mind he had to develop in order to fight his physical disability – he had been struck by polio at the age of four – he was an exceptional personality. He had had to become strong to fight against conventional opinions – people were not used to a violinist playing solo sitting down and very few people believed that he would be able to make a career as a solo violinist because it would be difficult for him to travel as well as to cope with all the side effects of his physical disability. I do not need to point out that he proved all the doubters wrong.

Among many unforgettable evenings, I had the pleasure, in 1970, of conducting his first concert with the Berlin Philharmonic Orchestra, when he played the Tchaikovsky Violin Concerto. I still remember the amazement of the public when he appeared on stage. I carried his violin behind him, and I felt that this was not the normal applause of an audience welcoming an artist on to the platform. There was an admiration for his evident courage, mixed with a sort of reticence, as if it would be out of place to applaud too loudly. As soon as he started playing, of course, everybody forgot that he was sitting down and that he suffered from polio; they were bewitched by his playing. In the last movement he broke a string. There are very few bars in this movement where the soloist does not play, but in a little gap of two bars he gave his Stradivarius to Thomas Brandis, who was then leader of the orchestra, who gave Itzhak his violin so that he could continue to play, and the colleague sitting next to Brandis gave Brandis his violin so that he could change the string on the Stradivarius. When that was done Brandis continued playing on Itzhak's instrument. I can still remember the expression on Itzhak's face. He wanted his violin back but, such was his mastery, one could not really hear the difference in the tone. On the other hand, I have not forgotten Brandis's joy at having under his chin this priceless Stradivarius – I think he parted with it very reluctantly before the end of the movement.

~

One of the most natural violinists I have ever come across was Nathan Milstein, who played with me very often during my years in Paris. He was able to produce the most individual and beautiful sound in the most effortless way imaginable. He held his instrument in such a way that it seemed to drop almost to his stomach and sat in rehearsals with a big handkerchief on his shoulder and a nonchalant expression in his face, as if this was the easiest thing in the world. Milstein's great lesson to me as a conductor and, I suppose, to many violinists, is that one should never force the violin and never try to go beyond the limit of volume and intensity that the instrument can take or provide. His great palette of colours stemmed also from the fact that he had a very individual way of fingering, which he always took great pride in saying he did intuitively and very differently from evening to evening. There were occasions in Paris when we would play the Mendelssohn or the Brahms Violin Concerto several times in one week and I was amazed by his gift of improvisation, changing fingerings and bowings from one evening to the next, naturally and effortlessly. Milstein has remained for me the supreme example of the pure violinist.

8

ISRAEL AFTER 1967

In the spring of 1967, when Israel's very existence was at stake and Nasser had closed the straits of Tiran, one did not need to be a prophet to realize that war was imminent. The situation was very clear and truly desperate and, like many other musicians, I could not stand the idea of being away from my family or my colleagues and friends in the Philharmonic. I decided to go back home. I arrived on one of the last normal commercial flights on 31 May 1967. Jacqueline insisted on coming with me, and we played concerts in Tel Aviv and Haifa every night. We played our last concert on 5 June, the eve of the war, in Beersheba, which is about halfway between Tel Aviv and what was then the Egyptian border. Driving back to Tel Aviv that night, after the concert, we realized how close to war we were as we watched the tanks going along the road in the opposite direction. Zubin Mehta arrived a few days later.

It was only because the Israeli air force was able to destroy the Egyptian air force on the ground within hours that it was possible for Israel to emerge victorious. At the time, though, the outcome was certainly not clear – but it was crystal clear to everyone in Israel that this was a fight for the country's very existence.

If you fight for survival, you must believe that you will win, but the odds were against Israel, as they had been in 1948. The best proof of this was the way in which public opinion changed within a week. Until the day the war started, public opinion in Europe (I do not know about the USA, as I was not there at the time) was almost totally pro-Israel. The fact that the Israelis managed to take care of themselves, and to survive so successfully, somehow made public opinion turn against them practically overnight.

After the 1967 war, which ensured the survival of Israel and the survival of the Jewish nation in the Middle East, a grave problem arose due to the fact that so many Arabs were now under Israeli control. Having accomplished their own transition from a minority to a majority, the Israelis now had to deal with a minority within their own nation. It was a problem the Jews had not experienced for thousands of years. I am not convinced that this new transition was as smooth and perfect as that from minority to majority. It is probably impossible to expect anything else from people who have suffered throughout history from the intolerance of others – a mild definition of anti-Semitism, when you think of the pogroms in Russia and the excesses of the Spanish Inquisition, not to mention the atrocities of the Nazis. However, even though the Arab minority dreamed only of destroying the Jews, there was a need for tolerance which was not realized either by Israel or Israeli politicians.

I am no politician, nor have I any 'magical' solutions to offer, and it is not my place to advise Israel's politicians. I can only express my very personal, Jewish opinion that a way must be found, there must be tolerance. But we have been part of a persecuted minority for many centuries, so that taking the needs of our neighbours into account may be expecting too much of Israelis too soon.

Yet I think such tolerance is essential for the very survival of the Jewish state. And tolerance is by no means foreign to Jewish thinking or Jewish philosophy. The Bible and the Talmud teach us not only how to deal with ourselves but also with our neighbours. But developing the kind of tolerance I refer to would require a conscious effort to change many concepts and attitudes which are the result of the Jews' long existence in the Diaspora. Jewish humour, often at the expense of non-Jews, expressions such as *goyim naches* (good enough for the non-Jews), is acceptable as a means of self-defence, even admirable, in circumstances where the Jew is in a minority. But as soon as the Israeli Jew is in a position to control the lives of a minority – and I say this without entering into any discussion concerning the degree of animosity felt by that minority – he can no longer use an expression like *goyim naches*!

The next stage in the history of Jewish development, coexistence with the Arabs, is something which I hope will come with the next generation of Israelis. I believe that events since 1967 have shown that some kind of coexistence is necessary for the survival of both the state and the spirit of Israel. This is one of the most vital developments for the future. The Jewish state is situated in the Middle East, and it has a responsibility to the area and to the culture and development of that area. When the State of Israel was founded, not enough was done to ensure that it would one day become part of the Middle Eastern community of nations. In the schools for instance, the second language has never been Arabic but always English, the third sometimes French, sometimes Arabic. We live surrounded by Arabs and must not forget that they have made an enormous contribution to the development of civilisation. There was Arab poetry in the Middle Ages; the Arabs have a rich culture; scientific discoveries emanated from the Arabs – words such as chemistry and algebra are evidence of this.

Once the principles of coexistence are worked out, Israel could and should play a major role. Israel could be one of the leaders, if not the main leader, of the Middle Eastern community of nations. I believe it is essential for Jewish, or rather Israeli thinking not to be directed exclusively towards Europe and the West. Israel should instead create a fusion of East and West. And part of the local Middle Eastern culture should be incorporated into the country's education – starting with Arabic as the compulsory second language, thereby further developing the Middle Eastern nature of the State of Israel.

In a way this has already been accomplished in the field of gastronomy – all Israelis eat hummus and falafel, and all the other delicacies of the Arab world. They have adapted their eating habits, while continuing to eat gefilte fish and other typically Jewish food. It ought to be possible to bring about the same kind of adaptation of cultural and political values. The Arabs must be assured that the State of Israel is not simply an artificially implanted Western state, and that it does not consist exclusively of people from Warsaw, Berlin, New York, Moscow and Buenos Aires, but of people who have become part of the Middle East.

To my mind this is the only way for Israel to approach the problems of coexistence. The country must not remain an island totally independent of its neighbours. At the moment, while we are still in a state of war, it is not possible to realize this aim, but when the problems of coexistence *are* solved, we should be ready in Israel. I am no expert on defence, and I do not wish to express an opinion on things I know nothing about. What I do know is that the only way Israel can remain faithful to the idea of a Jewish state, the idea that inspired Ben-Gurion and his friends, is to become an organic part of the Middle Eastern community of nations. It was to this goal that Teddy Kollek dedicated all his energies as Mayor of Jerusalem. Culture, language and knowledge are not things that can be added after peace is achieved. We must be prepared sooner rather than later.

History shows us that Jews and Arabs can coexist and, even more than that, inspire each other. (I am, of course, thinking of Spain in the Middle Ages.) The mind boggles at the thought of what might come out of true, sincere and effective cooperation between Jews and Arabs in the Middle East. We could very well see a second Age of Enlightenment.

Paradoxically, Palestinian identity has actually been enhanced by the fact that so many Israeli politicians have refused to recognize its existence! I remember Golda Meir saying in 1970, when asked about the Palestinian problem: 'What do you mean by Palestinian problem? There are no Palestinians! The only Palestinians are the Jews now living in what used to be Palestine!' This was asking for trouble. Even from a strategic point of view, it was hardly an intelligent statement.

Whether the Palestinians will have a separate state, or a federation with Jordan or Israel, I cannot say. But I do know that there should one day be a community of nations in the Middle East – or what is really the Near East – consisting of Egypt, Israel, Jordan, Lebanon and Syria.

When I returned to Europe a week or ten days after the war in June 1967, one could no longer talk about the Jewish underdog, but one had to tread very gently. The terrible events of the Second World War appeared to have been suddenly forgotten, and at first there were veiled, and later more open allusions to Jewish imperialism. I realized again what a short memory we have. Within a matter of days the world had forgotten that the Arabs had initiated the war which they then lost.

∼

I had met David Ben-Gurion as a child when, in the early 1950s, he heard me play. At this time everybody was concerned with changing the image of the Diaspora Jew to the Jew of Israel, and this led them to make all kinds of gestures, some good and some bad, including changing their names to their Hebrew equivalents. Ben-Gurion was not his original name: he was born in Plonsk in Poland as David Grün. He was very keen that I should change my name, Barenboim, which is the Yiddish version of Birnbaum (pear tree), to a Hebrew name. He tried to persuade my parents to change to the Hebrew *Agassi*, meaning pear. None of us was very enthusiastic, and he said, humorously, that it would be better to make the change before I became famous, that the name Agassi would be far easier for people to remember than Barenboim, and that those who could not pronounce Barenboim would manage Agassi, and might even think it was Italian.

Ben-Gurion was both a pragmatist and a visionary. A great deal of what Israel represents, and has become, is due to his efforts. He was one of the great statesmen of this century, comparable to Winston Churchill. He was not merely a politician but a statesman, the difference being that a politician is concerned with pragmatic plans, whereas a statesman is a person with a strategy and a vision. The qualities of a visionary do not always harmonize with those of a politician.

Staging Wagner's operas one is faced with a similar problem, because of the seemingly irreconcilable mixture of symbolism and naturalism. *Der Ring des Nibelungen* is not just naturalistic, with water and fire; in fact the naturalistic element is often suggested by the orchestra, and does not inevitably have to be shown on stage. The characters and situations in Wagner operas, particularly in the *Ring*, possess a symbolic significance which is almost impossible to describe in a naturalistic way.

A statesman must possess this visionary quality as well as the attributes of the pragmatist, so knowing how to achieve his vision. Ben-Gurion had a vision of Zionism and socialism. Not only did he provide the impulse to create the State of Israel, but he was also able to guide it along those lines. The Israel I remember from my childhood and adolescence was very much the outcome of his vision and his creation.

One of the most extraordinary things about Ben-Gurion, in addition to the role he played in the history of Israel and that of the twentieth century, was that he always appreciated the need to create a Jewish homeland with due respect for everything that existed and could exist in the Middle East. He was a great fighter for the Jewish cause, but also a great moderator when the danger of excesses began to raise its ugly head. He proved that in his relations with the British Mandate, and later in his relations with the Arabs, and the way he wanted relations with the Arabs to develop. Even in 1967, immediately after the Six Day War, although he was already an old man and no longer in government, he continued to develop some very original and forward-looking attitudes. After the war, Ben-Gurion said something which was extremely far-sighted. (It was not heeded, of course, or could not be heeded in the state of euphoria existing at that time.) He said that he would return all the conquered territories in exchange for peace. This was a utopian idea, because none of the Arab countries wanted to live in peace with Israel. He also said that he would destroy the old walls surrounding the city of Jerusalem. The whole world would have been up in arms against such an act, but it would have ensured that Jerusalem would never again be a divided city. The wall around the old city of Jerusalem is both a physical and a psychological obstacle. We know the significance of the Berlin Wall, which existed for less than thirty years. The wall in Jerusalem has been there for centuries.

Ben-Gurion had a vision of unity and coexistence in the city of Jerusalem. Unfortunately, with the euphoria of military success and the triumph of survival which swept the country immediately after the 1967 war, his ideas and visions were not popular. He no longer commanded the people's attention. With his departure, political life in Israel entered into a period of turmoil, with grave political consequences both for Israel and for its relations with the Arabs.

Nowadays, a prime minister in Israel needs three main qualities. First, he has to be able to deal with the population of Israel, and dealing with two or three million Jews at one time is no easy task. (There is an old joke that, where there is one Jew, there are at least three political parties!) He has to be able to govern, always remembering the Arab minority. Secondly, a prime minister in Israel needs to be able to deal with the Jews outside Israel – not just the Jewish lobby in Washington, but all the large Jewish communities in North and South America, and Europe. The Soviet Union was not accessible in Ben-Gurion's time, but some kind of dialogue was possible. He was able to communicate the fervour of his commitment without stepping on ground that was difficult for Jewish communities in the Diaspora to accept. In the 1950s, one used to say that a real Zionist is not somebody talking about Zionism in Rio de Janeiro, Washington or Paris, but somebody who goes to Israel and makes a practical contribution to building the state. And the third quality an Israeli prime minister needs, and will need more and more, is the ability to deal with the Arabs and with the superpowers. In the 1950s, we also had to deal with Britain and France. There was de Gaulle in France, and we must not forget that the British had only left the Middle East in the late 1940s. Ben-Gurion was excellent at dealing with all these complications. The main difficulty in dealing with the Arabs was their total unwillingness to negotiate with Israel as a state. Although there was no hesitation in Ben-Gurion's policies, in his strategy and vision for Israel as a Jewish homeland, he always conveyed the feeling that the Arabs had rights that had to be respected. This was certainly not an easy thing to do, because the country was in a state of war with all Arab countries, and the official Arab aim was to push the Jews into the sea. So it was not just war but a question of survival.

There are no bounds to my admiration for Ben-Gurion and the way he managed to balance his vision of Israel and his vision of the Middle East. I think his constant evolving of new ideas, his constant alertness to the aspects of conflict, were due to his great interest in, and preoccupation with philosophy and philosophical problems.

He was an extremely well-read man; he developed an interest in Far Eastern thought and Buddhism, and practised yoga. He was fascinated by the figure of Don Quixote, and dreamed of learning Spanish well enough to read Cervantes in the original. At a time when the very survival of the country and the people were at stake, it was hard to understand how he could concern himself with issues not directly related to the conflict in the Middle East. His philosophical curiosity was often misunderstood or, rather, not understood at all by many Israelis who were only able to deal with their own problems or, at most, the problems of the State of Israel. He became a great example for me, a symbol, somebody totally committed to the cause of his people, yet with an ability to think pragmatically and with the curiosity to interest himself in such far-removed things as

Buddhism and other philosophical literature. He had no particular interest in music, but he understood its importance for many people and, in a detached way, he encouraged cultural institutions and in particular the Israel Philharmonic Orchestra. Although he was a very rare visitor to the concert hall, he was present at the opening concert of the orchestra in its new home, the Mann Auditorium.

9

LIEDER AND GUEST CONDUCTING

With the one exception, in Bayreuth in 1963, I did not accompany singers in public until 1969 – the year when I gave my first recital with Dietrich Fischer-Dieskau. I subsequently worked with him regularly for nearly twenty years. I had been a great admirer of his since I first heard him in Vienna in 1952. He attended a recital Jacqueline and I played in Rome in 1968 and afterwards wrote us the most touching letter of appreciation. At that time I was trying to set up a London festival devoted mainly to chamber music called South Bank Summer Music. The idea emanated partly from me, partly from the Festival Hall authorities, and I was responsible for it for three years, from 1968 to 1970.

There is, of course, already another summer festival in London, the largest music festival in the world – the Promenade Concerts, with their wonderful tradition, which take place in the Royal Albert Hall. But at the Festival Hall, which is the home of symphonic music during the year, and at the Queen Elizabeth Hall, no music at all was played in the summer. The season finished at the end of June or the beginning of July, and then there was no music in London except for the Proms, which have their own audiences and are dedicated mainly to symphonic music. The authorities were undecided what to do with the Festival Hall – apart from a period allocated to a ballet season – or with the Queen Elizabeth Hall, and they asked me if I had any suggestions. So we worked out a scheme for a chamber music festival on the South Bank. As Fischer-Dieskau had been so delighted with our concert in Rome, I asked him whether he would consider singing. He agreed, and we gave our first concert in London – it was Schubert's *Winterreise*.

This was the beginning of a long collaboration, with many concerts all over Europe and in the USA, as well as several recording projects. It is thanks to him that I came to know a lot of musical literature I had not known before, particularly works by Hugo Wolf. We recorded all the songs Wolf wrote for male voice, all the Brahms songs, Mahler, Mozart, Liszt and Schubert.

When I was in Salzburg as a nine-year-old, I only spoke Spanish, so in those days I learned German with an Austrian accent. But then I had no opportunity of speaking it for years, and in Berlin I found myself surrounded by English-speaking people most of the time. My work with Fischer-Dieskau taught me a great deal about the German language, how to put together language and music, the understanding of the word and the sound of the syllables that go with the music. He taught me simple things – for instance, when consonants are followed by a vowel, the consonants have to come before the note.

Fischer-Dieskau is one of the few singers who takes an active interest in contemporary music. His fastidiousness and meticulous preparation were astonishing in the performances of Stravinsky's *Abraham and Isaac* (in perfect Hebrew!) and in works by Lutosławski and Aribert Reimann, which I was fortunate enough to perform with him. I also remember doing a recording with him of *Il matrimonio segreto* by Cimarosa, and it was fascinating to see how he managed, with his mixture of intuition and German thoroughness, to capture the comic aspects of the character as well as the Italian language.

～

It can be very useful for a pianist to know the Lieder literature, and to play it. First of all, the human voice is the most direct musical instrument. When you play music that has a text, like the German Lied, you understand what happens to the music when a vivid word or striking idea comes from the text. For instance, when the word *Tod* (death) is used in Schubert's songs, something unusual happens harmonically and rhythmically. It is not really important whether this something was a conscious or subconscious act on Schubert's part; the important thing is that it is special. And when you find similar patterns in Schubert's sonatas or impromptus, the experience is that much richer. In other words, there is much to be gained from dealing with different works by the same composer.

All Latin languages have a tendency to go forward – French is an extreme example, where the accent is at the end of every word – whereas German does not push itself forward but rather pulls itself backwards. This derives from the actual sound of the language. Mozart is a very good example, because Mozart wrote German opera and German songs, and Italian opera too, as well as some songs in French. The nature of the up-beat – the note or the group of notes which come before the main bar – also varies according to the language. When you say *das* or *die* in German, both sounds are longer than *il* or *la* in Italian. *La luna* goes forward, but in German you say *der Mond*. In the latter, there is a broadness both in the article and in the noun.

Characterization is clearly of great importance in a Lied. When the piano plays the introduction, an interlude or a closing section, the whole atmosphere should be expressed in it. Sometimes it may be just half a bar – in Schubert's 'Gretchen am Spinnrade', the spinning wheel is first set in motion through the piano. By playing Lieder, the pianist can develop gifts of characterization – sometimes by very small rhythmical patterns or modulations – which completely change the atmosphere.

Another factor, which applies also to chamber music with piano and strings but is all-important to the voice, is the use of the pedal. Although the voice is independent of the piano part, as soon as there is any over-pedalling in the accompaniment, both the text and the voice are blurred. Also important is the fact that a sustained vocal line often needs a certain dryness in the piano part to compensate – as a contrast to the mellifluous legato vocal line.

The question of projection from the stage to the auditorium raises a number of interesting points. If the soprano part in an opera says 'piano', a light soprano may be too light and a heavier soprano may come through better – it depends on the role. In Mozart, for instance, the difference between a Donna Anna or a Fiordiligi, and a Susanna or Barbarina, is obvious, yet often, from a purely musical point of view, the difference is not made. That has to do with the nature of the voice as well as with projection. When you play in a hall which is too large for a certain musical idiom, whether it is a Lied or a late Brahms intermezzo for piano, the pianist or the singer adopts a kind of artificial projection so as to get the sound across. The effect can be far greater if, instead of trying to project to the last seat in the auditorium, you draw those thousands of people towards you, on to the stage. Fischer-Dieskau has an uncanny mastery of this art of 'going out' to the audience and 'drawing it in'.

Naturally, the singer's understanding of the text must be the same whether he is singing Wotan or the *Winterreise*. The difference lies in the fact that, in opera and oratorio, the singer is used to getting the cues and the musical direction from the conductor. With the Lied, it is the singer who has to take the musical initiative and lead the way.

Opera singers are often unable to do justice to Lieder because their expression is customarily linked to some movement on the stage or to instructions from the conductor. The singer who can do both is very rare. I think it is a pity that so many singers devote all their time and energy to singing opera, and not enough time to singing Lieder, or that they only begin to do so late in their careers, when many habits are already established. I also think it is a pity that there are so few pianists who accompany Lieder. I played recitals with Janet Baker early on, and then with Jessye Norman. There is a lot in vocal music – whether it is Lied, opera or choral music – that has an almost onomatopoeic effect. And this can be brought out only through careful thought about the elements of sound in a language. A great singer may know the language of music on the one hand and the sound of the spoken language on the other, but only the combination of the two can do Lieder full justice.

~

Towards the end of the 1960s I started conducting the major symphony orchestras more regularly: I went to New York for the first time in 1968 with the London Symphony Orchestra, conducted the Berlin Philharmonic in 1969, and some of the great American orchestras, Chicago, Cleveland, New York and Philadelphia, in 1969 or 1970. I also continued to work with the London orchestras, first with the New Philharmonia and later with the London Philharmonic. I never seriously considered a permanent post as musical director because I felt it would take up time that I wanted for conducting different orchestras as a guest conductor, for piano playing and, later on, for opera. Then George Szell engaged me to conduct the New York Philharmonic regularly. Szell was the Music Advisor before Boulez became Music Director.

I had met Szell, as a child in Salzburg, during the conducting class in 1955 when Markevich could not come to Salzburg because he was ill. The Mozarteum was put in a very difficult position because all the students and the orchestra for the course were there but there was no guiding spirit. It was a great stroke of luck that they were able to get the different conductors who were conducting at the Salzburg Festival that summer to come to the class and give us a whole day of teaching. Mitropoulos came, and Szell. There were others too, I suppose, but those are the two who remain in my memory, especially Szell, because it was my turn to conduct the day he came to the class.

He was very stern and strict, not unlike Klemperer in that he almost enjoyed putting people in difficult situations to see how they would extricate themselves. He remembered me as a pianist, from the occasion a year previously when I had auditioned for him after a recommendation from Furtwängler. (After Furtwängler had heard me and invited me to play with the Berlin Philharmonic, which my father had refused, he suggested that I should play for George Szell who would be able to help me play in America.) Szell was therefore rather surprised to see me now as a conductor. He was naturally very sceptical, and the first thing he said was, 'What are you going to conduct?' I said, 'Well, I have prepared Beethoven's Fourth Symphony,' which was one of the works that we had had to prepare for the class. But Szell said: 'I want to see what you will do with the Fifth Symphony.' The beginning of that symphony is a nightmare for almost every orchestra and conductor just to keep together. It was almost sadistic on his part to throw me straight in the deep end, but I suppose he wanted to show me that conducting is not just a trick that anybody can perform. I tried to conduct it with, of course, no success at all. The whole thing broke down in no time and I earned very stern, strict words from Szell who, in a nutshell, told me to stick to the piano and become a serious musician. I think he thought my interest in conducting was very light-hearted. It was therefore with both great pleasure and great trepidation that, before I walked on stage for my first concert as a conductor in Carnegie Hall with the London Symphony Orchestra, in 1968, I was told that Szell was in the audience. I was worried because I knew that he had a very good memory and would remember the incident at the class in Salzburg, even though it was thirteen years before. But later I was very pleased, precisely because he had been so stern with me, when he invited me to conduct the New York Philharmonic Orchestra regularly.

My last meeting with Szell took place when I played Bartók's First Piano Concerto with Pierre Boulez in March 1970 in Cleveland and Szell came to the concert. He was already unwell and it was only a few months before his death. He was very complimentary to both of us; he knew the piece very well – he had conducted it with Rudolf Serkin and even made a recording of it – and he said it was one of the most difficult things he had ever conducted and he was very pleased with our performance. I had the honour of sitting with him in his box after the intermission when Boulez conducted Mahler's Fifth Symphony, which was one that Szell had never conducted himself. I sat with him, with the score, listening to Boulez conducting. I never saw him again.

During the last days of July 1970 both Szell and Barbirolli died, thereby leaving not only the musical world much poorer, but also two orchestras without a music director. Both of them had been much more than normal music directors. Szell had been a great teacher, a pedagogue in the highest sense of the word. In Cleveland he had managed to create an atmosphere of great seriousness in the orchestra and in the city. Sir John Barbirolli had been a great, paternal figure in Manchester where he had come after leaving the New York Philharmonic in the 1940s. Szell had drilled his orchestra to perfection and trained it to play as the most exquisite string quartet, with a high degree of articulation, homogeneity of attack and perfect intonation; and Barbirolli had trained the Hallé Orchestra to produce a very expressive sound, especially in the strings, the famous Barbirolli sound which made up for whatever technical deficiencies the orchestra may have had.

Both orchestras approached me to ask if I would be at all interested in becoming music director. While I was extremely flattered, I felt that I was in no way ready. I did not have the repertoire, I did not have the knowledge nor, frankly, the shoulders to take on such a tremendous responsibility. Moreover, the problem with Cleveland was that I had never conducted the orchestra. I had played with it twice, once with Robert Shaw who was at the time the Associate Conductor, and then with Boulez in 1970, but I had never conducted it. So on top of the feeling of awe that I had for the orchestra and the work that Szell had done there, it was really impossible for me to imagine, to even think remotely of working there in a permanent capacity without having conducted the orchestra. I did, however, go there as a guest.

My first performance with the Cleveland Orchestra as a conductor was in February 1972, with Clifford Curzon playing Liszt's Second Piano Concerto. We also played the overture to *Le nozze di Figaro* and Bruckner's Seventh Symphony. We performed the same programme a couple of days later at the Carnegie Hall in New York, and in January 1973 I conducted Stravinsky's Concerto for string orchestra, Schubert's Ninth Symphony and Lalo's Cello Concerto with Jacqueline du Pré and later the Mendelssohn Violin Concerto with Pinchas Zukerman as soloist.

I remember a rehearsal with the Cleveland Orchestra for Brahms's Second Symphony. I was hesitant about bringing my own marked parts for the orchestra because Szell had been such a meticulous worker and, as I had only a few rehearsals for the concert, I thought that it might be better to use the parts that the orchestra were used to. It also crossed my mind that I might learn quite a lot from whatever markings Szell had made. But, in the end, I decided that it would be more practical to bring my own parts since I knew exactly what was in them and could get the results I wanted in the limited time available. I felt something akin to a culture shock when I stood in front of the orchestra for the first time, not only because of its sheer technical perfection but because of the feeling that every musician knew the entire score, knew exactly what to listen for and also the exact dose of volume and articulation. And the orchestra had a transparency of texture which is legendary. It was an amazing experience.

After this first rehearsal I said to the manager of the orchestra that, although when they had first approached me about coming to Cleveland on a more permanent basis I had not felt ready for it – and in some ways I still did not feel ready – I would have liked to have been able to reconsider my decision in view of the high musical standard which was being presented to me. But the discussions with Lorin Maazel had already gone far enough that they were nearly ready to announce his appointment as the successor to Szell, so that was the end of that.

It probably was a blessing in disguise that I did not go to Cleveland because I really did not have the experience required for such a major musical position. There is nothing worse than getting by only on one's talent. To stand in front of an orchestra of this calibre, to lead a hundred highly qualified and excellent musicians, one needs the combination of talent, experience and also musical and personal maturity. Quite apart from my feeling inadequate to lead such an orchestra, I had grave reservations about committing myself to a permanent position at that time, feeling that as a guest conductor I could get invaluable experience and also continue to develop my piano playing.

With Szell I had discussed my various musical activities – piano playing versus the chamber orchestra and the symphony orchestra – and told him that the one thing I did not want was a permanent job and the administrative weight of it. He said something I have never forgotten, which is very true: 'You are wrong, because one makes better music with one's own orchestra, even if it is third- or fourth-rate, than as a guest with a first-rate orchestra. There is something in the development of the work, the regular relationship between conductor and orchestra that can never be established as a guest conductor.'

Another orchestra I conducted frequently in the late 1960s was the Hallé Orchestra in Manchester, not the most perfect instrument in the world but one with a wonderful ability for making music. All the qualities I respected and admired so much in Barbirolli were in evidence there, and my association with them was artistically very close. In retrospect, I think that I acquired a tremendous amount of practical conducting experience through my work with them. It was with them that I had the opportunity of conducting for the first time such works as Beethoven's Ninth Symphony and several Bruckner symphonies.

In Boston I conducted less often. I was always very aware of the difference in mentality and in motivation between musicians in Europe and America. Like all generalizations, this has its dangers, but over the years I have found that one of the greatest sources of pride to American musicians is their flexibility. They can play in a certain way for a conductor one day, and the next day play the same piece for a different conductor in an entirely different way. They are completely open-minded and totally devoid of any musical arrogance.

The few great European orchestras each have a particular way of making music: they adapt to the conductor they are working with, but there is something basic – an *Urmusizieren* – that really comes from the stomach and which cannot change its essence.

I have often wondered why the motivation of orchestras differs. It may be due to the fact that most of the music American orchestras play is imported, and therefore they can achieve the same closeness – or lack of it – to Debussy as to Beethoven, Tchaikovsky or Verdi. No matter how much they try, the Berlin Philharmonic will react differently to Debussy's *La mer* than to a Bruckner symphony – and so, conversely, will the Orchestre de Paris. A certain inevitable closeness derives from association with a musical idiom, and from the historical and cultural development of one's own country. Too much has been said in recent years about the sound of this or that orchestra. A great orchestra should have its own sound for Beethoven, a completely different sound for Debussy, and a different sound again for every individual composer – it should never impose its own sound on the composition being played.

Another observation I made during the years I spent mostly as a guest conductor – between 1968 and 1975 – is that there are certain musicians, certain countries, even certain nationalities, that have a natural aptitude for organized, day-to-day work. What you set yourself to do today must be completed in preparation for the next day, so that tomorrow you start where you left off today. This is a very German, but it is also an Anglo-Saxon characteristic. Latin musicians in general, but French musicians in particular, are different. When I conducted in Paris (as a guest from 1971) and rehearsed a particular movement in detail, I would find the next day that we had to start from the same point we had started at the day before. On the other hand, the French musician has an unlimited capacity for enthusiasm and, when it strikes him, there is a generosity of giving and performing which is very rare in other orchestras.

~

The first time I heard the Chicago Symphony was an artistic revelation to me – it was in 1958, with Fritz Reiner conducting. I had never before heard an orchestra of that calibre – at that time I had not yet heard the Berlin Philharmonic live. I had heard the

Vienna Philharmonic in Salzburg as a child, but nothing I had heard in Europe or elsewhere had prepared me for the shock of the precision, the volume, and the intensity of the Chicago orchestra. It was like a perfect machine with a beating human heart. But it was not just a cold and perfect instrument, it had tremendous vitality. The shock was augmented by the fact that for the first time I was hearing *Ein Heldenleben* by Richard Strauss.

I played with the Chicago Symphony for the first time under Solti, before he was appointed Music Director, in 1965. I also played Bartók's First Piano Concerto with them under Boulez, in 1969. When I started conducting them, I felt that it was essential to give the very best of myself. There was great mutual respect – they knew how much I admired them. In fact, my regular work with the Chicago Symphony from 1970 onwards became one of the main pillars of my musical life. I conducted six weeks every year, and, for the first time, I was able to form a relationship with an orchestra of high quality. We played quite a lot of twentieth-century music (I conducted the first performance by the orchestra of Schoenberg's *Pelleas und Melisande*), several of Lutosławski's orchestral pieces and *Métaboles* by Henri Dutilleux, and we also did complete cycles of the Bruckner and the Schumann symphonies. We covered a lot of repertoire, much of which was unfamiliar to them. I remember particularly breathtaking, brilliant orchestral playing in *Falstaff* by Elgar.

Here was a combination of the highest possible musical standards with a very warm and touching personal relationship with the musicians that became increasingly important to me. Whenever I stood in front of the Chicago Symphony Orchestra I felt that, whatever I was able to give, it was not enough, that they deserved more and better. I have seldom felt in a collective group this kind of professionalism and constant striving for quality. You really had the feeling that to the last person they were intent on showing that they were the great orchestra that they were, but also there was a real sense of responsibility toward the music, to producing their highest possible standard of orchestral playing.

I found it inspirational. Every day I went to the rehearsals with enthusiasm and the ardent wish to make progress. You can see why, when this happened six weeks every year, it became a very important part of my life. In those days I never thought that I would one day become the Music Director of the Chicago Symphony, but I knew from the very first moment that this was an orchestra with which I would like to continue making music for the rest of my life. It was an ideal situation, with Sir Georg Solti as Music Director conducting ten or twelve weeks a year; Carlo Maria Giulini as Principal Guest Conductor, conducting eight weeks, and me with my weeks, in the most august company! It was only in 1980, as a result of Jacqueline's deteriorating condition, that I had to curtail my activities in the USA, and it was painful for me to stop going to Chicago so often.

10

FRANCE

After a few years of appearing regularly as a guest conductor, I began to understand the point George Szell had made to me in New York. Thus, when I was offered the music directorship of the Orchestre de Paris some time in 1973, I decided to accept it. It was an unusual post because it was a very new orchestra – only six years old. It was also a mixture of talents. There were a great number of wonderful players, but others were less good. Moreover, the orchestra had been through a difficult time emotionally.

It was founded by Charles Munch at a time when he was already a sick man. Very much a father figure, adored by the musicians, he died tragically, shortly after the orchestra's creation. Then Herbert von Karajan became Chief Conductor, and Georg Solti after him. For an orchestra at the beginning of its development, it had the luck to work with some of the great musicians of our time, but neither Karajan nor Solti really saw their activities there as the principal part of their professional lives. Karajan had the Berlin Philharmonic and all his other activities to think of, and Solti had the Chicago Symphony Orchestra.

When I joined the orchestra, I found musicians who must have been disappointed that a much younger person, without the experience of my predecessors, was taking over but, at the same time, there was a desire for some kind of solid relationship and I felt very attracted by this. Both rationally and emotionally I felt an immediate attachment to the orchestra, and, from the start, I considered it to be my main professional activity. All my other interests would have to take second place. In spite of some understandable difficulties, we managed in fifteen years to do a lot of very good work together. We built up a repertoire with many German classical and Romantic works which they had not played before – a lot of the Bruckner symphonies were played in France for the first time by the Paris Orchestra. There was a whole Mahler cycle with Kubelík and a tremendous amount of contemporary music in a memorable collaboration with Boulez, who regularly came and conducted. When we first played Bruckner's Ninth, the brass constituted a real difficulty. We had fourteen rehearsals, and little by little I realized that only through the perspective of colour could they get close to this music. They began to understand that the brass sound in Bruckner is often similar to the sound of an organ, and that this organ quality requires that the horns, trombones, tuba and Wagner tubas blend into one sound.

I received from the Orchestre de Paris the gift of enjoyment of French music, but also an insight into French music which I did not have before. The difference in the difficulties presented by Beethoven and Debussy is obvious: with Beethoven you often need to build up a crescendo over a long time and, if you arrive at a forte or a fortissimo too soon, the rest of the crescendo is gone. With Debussy it is often exactly the opposite: there are sudden flashes of crescendo or diminuendo that happen very quickly – sometimes on one note only – and if you miss them you achieve only a very thick sound that simply does not suit the music. The best musicians in the Paris Orchestra acted as a wonderful 'laboratory' for me: they demonstrated how music can come to life – how to treat it with the seriousness and depth it requires – not just as an exercise in orchestral colour, which is a viewpoint frequently met outside France. With Debussy it is not just a question of ethereal, almost bodiless sound; his music also requires a tremendous strength in the structure of the phrases, which are far shorter than in German music, and great control in the swiftness of dynamic changes. All in all, I consider that my years in Paris were a very positive experience, because I think I was both giving and receiving. And, of course, to be responsible for one hundred and twenty musicians for the first time was very enriching.

In Paris, the engagement of guest conductors is the responsibility of the music director. I remember attending an unforgettable concert in London with the Bavarian Radio Symphony Orchestra under Rafael Kubelík, playing Mahler's First Symphony. I was so taken with his interpretation that I asked him then and there whether he would be willing to commit himself to come to Paris regularly every year and do a complete Mahler cycle. I thought it would be a wonderful opportunity for the Orchestre de Paris to get to know Mahler's works through him. Kubelík asked, 'Why don't you do it yourself?' and I explained that, when the orchestra played Mahler's works in sequence for the first time, they should be conducted by someone who had devoted much of his life to their study and execution. He was convinced by my argument, and he came to Paris and conducted most of the Mahler symphonies – not all of them, because he was by then already a sick man. Boulez also conducted the orchestra regularly, not only in contemporary music but also in twentieth-century classics. Mehta came regularly, too, bringing with him a great variety of repertoire, including the orchestra's first performance of Schoenberg's *Gurrelieder*. And then there was Carlo Maria Giulini, who also had a very close relationship with the orchestra from the very beginning. He always provided moments of great inspiration. Solti came fairly regularly, not as often as we would have liked owing to his other commitments, but he kept a paternal eye on us. It always gave me tremendous pleasure and great confidence when Solti had very positive things to say about our progress.

~

Conducting is as much a profession as playing an instrument. But a great part of the audience simply does not know what a conductor is doing. When an audience hears a really great orchestra like that of Chicago, Berlin or Vienna playing a repertoire piece, they often cannot tell what the conductor's contribution amounts to. Why should a wonderful orchestra that knows the music by heart need a conductor? An audience can grasp that when a violinist plays the Tchaikovsky Violin Concerto, he must, first of all, be able to manage the notes. This is not all, but it is a starting point. With a conductor, the starting point is far more difficult for the audience to understand.

When an audience hears a violinist, they see his fingers and his bow moving. But when a conductor stands in front of the orchestra, all sorts of extra-musical considerations come to the fore: personality, charisma, often blatant sex appeal, things that have nothing to do with music.

What is so difficult about conducting and what is so difficult about becoming a conductor? An instrumentalist must be able to play his instrument, and to have the physical power and manual skill to manage and control his instrument. But how do you control an orchestra? An instrumentalist can always practise; he has a piano at home, or a violin, or a cello. Where should a conductor practise? He cannot learn the music or the notes in an abstract way. Imagine a pianist who has no piano, and who has to learn a Beethoven sonata merely in his head. It is impossible.

There are different ways of becoming a conductor. The old way was for an opera house to use a répétiteur, or someone to conduct from an instrument, or – better still – musicians who were also composers. Many great conductors in the past were also composers, composing conductors or conducting composers. It is not really important whether Furtwängler or Klemperer were great composers or not, but the very fact that they composed gave them an understanding of the construction of a piece which non-composers lacked. If you come from the field of opera, you can also learn a lot as a répétiteur which can then be used for symphonic music.

The manipulation of sound is very hard to learn, and particularly difficult for a conductor, who has no physical contact with the sound. The conductor should really know the orchestra, and what the instruments can do, how the music moves from one group to another and practically walks around the orchestra. If the first violins are the main instruments in the first eight bars, and the oboe comes later, the music moving from one to the other, you must work with the strings. A wind instrument can play alone, whereas there are sixteen first violins, each with its own individuality, and this has to be organized. By organization I mean that each player not only plays his part as best he can, but also listens to his neighbours, trying to match their way of playing. That means, first of all, clear intonation and a similarity of attack, sound and articulation. It is the homogeneity of the group that facilitates the overall expression. This principle applies to the whole orchestra. The conductor should be able to listen to the sounds that are produced by the orchestra, as well as contribute to their precision and expression. Many of these problems are solved naturally by great orchestras like those of Berlin or Chicago. In their cases such problems are of course easier to solve than with third- or fourth-rate orchestras. But a conductor must know how to organize the sound of a lesser orchestra, otherwise he will not be able to influence a great one.

~

The only really polyphonic instruments are the piano, all forms of harpsichord or clavichord, the guitar, the organ and the harp. You can create an illusion of polyphony if you play Bach unaccompanied on a cello or a violin, but by nature these instruments are monophonic. Music, however, is polyphonic by nature, and harmony is possible only in polyphonic terms. I have often found it necessary to point out to both singers and instrumentalists the polyphonic nature of music – the relationship between the vertical and the horizontal, the horizontal being the separate lines of melody and the vertical the harmonies, the polyphony. If the relation between the horizontal and the vertical is incorrect, then the whole interpretation is incorrect.

To me, polyphony is the very essence of musical writing. It means that there are several 'voices', and it is difficult to integrate several instruments playing simultaneously, or several independent voices progressing at the same time on one instrument, say the piano. Are the different voices on the piano really independent? If you think of the *Goldberg Variations*, you can see the independence. The question here is whether different voices in a piano composition are totally independent, or if they are interrelated. If the question is enlarged in order to observe whether the instruments in an orchestra are really independent, it becomes immediately clear that they are not. If each instrument were wholly independent, it would follow its own speed and dynamic, regardless of the others, and would cause total disruption. It therefore follows that the different voices or instruments are interrelated. Here you could quote Spinoza who says: 'A body in motion or at rest must be determined to motion or rest by another body, which was also determined to motion or rest by another and this in its turn by another and so ad infinitum.' Bodies, like instruments, are not distinguished from each other in respect of substance. Since music is governed by its own unifying cosmos, the different voices or instruments react like bodies, and this accumulation constitutes a totality.

But how can a voice determine the motion or rest of another? Is there some kind of hierarchy which determines the importance of one and the subordination of the other? And if so, is it determined by the sheer power of certain instruments in an orchestra, or by the audibility of the discourse? If this were the case, each instrument would be required to play at full strength all the time. Therefore it must be the musical substance that dictates the dynamic hierarchy. It follows that a certain instrument or instruments must dominate. It is thus imperative to establish a correct equilibrium between the different instruments or voices, so as to allow total audibility and to reflect the hierarchy of the instruments or voices. This in turn will give us a total weight that will influence the chosen tempo: in other words, the weight of the object in motion determines its motion.

One of the most important qualities required of an interpreter or of the conductor is the capacity to balance the different voices or instruments. The creation of true equilibrium means that the different voices are audible in such a way that they appear in proper perspective – all present, but some nearer than others. Each voice or instrument must be clearly articulated in itself – only then will it be in a position to relate to the others. The different voices may be affected in numerous ways, either by self-transformation or through contact with other voices. But the juxtaposition of the different voices will not alter the whole. This means that each voice must retain its individuality. The contact with other voices, creating a more complex individuality ad infinitum, need in no way compromise each separate individuality.

~

As far as orchestral playing is concerned, I learned most of what I know from Barbirolli. I knew Barbirolli in my capacity as piano soloist, and often watched him at rehearsals. He had a very special way of forming the string groups. What I learned was due to a mixture of his influence and that of Jacqueline. Barbirolli taught me more about the practical work with an orchestra, whereas Jacqueline taught me what can conceivably be imagined from a string instrument in the way of sound. She pointed out to me many possibilities that I would not have found out by myself.

A string player's bow can go in two directions – up or down. Whether one starts a certain passage up-bow or down-bow is important. More important still is the way the bow is distributed and the speed at which it moves. The bow has a much greater weight at its lower end, the frog, than at the point, which is the upper half, where it becomes thinner and lighter, and a good string player must be able to control this difference in weight. Each part of the bow has advantages over other parts for certain types of articulation. A natural weight is produced by an attack down-bow, starting at the frog, but one can also very easily start a note at the point, up-bow, because this is where it is easier to control the beginning of the sound. It is important to know how to divide this: one, two, or five notes in one bow, but when does the bow change, and in what way? One must not forget that in a symphony orchestra there are usually sixteen, sometimes fourteen, and sometimes eighteen first violins. This means there are fourteen, sixteen or eighteen people playing exactly the same notes at the same time. Imagine if those sixteen people sitting at a table were expected, at a sign from the head waiter, to lift a fork at exactly the same time, with the same speed and the same enthusiasm. This problem does not apply to the wind instruments, where each player only plays his part, the second oboe part being different from that of the first oboe. There must therefore be an element of musical organization in order to produce the string section sound.

For the articulation of phrases (which is the equivalent of punctuation in language), it is most important to have a disciplined way of bowing. Barbirolli understood this and developed his own bowing technique. He was able to produce the string sound he wanted from any orchestra he conducted. Obviously, when he conducted in Berlin, where he was a great favourite and the orchestra understood him particularly well, the success rate was higher than when he conducted a second-rate orchestra somewhere else.

I was very fortunate, too, in being able to consult Jacqueline, about some of these features which interested me enormously, and I indicate the bowings in the string parts myself to this day. If there are sixteen first violins, that means there are eight copies of the music to be made. I used to do them all myself, thereby learning each part in an individual way. When you think of the complexities and the amount of time spent on bowing a Mozart symphony, you can imagine how much time I spent putting together complete new bowings for the *Ring* cycle in Bayreuth! I have found that even very fine string players in orchestras or in chamber orchestras, or even soloists, do not think enough about bow distribution and bow speed.

If a conductor does not understand the importance of the string sound, he is simply accepting a standardized way of playing. Some orchestras and conductors take the easy way out, in the sense that, if something is marked 'piano' for one of the string sections, the leader of the section plays mezzo forte, and the rest of the section plays pianissimo. The sum of the fifteen pianissimos and one or two mezzo fortes is equal to a general piano. It has the advantage that it is easier to play together and, if the leader of the section has a particularly attractive sound, the other instruments simply provide a kind of aura round it. But I have always been against this principle. I consider it musically wrong. I think that sixteen people, playing expressive piano, have a completely different sound from one or two playing mezzo forte or forte and the rest playing pianissimo, just providing a cushion as it were. The latter has less quality and less intensity.

The problems of the wind section and its organization by the conductor are completely different. They have to do with the physical aspects of each instrument: flute, oboe, clarinet, bassoon, not to mention the brass – horn, trumpet and trombone. Each has a slightly different mouthpiece, a different way of producing sound. It is therefore very difficult to get a homogeneity of attack from some of these instruments. It is hard to find the right balance between the individuality of phrasing, which is necessary when an oboe or a clarinet has a solo phrase in a symphony, and collective ensemble playing. The individuality of phrasing a major solo, as the oboe or the clarinet have in Schubert's *Unfinished* Symphony, must, a few bars later, be disciplined into chord playing, where one should not be able to distinguish the individual colours of the instruments. This problem is very obvious to a pianist playing a Mozart concerto. When the piano has the main theme, it requires very personal phrasing and articulation, with a maximum amount of imagination and fantasy. Later, when the main subject is in the orchestra, and the piano only has an ornamental, less important part, it is quite difficult to subjugate yourself. You often hear performances by people who have great individuality, and who project every note, even where their part is secondary.

Then, of course, there is the problem of intonation. The piano is either in tune or out of tune and it is the job of the piano tuner not the pianist to see that it is perfectly in tune. Each note the wind player plays, however, may be either too flat, perfectly in tune, or too sharp. There are notes that are slightly exaggerated, sharp or flat, when one instrument is played by itself, and this can be very disturbing to the ear, but in a chord with several instruments it is simply excruciating to the sensitive listener to hear a faulty intonation. It is essential for a conductor to detect faults of intonation, as well as faults of balance in wind playing. Certain notes may sound slightly out of tune if they are not properly balanced in the chord. The same problem arises with the brass group.

The difficulty is increased when you put everything together and add timpani and percussion. In other words, you have timpani and percussion, brass, woodwind, and strings, and you have to unite all these different sounds.

The main problem with the brass is, of course, the power of their instruments. A conductor must have profound knowledge of the necessary volume and 'dosage'. In other words, if the word 'crescendo' is written all over the score, it should not be played by the entire orchestra at the same time, since the weaker instruments will not be heard distinctly – the brass and timpani should start the crescendo later. This balancing, organizing, or even manipulating of the sound is essential for clarity in the orchestra. An equilibrium has to be found by the conductor between clarity and fullness of sound which can only come about when everybody is allowed to play with full intensity and volume.

There is something about the brass players which is almost frightening to a young conductor. Because of the instruments they play, these musicians are usually big, strong people who have the ability to kill any other sound by sheer volume. They can kill the woodwind and the strings – and also the conductor and the music! Lesser brass players often tend to play too loudly; they lack sensitivity to what goes on within the rest of the orchestra and are therefore insensitive to the music. With classical music – Mozart, Beethoven or Schubert – they usually have a harmonic role, playing tonic and dominant whenever the melody is to be played loudly.

Before Berlioz, composers did not consciously consider the colours of the different instruments in the orchestra. I am not saying that Mozart was insensitive to the colours – nobody ever wrote for the oboe or the clarinet the way he did – but within the general framework of an orchestra, colour was never considered as an independent element per se. It was Berlioz who started thinking about it in a new way. But before Berlioz and his fellow Romantics, the timpani and trumpets, especially, are often reduced to the less interesting role of playing the tonic and dominant. Owing, however, to the volume they produce, they are inevitably in the foreground. This is something which, consciously or subconsciously, affects the brass players' attitude and way of thinking. In classical works they do not usually have very much to do, and therefore their level of concentration is inevitably lower than that of the musicians who play constantly and without interruption. However, when you have good, sensitive brass players, they can, through one or two notes or a difference in attack, influence the colours of the whole orchestra. For example, in Ravel's *Daphnis and Chloe*, the crescendo of the trumpets makes you feel as if the entire orchestra were suddenly set on fire by just two or three notes from the trumpets. When the sound is properly balanced, and the attack is pure and not too hard, the brightness of the instrument can communicate itself to the rest of the orchestra.

The brass, therefore, have to be treated very carefully by the conductor. This applies to classical music: as you move on to the nineteenth and twentieth centuries, the music written for brass becomes far more elaborate and interesting. In Bruckner's symphonies the brass really convey the feeling of an organ, which has the ability to sustain a rather dark sound in a very broad way. In music from central Europe – in Dvořák, for example – the trumpets are the instruments that invite people to dance. In Latin countries, the trumpet is a premonition of death, not only in the Verdi Requiem, but also in Spanish music. Even when the music seems to be dancing, there is an element of fear. With Wagner, the trumpet has developed in a very individual way which has, consciously or unconsciously, influenced almost every composer since. On the one hand, he paved the way for Bruckner and Mahler and, on the other, he foreshadowed Debussy. When you think of the 'Todesverkündigung' ('Annunciation of Death') in *Die Walküre*, with the sound of the trumpets and Wagner tubas, you can hear Wagner's preoccupation with the brass. He actually developed the Wagner tuba – horns, trumpets and trombones were not enough for him. He wanted to enlarge the section with a special sound, and to give the brass as much colour and prominence as possible. This creates a feeling which the Germans call *feierlich* – a ceremonial atmosphere. It is not only festive; it has something to do with a 'ceremony of mourning'. This is where the difference between the German and the Latin use of the trumpet becomes obvious. In Mahler's Fifth Symphony, it is true, the trumpet is used in the Latin sense – but then Mahler is a special case. He is not part of the normal evolution of the so-called German tradition. He introduced many new elements. I find there is more of Berlioz in him than is generally realized. This does not only relate to the colours of the instruments but also to the spirit of the music – a certain sense of craziness that Mahler shares with Berlioz. One must remember that even Wagner would not have been possible without Berlioz.

It is very interesting to note what partners Wagner found for the trumpet. In the soft passages, especially, you often find the trumpets playing in unison with the cor anglais. This effect, the colour produced by the two instruments, was also something that Debussy used: if you think of *La mer*, immediately after the introduction, the trumpet and cor anglais play in unison. I do not think this is a coincidence. Wagner's orchestration was carefully thought out. Boulez once said, with the humour very typical of him, that one had the feeling Wagner orchestrated the way a butcher mixes minced meat – so many pounds of veal, so many pounds of pork, so many pounds of beef. This is an apt way of putting it. You can feel Wagner weighing the colours of the instruments. Of course he was mainly influenced by Beethoven, also considerably by Berlioz and Liszt, as well as, in a spiritual way, by Schumann.

In classical music you find the timpani in many ways having the same problems as the brass, always playing tonic and dominant, with the added danger that the classical composers did not write for chromatic timpani. They were therefore limited to two or three notes. The problem of timpani is that, played properly, they are capable of much more than simply acting as an element of emphasis and rhythm. Really good players have a certain imagination for sound – and for creating the illusion of more sustained sound – as on the piano. Timpani playing is not just a question of bringing the stick down and making a noise. It matters very much where the stick lands and with what degree of strength. A certain inner strength is created by playing every note with one hand. At the beginning of the fourth movement of the *Symphonie fantastique*, Berlioz wants the sextuplets to be played with one hand, the other hand playing only one out of every six notes. Timpani players often change that so that they play one note with the right, and the next note with the left hand, and this produces a completely different sound. The original score shows that the tempo must not be too fast. If Berlioz had intended the movement to be played very fast, he would not have given this instruction. I always ask the timpani players at the beginning of the second act of *Siegfried* to play with one hand. I have even gone so far as to ask the timpani players at the 'Todesverkündigung' in *Die Walküre* – which I take at a relatively slow tempo – to play the triplet with one hand only. The hand has to come down and go up on every note, so each note has a relentless quality. When you think of the second movement of Bartók's First Piano Concerto, each percussion instrument has a different colour. And there is Boulez, with marimbas, vibraphones and xylophones, and all their colours!

The element of sound quality and colour is very important in percussion instruments. Some twentieth-century piano music is less attractive to my mind because it is percussive in a limited sense – very little more than a bad imitation of a typewriter. One composer, who was not a particularly interesting orchestrator but who had an instinct for a very individual use of percussion instruments, was Liszt. His main contribution to orchestral sound was the use of the harp and the triangle. Compared to Liszt's First Piano Concerto, the use of the triangle in Brahms's Fourth Symphony seems rather primitive. In Brahms's Third Symphony it requires thought and sensitivity to achieve the balance between clarity in the timpani, and the feeling of tremolo. Tremolo, of course, comes from the word trembling, and it is a question of how fast one trembles. In Bruckner's symphonies, conductors and string players often see the tremolo alike and just play in an unthinking way, either very slowly or very fast, instead of using the different speeds that are possible in tremolo, and which are among the most expressive elements in music.

~

Regarding psychology, the orchestra is, of course, very sensitive, probably even touchy. There is nothing worse for an orchestral player, who knows his problems and has solved them, to hear a conductor say: 'There seems to be a problem that has to be solved.' I once saw a conductor's score inscribed with the mark: 'Bassoon too loud!' That is to say, the bassoon had not proved to be too loud at rehearsal, but the conductor had already imagined before the rehearsal that it would be too loud at that point in the score. He had lent me his score, and when I went to his rehearsal and the relevant passage came up, he interrupted and said: 'The bassoon is too loud.' Such dishonesty can completely undermine the conductor's work as far as the orchestra is concerned, and justifiably so. The orchestra is more likely to accept a certain indecision from the conductor than musical dishonesty.

One of the most delicate subjects in this area is intonation, and I had my share of problems with intonation at the beginning of my conducting days. Having grown up playing the piano, I did not always notice if something was not quite clean from the point of view of intonation in the orchestra. I knew what was not quite clean if a wrong note was played, and obviously I heard that chords were out of tune, but I could not always indicate which instrument was too low and which too high. In the 1960s I was present in London at a Boulez rehearsal of *Pelleas und Melisande* by Schoenberg. During a very complicated tutti part there was a chord, and Boulez said, 'This instrument was too high and that one too low.' And I was quite astonished. I had heard that it was not clean but I could not hear what was too low or too high. Boulez, on the other hand, knew exactly. He repeated it, and this time the chord was clean. I asked him, 'Pierre, how does one do this? I come from the piano, and I do not know exactly …' 'Yes,' he said, 'you need experience for it. For instance, if you do not hear a chord very clearly or very cleanly, just say what you are thinking at the moment – that this is too high and that is too low – you may be right, and then you will know if this is the case for the next time. Or you may be on the wrong track altogether, and tell a musician that he is too low, and he may say, 'I was not too low, if anything I was too high.' You mustn't be afraid of

saying something wrong, because this is how you will train yourself.'
And this is how I learned. I was not embarrassed, if I heard something
unclean, to say, this is too low.

At the beginning it often happened that a player replied: 'What do
you mean, too low? I was far too high!' Then I would say, 'Yes, you
are right.' This is how you train your ears. But you must be open
about it, and not afraid of making mistakes. It is rather like learning
a strange language. If you are afraid of making mistakes you will
never learn to speak it.

~

My concerts with Sergiu Celibidache in Munich were among the
main yearly events of my professional life in the 1980s. He had taken
over the directorship of the Munich Philharmonic in 1979 and
invited me to play with him every year. Celibidache not only had a
remarkable technical knowledge of the orchestra, and the gift of
balancing it; he was also consistent and uncompromising in achieving
his aims. He had also certain obvious characteristics: slow tempi,
a particular way of phrasing which demands very often a less than
full sound from the bass, and his particular way of ending phrases.
These characteristics are easy to imitate, and in so doing so-called
Celibidache disciples do him and themselves a great disservice. They
would be better employed trying to understand *why* he did things in
a certain way and applying this to their own work, for instance in the
matter of tempo. In a Bruckner symphony, for instance, his tempi
were fixed not just because he wanted an uninterrupted sound but
because he needed the slow tempo in order to express all he saw in
the music. His tempo was related to the substance of the music and
of the sound. What was important to him was the way one instrument leads into another, how the phrases all have one culminating
point, how he applied the principle of tension and of releasing
tension. With Celibidache you never found an accent in the wrong
place. There was not one instrument that was allowed to play in a
way that was not integrated with the overall sound of the orchestra.
And there was no musician in the Munich Philharmonic who was
allowed to play even one note in a mechanical, routine, unthinking
way.

Celibidache had one of the finest ears and one of the sharpest musical brains that I have ever encountered. I do not think I ever came away from Munich, after a week of rehearsals and concerts with him, without additional food for thought. Sometimes, unexpectedly, a new angle came out in the rehearsals or in the concerts. This constant preoccupation with phrasing and articulation was something that enriched every musician who came into contact with him.

11

OPERA

If I want to write about my career as an opera conductor I have to go back to the beginning of the 1970s. The first opera I conducted was Mozart's *Don Giovanni* in Edinburgh in 1972. At that time, the Director of the Festival was Peter Diamand. He had started his professional life very early, as secretary to Artur Schnabel, and he went through every conceivable stage of musical administration. Later he was Director of the Holland Festival for seventeen years, and then director of the Edinburgh Festival for thirteen. He had a great passion for opera, and he was very much aware of the limitations of repertory opera with its insufficient rehearsal periods.

In Edinburgh the work was done under the best of conditions, with the English Chamber Orchestra. We had an ensemble of singers who were there for the whole period without interruption, rehearsals and performances included. We had a theatre that was not technically ideal, but which was exclusively at the disposal of the production, the King's Theatre.

Peter Diamand had brought to Edinburgh every conceivable European opera company before deciding that the Edinburgh Festival should produce its own operas. This was a very courageous decision and it provided the public with some operatic performances of very high quality. He obviously had faith and confidence in my ability to conduct opera. I never regretted it, and shall always be grateful to him for giving me this first chance.

As my conducting of symphony orchestras developed, I said to myself, 'not opera as well, that would be too much.' The man who convinced me that I should conduct Mozart operas was Peter Diamand, who proposed that we should do *Don Giovanni, Le nozze di Figaro* and *Così fan tutte.* We performed *Don Giovanni* two years running, likewise *Le nozze di Figaro*, but unfortunately *Così* never got off the ground in Edinburgh. In 1967 I had had an offer from Rome to do a concert performance on the radio, but then the Six Day War broke out in Israel, and I cancelled it. It was a great pity because that was really the first opera I had studied properly.

Peter Diamand's original idea for Edinburgh was to do all three operas with Jean-Pierre Ponnelle, but at that time he was fully occupied in Salzburg. He and I had several meetings and talked about the operas, but it was only in Paris that we finally worked together. So Peter Ustinov produced *Don Giovanni* and *Le nozze di Figaro* was produced by Sir Geraint Evans.

Later in Paris I did all three Mozart–da Ponte operas with Ponnelle. Then we performed two of them as a co-production in Washington, one, *Le nozze di Figaro*, with surtitles. The surtitles were marvellous in many ways and the audience reacted very well to them. But there were some problems, especially when recitatives with a comic twist appeared before the character actually said his lines. It was also diffi-cult when more than one character was speaking at the same time. Surtitles must be presented as discreetly as possible, and only convey essential information. They must be poetically correct, and the timing is of paramount importance.

In Israel we did all three da Ponte operas in a cycle. As Tel Aviv has no opera house or theatre, we performed in a concert hall, and Ponnelle divided the stage so that there was a part for the orchestra to play in. The orchestra was a few steps down, and at the back, where the choir would normally sit at concerts, there was a small curtain that opened and closed. It was more improvised theatre than large-scale opera, but very beautifully done, without proper decorations but in costume, with just a few significant props.

As a student I was not able to attend opera performances very often, unlike some of my colleagues who studied in a city like Vienna, where there is a wonderful opera house. It was only when I started travelling that I began to go to opera houses like Covent Garden and the Metropolitan, and those in Germany.

My interest in opera was aroused through my work with voices, with Dietrich Fischer-Dieskau as a Lieder singer, and with Wilhelm Pitz as a choral conductor. But then, my entire musical upbringing and piano education were based on the dramatic element in music.

As I gained experience in the control of huge forces through choral work, I continued to play the piano, and was constantly in search of theatrical expression and of the inner drama of music. I remember listening to Furtwängler's rehearsals of *Don Giovanni*, and through my interest in so many of Mozart's works, his piano concertos and sonatas, his symphonies and the Requiem, I naturally wanted to move on to his opera. I also wanted to do Beethoven's *Fidelio*, but perhaps because of the Latin side of my upbringing, I was always drawn to the Italian side of Mozart, especially the da Ponte operas.

By the mid-1970s Jacqueline's illness had become more acute, and I considerably curtailed my activities in America. She was in a wheelchair by then – she came to Paris once in 1976 but that was really the last trip she undertook. It became very hard for me to stay away from her and from London for any length of time, so I lived in London and worked in Paris.

In 1978 I went to the Deutsche Oper in Berlin for the first time and it was here that Siegfried Palm, the Intendant of the opera house, first asked me to conduct *Le nozze di Figaro*, and then *Tristan und Isolde*.

Later I conducted *Fidelio*, *Aida* and *Der fliegende Holländer*. I had an ideal relationship with the Deutsche Oper in those days because we planned things far enough in advance to enable me to repeat the work I was in charge of on a regular basis for at least three years. The cast remained more or less unchanged, so there was almost a fixed company within the repertory theatre. I think that for the first three or four years both *Figaro* and *Tristan* remained in the same hands as far as conducting and singing were concerned.

I was, of course, far less experienced then, my knowledge of German was more limited and so was my knowledge of the Wagnerian world, but I have very positive memories of my work with Götz Friedrich in Berlin. We worked together on four operas: *Le nozze di Figaro*, *Aida* and *Tristan und Isolde* in Berlin, and *Parsifal* in Bayreuth in 1987. Friedrich was the first person who made me realize how easy it is for singers to wander around the stage without knowing where they are supposed to go or for what purpose. He had the ability of eliminating completely any senseless movement on stage.

When I had the opportunity of doing *Tristan* in Berlin, I became more and more involved with the score, like most conductors. I was greatly attracted to Bayreuth, particularly because of the acoustic conditions. I had been there in 1963 and I had heard quite a number of broadcasts from Bayreuth over the years, and Wolfgang Wagner had already invited me to conduct *Lohengrin* in Bayreuth in the 1970s. It was his idea that I should conduct *Tristan und Isolde* in 1981, and I accepted with great excitement and some degree of trepidation. I remember asking him whether it would be possible to do *Tristan* a year or two later, as I was already so involved with the Berlin production, but he explained that 1982 would be the centenary of *Parsifal* and then *Der Ring des Nibelungen* would follow, so that a new *Tristan* production would have to be done in 1981. Originally Patrice Chéreau was to have staged it, and I had a number of conversations with him and Wolfgang Wagner. However, after the last *Ring* by Chéreau and Boulez, Patrice told me that he needed a break from Wagner and Bayreuth, otherwise *Tristan* would simply become the fifth instalment of the *Ring*, so regretfully he pulled out of the project.

It was then agreed that Jean-Pierre Ponnelle would produce it. Ponnelle had quite a bit of experience with Wagner, even though he had never staged an opera in Bayreuth. He was known mainly for his work with Monteverdi, Rossini, and Mozart, but he had done the *Ring* in Stuttgart and also *Der fliegende Holländer*, and *Parsifal*.

From then on, I began to get to know the working habits of Bayreuth. Wolfgang Wagner was always there, always available, at any time, for any discussion about casting, or rehearsal schedules, which gave me a great feeling of security. Pierre Boulez has had the same experience. Wolfgang Wagner suggested that Ponnelle and I come to Bayreuth for detailed discussions in 1980, the year before we were to do *Tristan*. I wondered at the time why it was necessary to go to Bayreuth for discussions, but over the years I have come to realize just how essential it is to prepare projects on the spot – audition the singers on the stage, because the acoustics of the theatre are totally unlike anything else in the world, and not only because the pit is covered, something which has a great influence on the relationship between orchestra and singers. Even from the stage, the acoustics are completely different. The theatre is not very large, which enables the singer to fill the auditorium with sound. There is no need to force the voice, as in some other theatres. The advantage of the covered pit is obvious. It eases the relationship between voice and orchestra, and the mixture of the sound is ideal.

In Bayreuth you can discuss projects and problems differently from the way you do at normal theatres. It is not just because you are in Bayreuth; it is the fact that everything there is open-minded. Nothing is ever accepted just because it has been done this way before. I think this is most remarkable in a festival that has limited itself to only ten works by one composer for more than a hundred years. Wolfgang Wagner's conception of how to mount the productions and run the festival is a unique example of musical administration. Being a stage director himself, he obviously has his own ideas, and an unbelievably intimate knowledge of the works and the texts. Yet he has given every stage director – in my case, first Ponnelle and later Harry Kupfer and Heiner Mueller, each with an aesthetic concept entirely different from his own – not only the feeling that they could realize their artistic visions without interference, but also that they would have the means to do so. I know of no other institution allowing such unlimited freedom to its artists. The fact that the financial rewards are so exceedingly low works almost to advantage in Bayreuth. The combination of total openness and willingness to experiment with any new idea, and therefore un-limited scope for artistic creation and very limited means for personal reward, somehow makes for high creativity among all concerned.

Wolfgang Wagner's main interest is, of course, concentrated on the theatrical, rather than the purely musical side. But he realized, for instance, that I was very particular about the scores that were used, that I had my own ideas about the bowing of the string parts, and that it was not just arrogance if I wanted my own bowings marked in the orchestral parts. I always had his full cooperation as far as new parts were concerned: he provided completely new parts for the *Ring*. There was a kind of workshop atmosphere about it all.

The orchestra consists of musicians from many different opera houses, mostly in Germany, although there are others as well. In the last few years its quality has been greatly enhanced by the presence of some excellent East German musicians from Dresden, Leipzig and East Berlin. Most of the musicians play at opera houses all year round and practically know the works by heart. They come to Bayreuth simply because they are interested in playing there. It would not be unnatural, since they play opera full-time, to find a sense of routine in their playing, but I experienced a tremendous curiosity on the part of the orchestra members, which meant they were prepared to tackle things anew every time. All in all, when you consider the organization of auditions, the discussions with the stage director, the planning of the stage sets, and every opportunity to try things out a long time in advance, you feel a great confidence when working at Bayreuth.

I have specialized in Wagner through my work in Bayreuth, and in Mozart because I started the Mozart Festival with Ponnelle in Paris in 1982. In Paris I also conducted *Fidelio* and Berlioz's *Béatrice et Bénédict*. My only wish is that I would have liked to have had the chance of exploring Verdi at greater depth in Paris, to have put on a Verdi series – especially *Otello*, *La Traviata* and *Falstaff*.

~

It can be hard for a stage director to achieve what he wants if, on the musical side, the phrasing, the articulation, the intensity, the tempo and the volume are wrong. A lot of difficulties arise if there has been too little attention paid to the clarity of the text, and to coordination between the sound of the language and the sound of the music. The same applies to the articulation in music. It is like speaking without punctuating your sentences – using no commas or full stops or colons: what you say would be incomprehensible.

Too much emphasis is laid on the physical position of the singer on stage. Lying on the floor or kneeling may coincide with an extremely difficult musical or vocal passage. The priority is not position, but timing. When does a singer get herself or himself into the position suitable from the point of view of breathing, and when does he or she make the necessary movement on the stage? The tension between singers and stage director is, as so often in life, due to a kind of stubbornness on both sides. The solution may simply be a question of timing a certain movement or action – a few notes earlier or later the same movement becomes easy, and even helpful to the singing. If a singer comes to rehearsal with the attitude, 'Here I have to stand', and the stage director comes to the same rehearsal with the idea, 'Here he has to kneel', tensions are unavoidable. This

143

is one of the reasons why a conductor should be present at as many stage rehearsals as possible, not just to discuss the overall concept with the stage director, but to be able to help with the timing of certain movements. I have found that stage directors who are open-minded about this are only too glad when the conductor is present.

At the same time, I have always welcomed the presence of the stage director at the music rehearsals. I think the music and the action should be worked out at the same time, regardless of the fact that they sometimes go hand in hand and are at other times opposed to each other. This is the only way of achieving that ideal state of hearing with the eyes and seeing with the ears. You cannot separate the two. Sometimes it is the juxtaposition of action and music that creates the full expression. An opera cannot be produced with a stage director who has absolutely no feeling for the music, and does not understand the element of timing introduced by music. When you have a spoken text only, you control the speed of every syllable, but in an opera a great deal is controlled by the length of the music. So there is often a total discrepancy between the stage and the pit. The other extreme is when you have musical stage directors who try to do everything through the music. Then you may get merely a choreographic description of the music. Both extremes are equally poor. As a conductor one has to be interested in the scenic aspects of the production, for the impetus for the drama can sometimes come from the stage, with the music following, accompanying, or in juxta-position. At other times the roles are reversed and the motivation for the action on stage flows from the orchestra.

An opera conductor should not only be interested in the theatrical element, he should be the one to link it to the musical element. If a conductor is not interested in the theatrical aspect of opera, he might as well limit himself to symphonic music. I was fascinated by it from the very beginning, and spent a lot of time during rehearsals of the Mozart operas working out every possible inflection of the recitatives. One of the great advantages of the recitative secco – unaccompanied recitative – is that you are free to choose your own speed and dynamics. There are rarely any instructions for the recitatives to indicate whether they should be fast or slow, loud or soft. There are certain cases when there are sotto voce indications, asides by the characters. Normally there is a great amount of freedom, and it is up to the conductor to work on the recitatives, especially their speed, the amount of singing as opposed to speaking, and the question of volume. The recitativo secco features only the harpsichord (sometimes supported by continuo cello) apart from the human voice. Pauses can be used extremely expressively sometimes and a sudden underlining of a syllable, a word, or a sentence can have a far stronger dramatic effect than an entire tutti by the orchestra in a musical number. One also becomes aware of the need to relate the recitatives to the musical numbers. Sometimes there is meant to be a complete break between one and the other, but at other times the recitative prepares the entrance of the orchestra, the next musical number. In the famous duet in *Don Giovanni*, 'La ci darem la mano', for example, you often find that at the end of the recitative preceding it, Don Giovanni has already prepared the atmosphere and the volume of the duet. Therefore there must be no abrupt change in speed or volume.

Ponnelle started out as a stage designer. He was a very gifted craftsman and painter. By doing everything himself, he sometimes deprived himself of a dialogue with independent stage and costume designers, but at his best he achieved a total unity that was quite remarkable. There was an almost physical feeling of well-being about his work, and the certainty that no other way of doing it was possible.

Ponnelle knew me as a pianist, having attended my concerts in Munich, and I had seen some of his films. Among stage directors he was one of the most knowledgeable, musically speaking. You could see him at chamber music concerts whenever he had the time, or at symphonic concerts. He had an unlimited curiosity for everything, and he lived life to its fullest. He had the ideal combination of German education and Latin temperament. There was something refreshingly imaginative and improvisatory about him. Latin people who spend a lot of time living or working in Germany often arrive at a special fusion of these two seemingly antagonistic temperaments. One could cite Busoni, for instance, and later Claudio Arrau, Ponnelle and Giulini. And it was such a fusion, historically speaking, that made Mozart a unique phenomenon among the operatic composers of his time. There is nothing more Italian than the da Ponte operas that Mozart wrote, nor is there anything more Germanically inspired than *Die Zauberflöte*, which is why I always think of Mozart as one of the first pan-Europeans.

Ponnelle came to Bayreuth every year of his *Tristan* production. The way I worked with him was very similar to the way I worked with Harry Kupfer. The first production of Kupfer's which I saw was his *Der fliegende Holländer* in Bayreuth — it fascinated me. So when Wolfgang Wagner spoke to me about further projects, I mentioned that I wanted to work with Kupfer.

I have already stressed the importance of collaboration between the stage director and the conductor. If you have a highly intense musical score, yet there is no theatrical intensity, or if there is a highly intense level of acting and a low-level intensity in the music, the production as a whole just cannot work. Kupfer and I discussed this relationship from the very beginning, the fact that the motivation must come sometimes from the music and sometimes from the acting.

One of the aspects of Kupfer's work that captivated me, and made me want to work with him, was his unusual ability in dealing with crowds on the stage. There is only one example of this in *Der Ring des Nibelungen*, in the second act of *Götterdämmerung*, but in *Der fliegende Holländer*, his handling of crowd scenes was really remarkable. One had the feeling that there were thousands of people on the stage, yet that the movement and position of each one had been carefully thought out.

Another quality which attracted me to the idea of working with him was that he clearly understands the difference between intensity and volume. This applies equally to singing, speaking, acting and, of course, to music. In order to create a feeling of something static, there has to be a very controlled, slow movement conveying that illusion. If you permit the character on the stage to remain motionless, it is not aesthetically pleasing, nor does it express anything static — it is simply a lack of expression. We talked about the ideas which interested me, and found that we were really soulmates in this respect. He is able also to make singers produce moments of tremendous intensity without resorting to too great a volume, loudness, or shouting. Some of the most intense moments occur at very low volume.

In the first act of Kupfer's *Siegfried* in Bayreuth, there was a singer who found it easier to sing when moving about rather than remaining still, so we worked it out so that he could have a moment of rest, to control his breathing, before going on to the next 'assault'. The first act of *Siegfried* demands virtuosity in the best sense of this word. It is a word which can acquire a slightly negative sense when one says 'virtuoso', as if it were the opposite of deeply thought-out music making. I like to think of it as coming from the same root as the word 'virtue'.

~

My Bayreuth experience served as a model for planning the Bastille Opéra, for which I became responsible in July 1987. The first person to speak to me about the Bastille was Pierre Boulez who, along with his other interests in the project, was on the architectural board for the building. I was very hesitant at first, because I had already had more than preliminary discussions with the Chicago Symphony, and felt very uncertain whether I could undertake the Bastille project as well. In the end I decided it was possible. It was to have opened in January 1989, So from the autumn of 1988 to the autumn of 1991 I would have two seasons with the Bastille before starting in Chicago. There was such enthusiasm and willingness to collaborate on the project by all the artists concerned that I decided to take it on.

I signed a five-year contract as artistic and music director of the Bastille Opéra with the Minister of Culture of that time, François Léotard. The theatre was a new building with all the latest technological devices imaginable, and I was eager to be in on the ground floor, as it were, of an entirely new project. It was the possibility of a new vision of producing music theatre that fascinated me.

The decisions on the building had been made earlier, but we had to form an orchestra. There was a lot to do, so the first season was not to be a full one. Instead, between January and June of 1989, we planned to have something like forty-five or fifty operatic evenings, plus concerts, which we would gradually build on. The theatre was to have achieved its full 'cruising speed' by the third year. By that time I would probably have been conducting about forty to fifty evenings a year.

In March of 1988 I announced a schedule for my first three seasons. I wanted to create a situation where all the different disciplines would be given equal attention – the orchestra, the conductor, the singing, the stage directions, the set, and the costumes. In other words: neither *prima la musica*, nor *prima la parola*, no *prima* anything.

Theatre administration is very complicated. The repertory theatre, in spite of all its advantages, has shown that it cannot possibly sustain the quality one would wish. If you play fifty different operas on two hundred and fifty or three hundred evenings, there is inevitably a shortage of rehearsal time. The fixed-company system has the advantage that the works are well rehearsed for a series, but it is not entirely satisfactory unless it takes place at a festival. At the Bastille Opéra, I had planned a system which was to be a combination of the two. We had practically unlimited rehearsal time, for both the music and the staging. We had planned one cast for the first series of performances but each work would be repeated two or three times within a season, with only one or two cast changes. We did not want to work with a double cast from the beginning. The stage directors were all committed to this principle – Chéreau, Ponnelle, Kupfer, Carlos Saura and Peter Stein, who was going to do *Pelléas et Mélisande* by Debussy with Boulez. They all promised to be there for the revivals, so each stage director would have come for at least three years, adding a new production each year, and reviving the old one. If you plan two or three series of performances during a season, you save time on rehearsals because you never really need to revive a production from scratch. One of the problems with the quality of an opera performance is that it is rehearsed for the première and followed by a new series of performances. Then the work is practically abandoned, and has to be revived. During the course of three years, we would have had two, if not three casts for works like *Don Giovanni*, but all of them rehearsed with Chéreau, who was to do that production with me conducting.

I also scheduled *Tosca* and *Tristan und Isolde* for the first short spring season and planned to revive them in the autumn, adding five new operas and five again the next season so that by the third season we would have the possibility of mounting fourteen different productions. As we could have no ballet performances, because the government was going to turn the old opera house, the Palais Garnier, into a pure ballet theatre, we decided to have concerts between the opera performances. I therefore had already invited the Berlin Philharmonic Orchestra and the Munich Philharmonic to play there.

With Chéreau, Ponnelle, and Kupfer at the Bastille I had the three pillars of the stage. As conductors we had Boulez, Solti, Christoph von Dohnányi, Zubin Mehta and myself.

After the 1988 presidential elections in France, the political situation changed, and somebody close to the government and François Mitterrand was put in charge of the opera houses. This was Pierre Bergé, who was a very successful businessman and President of Yves Saint Laurent. He possessed neither an understanding of my artistic conception for the new opera house, nor an alternative conception of his own. He argued that the repertoire was not popular enough. The government intended the Bastille to be the opera of the people, yet the only truly popular opera scheduled was *Carmen*. He also felt that more performances would make the Bastille more popular and, presumably, he wanted to have more influence on the repertoire and on my work. He was tired of being in the position of businessman to someone else's 'artist'.

Bergé was always very polite and we communicated on very friendly terms. He liked to say that, although he was new in politics, he had always 'felt Left'. It never occurred to me that once I had accepted a job from a minister in Jacques Chirac's government I was going to be regarded as 'the Right's man'.

The battle started in the newspapers in autumn 1988 with a front-page article in *Le Monde* entitled 'Daniel Barenboim, Oui ou Non?' As a result the whole issue ceased to be an artistic problem and became purely political. It was inevitable that the situation arose where there was no place for both of us, and the political favour in which Bergé found himself gave him the power to relieve me of my duties.

So at the end of the spring of 1989 I found myself, for the first time in fifteen years, without an administrative position. I had terminated my connection with the Orchestre de Paris, I had been fired from the Bastille Opéra, and I was going to have quite a lot of time on my hands for a period of two years before I took over the music directorship of the Chicago Symphony Orchestra.

Since I had set aside so much time for the Bastille Opéra, I suddenly had time for activities that I enjoyed but which I had not really had time to concentrate on for many years. The only fixtures in my diary were my eight weeks with the Chicago Symphony, six weeks in Chicago and two weeks on tour, and of course the *Ring* in the summer at Bayreuth. At precisely the same time the Berlin Philharmonic Orchestra found itself without a chief conductor, and we were able to develop our already existing close musical relationship to a degree which I had not imagined possible. We played a great variety of repertoire in our numerous concerts in Berlin, not only the German classics, the Bruckner, Beethoven and Brahms symphonies, but also quite a number of contemporary works, among them the first German performance of Lutosławski's Third Symphony and Boulez's *Notations*, and we recorded Mozart's piano concertos, the three da Ponte operas and *Parsifal*.

Strangely enough, it was in Bayreuth that I had had my first conversation with Solti about the Chicago Symphony Orchestra. He was conducting the *Ring* in 1983, and gave me the first hint then that he was looking into the distant future when he would leave the orchestra. He felt that I would be his natural successor. He knew the admiration I had for the orchestra, and I think he also felt the affection the musicians had for me. With great charm he said that, since we had managed the transition in Paris so smoothly in 1975, a similar transition in Chicago would also go well at the time he wanted to leave. I found his attitude very flattering and I was very touched by the confidence he had in me. I knew that if Chicago were actually to offer me this position, I could not imagine a better predecessor than Solti, and so it was that later in the 1980s the dream I had never dared to dream became reality. I was offered the position of Music Director of the Chicago Symphony Orchestra, thereby, on the one hand, closing a very long and fruitful relationship with them as a guest conductor which had started in 1970 and, on the other, leaving me to hope for an even more fruitful association in the future.

With Rafael Kubelík and Georg Solti in Chicago, 1991.

With Harry Kupfer at the Staatsoper, Berlin, 1992.

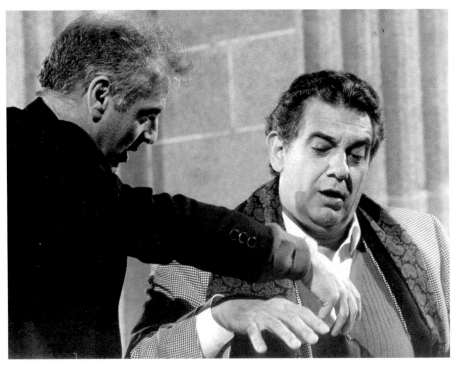

Rehearsing with Placido Domingo in Berlin, 1994.

In discussion with Sergiu Celibidache, Munich, 1995.

With Claudio Abbado.

With Patrice Chéreau in front of the Staatsoper in Berlin, 1994.

At the West–Eastern Divan workshop, 1999.

With Edward Said *(standing)* and Saleem Abboud–Ashkar
in Birzeit, January 1999.

With Yo–Yo Ma in Chicago, September 2000.

Conducting the Staatskapelle Berlin in 1999.

In Madrid, June 2000, with
Teresa Berganza.

At a performance of *Parsifal* in
Berlin in November 2001: with
Christian Franz, Andreas
Schmidt, Elena Bashkirova
(Elena Barenboim), Violeta
Urmana and John Tomlinson.

12

CHICAGO

Looking back now, I must say that the beginning of my time in Chicago was connected to many important decisions. In 1987, shortly after I had agreed to become Music Director of the Chicago Symphony, I received the offer to become Music Director of the Bastille Opéra in Paris. The question was whether it would be possible to combine the two, as I now combine my work with the Deutsche Staatsoper and the Chicago orchestra. I remember very well a conversation I had with Pierre Boulez in Paris, in which I asked whether he felt I could do both. In his usual pragmatic way he answered that I most certainly could, but it would likely be at the cost of playing the piano.

The question repeated itself when I was offered the position of Artistic Director of the Deutsche Staatsoper in Berlin, after I had begun the Chicago job in 1991. I came to the conclusion that accepting the position in Berlin would require a drastic reduction of my time as a pianist. It was clear that Chicago and Berlin would need a lot of attention, time, and effort, for this was work of great importance. The situation in Berlin was completely new, because it was only a few years after the Wall came down. And at the same time it was a new beginning in Chicago, after twenty-two years of a very successful and clearly defined partnership between the Chicago Symphony and Sir Georg Solti. I think it would have been easier if their collaboration had been shorter and less intense. However, out of respect for Solti and his accomplishments there in purely musical terms, I felt the need to step in very gently. I could not have imagined a more generous and fair transfer from one conductor to another. It was the second time I had gone through this process, having already succeeded Solti at the Orchestre de Paris in 1975.

Although I wanted to begin discreetly, it was difficult because I had very definite ideas about how the orchestra should sound. So I had to find a way of treading gently but firmly. I very consciously tried to see whether I could distinguish what was intrinsic to the Chicago Symphony from that which was a combination of Solti and the orchestra. I had known the Chicago Symphony since 1970, when I conducted the orchestra for the first time, and I had listened to all its recordings with various conductors. I now tried to determine what the character of this orchestra was throughout its history. I felt that 'that' – if I discovered what 'that' was – should remain untouched, and should be treated with utmost respect.

Some issues were a result of the collaboration with Solti, and those were the ones that I found less sacred. But if there was something that, over generations, had been typical in the music making of this orchestra, I wanted to maintain it. I still find there is a certain clarity of articulation, a rhythmic transparency, a particular purity of intonation, and a kind of phrasing that is extremely clean without being ornamental – and this I really tried to preserve. I always had the greatest respect for Solti and his way of making music. But his idea of sound was more angular and edgy than my own, and this was not something that belonged to the orchestra. It is strange and interesting to see now that when Solti and I played the piano together, we understood each other extremely well and made great music. But the way we got there was very different.

For me, the decision regarding tempo is the last one to be made. Solti, on the other hand, always insisted that he saw it as essential to check the tempo with the metronome, and literally to fulfil it. Therefore, the decision about tempo was made first, and he then saw what content he could put into this tempo. My way of proceeding is just the opposite. I start with the premonition of a tempo – one hears the notes and the music but not the tempo. The tempo is the speed that is required for everything to be audible – for the transparency, the clarity, and the volume that the tension of the music requires. It is a completely different way of thinking, and of preparing the music.

Singers, especially those who have not worked with me regularly, often come to me and ask what tempo I am going to take. I answer that I cannot tell until I have heard them sing, and I often give the same silly but illuminating example: when you are going on vacation and have no suitcase, what do you do? Do you go and buy just any suitcase and then decide what you can put in it? Or do you first consider what you need to take – shirts, tennis racket, rollerblades, books, whatever – and then buy a suitcase of a certain size? Most likely, you do the latter. The tempo is the 'suitcase', and the music is the 'contents'. If the suitcase is too small, you can't fit in all your belongings, and if the suitcase is too big, everything floats around. Once you arrive, it does not matter if the suitcase is brown and round, or square and black. The only thing that matters is whether you have what you need. The tempo is there to provide the correct speed for the content of the music; therefore, it is the last decision I make. For many musicians in the Chicago orchestra, this was a totally new concept, because over the years they had become accustomed to setting the tempo first, and then reproducing it in each concert. This is something that is foreign to me, and it took some time to work it out.

Solti had begun his work in Chicago in the autumn of 1969. I first conducted the orchestra in November 1970, at the very beginning of the Solti era. Between 1970 and 1980 I was a regular guest conductor there, but then I took a break from Chicago for personal reasons and did not come back for several years. By the time I took over as music director, twenty-one years had passed since I first conducted the orchestra. In the mean time, the orchestra had changed – many of the musicians were new – and you could feel the effect of twenty-one years of playing under Solti.

When you are the music director rather than a guest conductor, you work with the orchestra in a totally different way. When I came to Chicago as a guest and had four rehearsals followed by a concert, I tried to prepare the programme as best as I could in order to perform it at its highest possible level. As music director, however, I spend time in rehearsals developing with the orchestra a shared idea of sound, phrasing, articulation, and intonation. In the process, almost by chance, the programme gets prepared. It is a completely different attitude that you are allowed only when you are music director. It is your right and at the same time your responsibility to create a unified way of making music.

There is a wonderful anecdote that illustrates that. Fritz Busch, who was a great admirer of Toscanini, attended one of his concerts and was deeply impressed. He went backstage to congratulate Toscanini, only to find him pacing in a fury. Why was he so unhappy, he asked, after such a wonderful concert? – the orchestra, after all, had played exactly as he wanted. To which Toscanini replied that any professional orchestra playing with any professional conductor could do that – that this was neither interesting to him nor was it making music. He would only be satisfied when every musician in the orchestra felt exactly the same thing at the same time as he did.

It is not that difficult to make an orchestra 'just play'. It is fine when a professional conductor has a feeling for what he wants and the orchestra is able to follow that, but it is not necessarily making music. That happens only when the orchestra acquires a collective lung, and breathes the music as one. You can achieve this as a music director if you are able and willing to share your thoughts and your preoccupations. I find this way of making music more satisfying, but as a guest conductor you rarely have the chance to create that kind of feeling. This is why for so many years now I have rarely guest-conducted, except with orchestras I know very well.

All of my work in Chicago has more to do with the general concept of music making than with preparing certain pieces. I believe it is very important, both for the conductor and the orchestra, to remember that it is the musicians who produce the sound. The conductor can educate them and make them play better than before, but the musical impulse comes from the person who creates the sound. The baton is inaudible. There are musicians in every orchestra who feel that their duty is to prepare the music in a way that allows them to play each note to perfection. They believe that the music is made by the conductor, and that, of course, is not the case. This is not a demagogical and psychological analysis I am making, but a purely musical one.

I have written in great detail about the relation of sound and silence, and this is something that was not second nature to the musicians of the Chicago orchestra. Very often I had the feeling that the thought process about the music began after the first note was played, not before, which is why an attack was often edgier than I wished. Therefore, there was a flexibility of sound, phrasing, and tempo that was foreign to many of the musicians, especially those who had been with the orchestra for many years.

It was necessary to start from zero each time – in other words, not simply to rehearse a piece so that it was well prepared and could be repeated as often as possible. The conscious search for a perfect repetition of each performance makes life more comfortable for the musicians, but for me that kind of routine is the arch-enemy of music making. I tried to make the musicians start from scratch every day. The reminders of the previous day were still present, but the sound had to be newly created. That is why it is important to decide clearly *in each rehearsal* what it is that is to be underlined – where the high point is, where the low point is – and not fix it in cement, but let it happen the very moment the sound is literally brought into this world. This requires tremendous courage from each musician on stage, because it is much easier to sit back and try to reproduce something that has worked in the past.

The concept of listening to each other – not only to follow one another but also to create a continuous interdependence between the instruments – is the most important quality required for playing in an orchestra. It is at least as important as individual excellence, if not more so. I was preoccupied with the desire to create this very early on. By not only tolerating, but also demanding individual flexibility and creativity, I took a certain amount of security away from the orchestra in the beginning – for example, when it is dangerous to play too softly because a note may crack in the brass section, or when it would be easier for the strings to play together if you place accents on every beat of the bar. Many musicians would rather do this than risk not playing together, but this is totally foreign to me. Music is not about playing it safe. Music is about courage, and courage means risk. In some works, the element of effort is also an intrinsic part of the music. Trying to play Beethoven in an easy and flowing way goes against the nature of his music. Having the courage to take a crescendo to the maximum before a subito piano, and then drop off just before the piano requires tremendous energy and effort, which is inherent in the music. In more virtuoso music, on the other hand, effortlessness is an attribute. When a violinist plays Paganini's Caprices, it must sound effortless because that is part of the music's nature. But in Beethoven's Violin Concerto, you have to feel from the very opening that the violinist strives upwards with the energy that is required for each octave. That struggle is an integral part of this music.

It is very difficult for an orchestra that possesses unlimited technical prowess, as the Chicago Symphony does, suddenly to be confronted with the idea that certain things require effort. The musicians' training and preparation, from the very beginning, taught them that their goal is to reach the point where everything is effortless. I must say, though, that I found a great majority of the orchestra members to be very open-minded. Yes, some of them thought I was a strange bird, but the orchestra in Chicago is totally devoid of musical arrogance. These ten years have given me a sense of deep satisfaction, because I constantly feel that there is a real give and take. I have been able to give the orchestra something of myself and of what I believe music is about, and they have been able and willing to give me a lot of themselves in the seriousness of their approach, in the excellence of their playing, and – at least as important – in their openness and willingness to do anything that was considered desirable.

When I started in Chicago shortly before the orchestra's centenary in 1991, I invited two former music directors to join me in reproducing the programme of the orchestra's inaugural concert, on 16 October 1891. The two were Sir Georg Solti and Rafael Kubelík, and the programme was Wagner's *Faust* Overture, which I conducted; Beethoven's Symphony No. 5, which Solti conducted; Tchaikovsky's First Piano Concerto, which Solti conducted and I played; and Dvořák's *Husitzká* Overture, which Kubelík conducted – it was his only contribution, since he was already in failing health.

I remember Kubelík telling me that I needed to change the seating of the orchestra. Under Kubelík's baton, the orchestra always sat with separated first and second violins. Then under Solti the violins sat together on the conductor's left with the cellos to the right, on the outside. When I came, the violas sat on the outside instead, which made many musicians unhappy. The cellists were especially disappointed, because they were used to sitting to the conductor's right, and they felt they had more room and independence that way. I felt that the sound and balance in the strings was not right, however, and opted for the more traditional 'German' seating, with the violas outside and the cellos inside, facing out, giving a fuller picture of the bass.

I had always had doubts about dividing the first and second

violins. First of all, with the second violins on the conductor's right, they would be playing in the wrong direction – that is, with their instruments facing away from the audience. And second, the problems of the ensemble, especially in unison or octave passages, would be greater because of the difficulty in hearing from one side of the stage to the other. Later, after we rebuilt Orchestra Hall to correct this deficiency, I became more and more convinced that the advantages of separating the violins were greater than the dis-advantages and that Kubelík was right. Now the violins sit as he first suggested, with the cellos and violas between them and the basses behind the first violins. Actually, the communication between the violins is better when they are seated on opposite sides, because in passages of unisons or octaves you get the sound from the whole width of the stage, which makes up for any lack of direction. Most importantly, the proximity of the cellos and basses to the first violins gives the whole string section a fuller and more harmonic sound, and in addition the violins sound rounder and more beautiful in the high register when the bass is next to them, almost like a support.

I did not want to impose that arrangement on other conductors, however, and so the seating changes every now and then, according to the guest conductors' wishes. When I led the world première of Boulez's *Notations* VII, knowing his preference for seating the violas outside and having the violins together, I asked Pierre if he wanted me to change the seating arrangement. It was very interesting to find that he left the decision to me. Actually, there was an interplay of the violins which we got right even though we separated them, and we probably would not have got it right had we placed them together.

The other change that I made regarded the horns, which are often seated to the left of the conductor. Orchestras like that, because when the horns are seated on the right they blow into the orchestra and that is uncomfortable for some sections. I believe, however, that the horn is not a pure brass instrument, and that it represents a transition from woodwinds to brass – from oboes and bassoons to trumpets and trombones. Therefore I need to integrate them completely, which means placing them on my right. I find it intolerable to have them to the left, because they blow outside the orchestra and you cannot integrate their sound with the rest of the orchestra.

Any desire to make a change is influenced by the time that you spend with the musicians, as well as by the choice of guest conductors. I am in Chicago for twelve weeks each season, in addition to touring with the orchestra. The quality of guest conductors is therefore of major importance to the orchestra, because it ensures the continuity as well as the quality of the work. We have been extremely fortunate to have Pierre Boulez as our principal guest conductor. I asked him to take this position not only because of the respect I have for him, but because I felt that he, more than anybody, could put a strong accent on the classics of the twentieth century, keep the curiosity for new music alive, and do it all with the greatest assurance. I know him as someone who never merely pays lip service to a cause, and who does everything with total honesty and commitment at the highest possible level.

The orchestra has developed a deep bond with Boulez over the years. He has introduced new music and conducted nearly all of the so-called classics of the twentieth century – together we have basically done a complete survey of the Second Viennese School. In addition to Stravinsky, Bartók, and Ravel, he has also become more and more interested in repertoire which had never interested him before, such as the Bruckner symphonies. For his seventieth birthday in 1995 we gave him a score of Bruckner's Symphony No. 8, signed by each member of the orchestra, because that was the first Bruckner symphony that he was to conduct, with the Vienna Philharmonic. I find this quite remarkable, especially when I remember his coming to a concert of Bruckner's Eighth that I conducted with the Orchestre de Paris some twenty years ago. He made some rather critical remarks about the work, and when I pointed out to him a very attractive juxtaposition of duple and triple rhythm at the beginning of the slow movement, he said that I would find a more interesting example in the second act of *Tristan und Isolde*. Boulez is always open to new ideas, and that is a great inspiration for everybody, especially when you consider what drives him to conduct Bruckner for the first time in his seventies! He has since conducted Bruckner's Fifth and Ninth Symphonies in Chicago. It is a sign of his ever-expanding horizons and his belief in curiosity as the most important element of progress.

I find it extremely important for a symphony orchestra, especially one like the Chicago Symphony, to perform operatic pieces, and I have done several in Chicago since I became music director. It may be more important for an opera orchestra to perform symphonic works once in a while, because an orchestra that normally plays only in the pit needs the opportunity to be on stage and in contact with other kinds of music as much as possible. But a symphony orchestra gains immeasurably whenever it plays opera. It gains a flexibility of listening, because the musicians need to listen to the voices on stage in addition to each other. And the musicians must get acquainted with the expression of the voice and of the text as well. When you understand the relation between musical means and the meaning of the words, you obviously have a much richer sense of association. I have done *Elektra, Fidelio, Tristan und Isolde*, the second act of *Parsifal*, and semi-staged versions of the three Mozart–da Ponte operas in Chicago. The orchestra had a long tradition of playing opera before I came – *Das Rheingold* and *Moses und Aron* with Solti, for example – and since I became music director they have done *Otello* and *Meistersinger* with Solti, as well as *Moses und Aron* with Boulez, which we then took on tour to Berlin.

In the late 1990s, Orchestra Hall underwent major and very necessary reconstruction. Although there were many reasons for re-building, we mainly needed to improve the acoustics. The stage was too wide and not deep enough. It had a wonderful directness of sound, but it was very dry and did not allow the orchestra to correctly balance itself. It was also necessary to create a better working environment for the orchestra itself backstage. There were no practice rooms, and there was not enough space for the rather large administration, which is an essential part of any American institution. The fact that there is little public funding means that the orchestra depends on private support, which requires a whole fund-raising apparatus that needs to be a combination of heavy artillery handled with silk gloves. I don't know whether the quality of the silk is more important than the quantity of the artillery, but in any case, it is a major operation requiring space.

The pluralistic nature of American society is mirrored more and more in this orchestra, which is normal, because an orchestra is like a miniature version of society. It has been a source of tremendous pleasure for me to see how many young musicians with great talent have come to an orchestra with such a strong tradition to absorb what we have to offer – whether it is our Chinese concert master, the Chinese musicians from the mainland, or those from Taiwan. It is very important not to oppose other identities, but to encourage their development. There are plenty of reasons to be pessimistic about the world today. One unquestionably positive step in the last fifty years, however, has been the realization of the necessity for and possibility of pluralistic identity.

13

BERLIN

When I began negotiations to become artistic director of the Deutsche Staatsoper in Berlin in 1992, the plans there bore a great similarity to those for the Bastille Opéra in Paris, for this was to be a completely new beginning. I believed that it would be very valuable work, although there was a lot of cleaning up to do. Taking over this position meant the possibility of combining a fresh start with an old tradition.

The Staatskapelle, the orchestra that I found at the Staatsoper, was comparable to the most wonderful antique furniture, its beauty covered by layers and layers of dust. I knew that the quality was very high and started to clean it up. In purely musical terms, I uncovered the intonation, a unity of attack, and ensemble playing that had a unified purpose. Little by little I realized that my estimation of the orchestra's high quality had been right, and everything fell into place very quickly. The musical substance of the orchestra was very strong – not only the attitude in general, but its preoccupation with the correct issues: phrasing, the search for sound, and an innate musical rightness.

The 'daily hygiene', however, had to be initiated. It was an unusual atmosphere. I was dealing with people who had lived in a totalitarian state for many years. They had been without freedom and contact with the outside world for so long that their behaviour showed apprehensiveness on many levels. The most difficult aspect of a totalitarian state is not necessarily that some things are forbidden, but that fear becomes the guiding emotion of everyday life. Fear of communication with friends and families, fear of being found out – not, as is often naively thought, in a Machiavellian way, for reporting someone to a higher authority, but for exchanging information for a hospital bed for a sick mother, for example. Can you blame someone for making such choices? Although some musicians thought they could forget all that when they came to the opera house, in general there was apprehension and insecurity about the future, and it took quite some time for those feelings to disappear.

The musicians' feeling for tradition had survived, which is not surprising when you consider the circumstances in which they had been living for so many years. People had very little contact with the outside world – or rather with what we call the Western world – which means the lack of an influence that could have destroyed this tradition. The musicians' attitude toward making music was – and still is – exemplary and without parallel in other orchestras I know. They confront a Beethoven symphony, for example, with a sense of awe, and have deep respect for creations which contributed so greatly to the development of music and culture.

I have tried to maintain what I believe is the essence of the Staatskapelle Berlin, just as I tried to do with the Chicago Symphony. It was the same with the singers who were already members of the ensemble when I arrived, and with the chorus. I actually had my first contact with the Staatsoper through the chorus, when I recorded *Parsifal* with the Berlin Philharmonic Orchestra in 1989. Someone recommended we use the chorus of the Staatsoper, because they had done the piece with Harry Kupfer and knew it by heart. It was the first contact between the Berlin Philharmonic Orchestra in the West and the Staatsoper in the East.

One important first step was to widen the repertoire and add contemporary music. Now, in addition to a complete Wagner cycle, we have also played Boulez and Carter. It is of great importance to recognize that the Staatskapelle is not exclusively an opera orchestra, but also a symphony orchestra with a very long tradition. In fact, it is the second oldest orchestra in the world. The orchestra's musical 'hygiene' began with two very important parallel cycles: a Wagner cycle in the opera house and a Beethoven symphony cycle in the concert hall. These two projects, each in its own way, required the maximum discipline and preoccupation with the art of orchestral playing. They made the orchestra grow and develop significantly, and I am convinced that this was the right way to proceed. Later on, we added a Mozart cycle, *Fidelio, Wozzeck, Elektra,* Busoni's *Brautwahl,*

Schoenberg's *Von heute auf morgan*, *Aida*, and *Otello*, as well as world premieres by Carter and Birtwistle. And, as we had planned from the beginning, we performed the ten Wagner operas in 2002, as a sort of résumé of the first ten years of work.

An opera house, especially one that has endured so many years of a totalitarian state, is a very complex institution. The bureaucratic and administrative issues alone were an immense load. The Stasi informers had to be dealt with, for example, even though there were amazingly few cases of discoveries for an institution that employed more than 1,100 people. It was very difficult on a day-to-day basis in the beginning, but the attitude of the people made it special. Perhaps this results from the fact that going to the opera house was a privilege for those who worked there, whether it was the orchestral musicians, the singers, the ballet dancers, or the chorus members. Those who were, deep in their hearts, in disagreement with the regime felt a sense of freedom – they could breathe freely and let out what was inside. Those who believed in a party system had the special pride of belonging to such a wonderful institution. So, no matter what anyone believed individually, the motivation was morally very strong. This is much less often the case in free societies.

At the Staatsoper, in comparison to many other opera houses of the former German Democratic Republic, I succeeded in a relatively short time in merging those who had been there for years with those I brought in. One feels the spirit of an 'ensemble' at the Staatsoper, and to maintain that I wanted to keep most of the musicians of the orchestra and chorus. I did not intend to fire anybody because of the political change, and I made that very clear both to the orchestra and to the authorities. I had too much respect for all that they had been through, and I felt this was morally the correct choice.

However, changes were necessary. Certain positions in the orchestra needed to be improved, and I spoke with the musicians very openly and honestly once I got to know them better. The quality of the musicians varied, and the level I was aiming for was not met by all. One factor worked in my favour: the economic situation was better then than it is now. Therefore I was able to obtain what I call 'joker positions'. Sections which did not have a single musician of the quality demanded of a first-chair player were enlarged by one additional musician to strengthen the group until someone retired. We managed to achieve an immense sense of musical justice that way. Very frank discussions, extraordinary insight, and honesty made this all possible in the orchestra; it was less of a problem in the chorus because it was more homogeneous to begin with.

As opposed to international opera companies, the Deutsche Staatsoper is an ensemble company, like other German opera houses. People are contracted to the house and essentially have to sing whatever they are told. In addition, guests are invited to come for specific pieces. I knew that we had to merge these two approaches. The Staatsoper needed to maintain an ensemble, but the ensemble itself needed to be rejuvenated. Over these last few years, great singers such as René Pape and Dorothea Röschmann have come out of this ensemble. On certain occasions we also have had the most wonderful guests, such as Plácido Domingo.

The key was to find a common ground and create a flexible ensemble. This 'flexible ensemble' would include permanent guests who felt that the Deutsche Staatsoper Berlin was their artistic home, where things would be done for them but where things were expected from them in exchange. Deborah Polaski, Siegfried Jerusalem, Waltraud Meier, John Tomlinson, Günter von Kannen, Graham Clark and Falk Struckmann, for example, have sung in Berlin with great regularity and therefore are part of the ensemble in every sense but the formal one. I was not interested in only having festive gala evenings. I wanted to create a special style of music making, singing, and acting on a regular basis. I am a great believer in cyclical thinking, which I learned to value very early on. This is the artistic reason that I prefer a Wagner cycle or a Mozart cycle. When artists appear in a cycle, it allows them to become more attached to the house. They give a lot to a company and receive a lot from it in return.

I have also been fortunate to have had a succession of very talented assistants, including such conductors as John Fiore, Asher Fisch, Philippe Jordan, Antonio Pappano, Christian Thielemann, Sebastian Weigle, and Simone Young. I never look for an assistant whose only function is to make my life easier. I choose individuals whom I feel have a lot of talent, who will learn in the process, and who are able to bring their own creativity to the work. Many of my assistants stayed only for a short period of time because they were so talented;

they needed to go out and make it on their own. I feel it is my duty to encourage them, and I am very happy to see what has become of them. My career as a musician began very early, and I have accumulated a lot of experience over the years. I want to pass on not only my practical experience, but also my way of thinking. I don't give tips to my assistants unless they have precise questions about certain issues – do I conduct something this way or that way, for example. My higher goal is always to make them think for themselves musically – to learn, to listen, and to observe the phenomenon of sound. This is the only way to grow.

This brings me to an important topic. I separate 'listening' from 'hearing' because they are two different things that have to be learned. An orchestra produces a multitude of sonorities. The ear has to identify very quickly what is important and what is less important for balance and intonation, for thickness, for colour, and for so many other things. To succeed in doing that you need to be able to observe how sound operates once it is brought into the physical world. I am very consciously trying to pass that knowledge on, and this is why each of my assistants has developed in his or her own way, and conducts in a very individual style. They are not copies of me or of each other.

It was always important for me to give these musicians credit early on, and to let them conduct their share. I replaced mediocre older conductors with younger ones, which I didn't think was risky because I don't believe in mediocrity. Celibidache once said that mediocrity is very dangerous because it is contagious. My way of avoiding this during the last ten years in Berlin has been twofold: to get the very best conductors, such as Abbado, Boulez, Mehta, Solti and Michael Gielen for opera and concert performances of the Staatskapelle, or to give performances to young conductors who have the potential to grow. There were no failures in all those years. Unfortunately, some of my colleagues think only of the short term when they are looking for an assistant to help them prepare an opera or a concert. I would always opt for someone who has more talent and less experience. It is sometimes more difficult and creates tricky situations, but it is definitely more satisfying in the long run. An orchestra tolerates inexperience but not lack of talent.

My attitude is the same where singers are concerned. The singers

I choose are either already of great quality and fame, or they are young, with the potential to get to the top. The middle ground is not a choice. It is very important to learn how to listen to singers in audition, just as it is with orchestra members. It is essential to determine where they are on their path – are they at the beginning or the middle, or have they already reached the end? In other words, how much potential is there for development? Musicians with the right potential and a willingness to grow will achieve something far more interesting than those who have already reached the limit of their possibilities. If I take someone knowing that he or she gave the maximum of his or her potential in the audition, the maximum has to have been very high.

In the Chicago Symphony, for example, we now have one of the world's great oboe players. Yet he had never played in an orchestra before. In many ways it would have been much simpler to take someone from another orchestra with lots of experience. The fact that during all these years Alex Klein has played the most difficult pieces for the first time took tremendous effort on his part and on ours as well. However, the potential was so obvious when he auditioned that we immediately chose him. Now he is one of the best, and there are not that many.

This is why it is extremely important to develop the ability to listen. When you are reading, whether it is a book or a musical score, you have to read between the lines in order to get the full meaning. When you hear someone in an audition, you have to listen not only to the note they play at that moment, but to where their talent leads. This, too, is reading between the lines – it is seeing and foreseeing at the same time. When you view an audition as a final result, it is like reading single lines instead of the poem as a whole.

At the Staatsoper, we have successfully introduced Baroque music and we have invited many important guests over the years. It all adds to the colour of the house. Many people believe that an artist running a house may succumb to the dangerous, perhaps unconscious tendency to keep other good artists away. I believe that a music director does a great disservice to a company if he prevents musicians who are his equal or those better than himself from appearing. When you are in a responsible position, it is absolutely essential that every decision is made with regard to how it serves the house in the long run. Short-term decisions are for politicians, not for artists. Politicians need to be reelected, and they need to have a great capacity for compromise. An artist who is willing to compromise on artistic issues automatically slows down his own possibilities for development. This is really the main difference: the greater the politician's ability to compromise, the further he will advance. The greater the artist's ability not to compromise, the further he will advance instead.

14

STAGE DIRECTORS AND BAYREUTH

Rafael Kubelík once told me that he was going to record all of the Beethoven symphonies. There were already many recordings available with one conductor and one orchestra, but he planned on using different orchestras, in order to pick the specific sound of the orchestra that he found the most suitable for each symphony. I think the outcome would have been entirely different, and had much less variety, had he recorded all the symphonies with the same orchestra.

In Berlin, I preferred to have one team for the complete Wagner cycle and happily did it with Harry Kupfer, because I greatly admire the way he directs people on stage – his 'Personenregie' – and his ability to articulate text and to put it across. I see a great similarity to my way of handling music – knowing, for example, exactly when new ideas start, and which word it is that changes the direction. This is more important to me than a customized way of singing and staging, because I abhor generalization.

Stage directors are often criticized or given credit for the wrong things. At the highest level, a director's work is incredibly complex: he has to know and understand the text, be able to articulate it, and give direction about where to move and how to move. In the end, the stage director is responsible for the visual effect of the opera, even though someone else designs the lighting, the sets, and the costumes. The depth of his work lies in his direction of the acting singers or the singing actors – whichever way you prefer to think of it – and very few people in my experience have an equally developed ear, eye, and psychological understanding. I would rather have a fascinating presentation of the psychological relationship between the characters, at the expense of the visual realization, than have a beautiful tableau on which people move aimlessly. After my experience with the production of the *Ring* with Kupfer in Bayreuth, I knew that this aspect, which is equivalent to phrasing and articulation in music, was very important for the Wagner cycle in Berlin.

I have worked with a few directors who have shared my way of thinking – Harry Kupfer, Patrice Chéreau, Jean-Pierre Ponnelle, Götz Friedrich, and, in a different way, Heiner Müller. However, the balance between brain, heart, eye, and ear has rarely been as satisfying as with Patrice Chéreau. We became very close friends during our experience at the Bastille Opéra. After the plans there collapsed, it was clear that we still wanted to work together. We had already begun work on *Don Giovanni*, which was to open the Paris house, and we found that we were soulmates in our understanding and sensitivity for music theatre.

We were next asked to do a new production at the Théâtre Chatelet in 1992. I am not sure whether it was to be *Wozzeck* from the very beginning or whether the idea came later, but *Wozzeck* was a work that interested both of us very much. I had been present when Mitropoulos conducted the piece in Salzburg in the 1950s, and had very powerful memories of it. I threw myself into the preparation of *Wozzeck* with great enthusiasm. There were ideal conditions to prepare the project. We had wonderful rehearsal facilities outside Paris and we started rehearsals in two independent ways. First we would do a scene musically, with just the piano, during which Patrice would be present, asking questions and making remarks. And when that scene was musically prepared, we moved to the other side of the room, where there was no piano, and he would then rehearse the scene in a 'dry' form, as if it were spoken theatre. Since we were both always present, we were able to interact to an unusual degree. At a certain point we had two performances on the same level – one purely musical and one purely theatrical – which we then painstakingly put together. This whole period will always be a unique memory for everyone involved, because we learned not only important lessons about the piece, and about musical and theatrical performance, but also about each other.

The second opera I did with Chéreau was *Don Giovanni* in Salzburg, in the summers of 1994 and 1995, which was my only sidestep during my many years in Bayreuth. In retrospect, the *Don*

Giovanni was not as complete an experience as the *Wozzeck* for a variety of reasons, including the size of the Festival Hall in Salzburg. It is a great shame that a festival in the 'city of Mozart', where Mozart played such an important and central role, does not have an adequate hall for Mozart operas. The Festival Hall is so huge and wide that the kind of performance Patrice and I would have liked to present was very difficult to produce. Fine details, for example, could not be seen beyond the first few rows, and the problems of coordination between stage and pit were enormous. I still dream that one day Patrice might attempt this work a second time, because he has a particular insight into the world of Mozart and da Ponte.

Unlike most directors, Chéreau is a very fine actor, which enables him to give singers especially clear directions. He possesses a very unusual combination of a strict sense of discipline – the Cartesian side of French thinking – with great flair, imagination, and a capacity to tell a story in a particularly lively and interesting way. I have seen him in private moments simply observing people in various situations which he would later incorporate into a rehearsal. And although he is not a musician himself, he is extraordinarily musical. He has a very perceptive ear and a great memory, which allows him to recall details. For example, he noticed that the interval Marie sings when she sees the soldiers is exactly the same interval as in the difficult discussion with Wozzeck in the second act. On top of that, he has a particularly imaginative eye. His ability to put all these elements together in total harmony, and his ability to tell a story with all the psychological ramifications, with a very strict understanding of style and discipline, and with sensitive ears, is unique. I find it rather tragic that he has no interest in any new opera productions at this point, and I hope that he will change his mind, because he has given us great gifts in the past.

~

The years I spent in Bayreuth since 1981, when it became a central part of my activities, have had a very positive influence on my later work in Berlin. Bayreuth gave me a chance to learn about the relationship of the music, the pit, the stage, and the organization itself. Bayreuth had a skilled leader in Wolfgang Wagner, who had a total overview of all aspects of the Festival, from the cleaning personnel in the canteen to the most important singers and stage designers. It was here that I learned about the necessity of being concerned with all the different people involved in an opera company.

When Chéreau pulled out of staging *Tristan und Isolde* at Bayreuth in 1981, I was very happy to have Jean-Pierre Ponnelle take over. This was my second opera production of *Tristan und Isolde*. The first had taken place at the Deutsche Oper Berlin with Götz Friedrich, and Ponnelle had a completely different aesthetic and focus. The two had a tremendous respect for each other, and I remember Ponnelle coming to Berlin for the dress rehearsal of the Friedrich production, and leaving after the first act because he found it so interesting, consistent, and intelligent that he did not want to be influenced. That was the greatest compliment he could have paid Friedrich.

It saddened me tremendously when Chéreau cancelled for *Tristan und Isolde* at Bayreuth again, this time for 1993, for reasons which I do not completely understand to this very day. It was very difficult to replace him, especially for the second time, for the same opera, in the same place! That is when Heiner Müller, with whom I had indirect contact in my days at the Bastille, came into the picture. He was supposed to write an opera with Boulez, and I was familiar with him personally, as well as with his writings. The idea of having such a great poet staging *Tristan und Isolde* appealed to me, because I thought he might be able to bring a certain special aspect to the work. Composers who conduct – even less gifted composers – and conductors who compose bring a unique element to conducting. Artists like Furtwängler and Klemperer, who both composed, had a special strength when they conducted. I felt that Müller, who had created so many interesting texts of his own, would bring a similar understanding to the text of *Tristan und Isolde*.

I met with Heiner Müller in the former East Berlin in the spring of 1990, and asked him to take over *Tristan und Isolde* in Bayreuth. At first he thought I was crazy, since he had no experience of staging opera and had little knowledge of music in general and of Wagner in particular. However, the idea intrigued him, and after a discussion with Wolfgang Wagner, he agreed to stage the opera in Bayreuth. I was extremely surprised as the first performance approached, because he was much more of a visual person than I had expected, and together with Erich Wonder, the set designer, he had developed a presentation of the work which heightened the claustrophobic nature of the drama to a remarkable level. The first act was an especially unforgettable experience, because one could almost physically feel the oppressiveness of the situation. In a way that I had never seen before, Müller's realization gave the impression that there was no way out, just as there is no way to escape the chromaticism of the score, itself a musical maze of half resolutions ad infinitum.

Müller had some difficulties with the singers in rehearsal, because he was unwilling or unable to give them what they expected from a stage director. He had two wonderful protagonists in Waltraud Meier and Siegfried Jerusalem, who were both singing their roles for the first time. It was as if the high level of the performance was achieved in spite of the circumstances. In the end, almost against all odds, this combination of the creativity of these two singers and Müller's vision of the work made for a performance that has now become legendary.

Müller had the extreme need to appear tougher and more cynical than he actually was. He abhorred showing any kind of warmth or sentiment, and I never figured out why. He was absolutely devoid of artificiality, and he had a special kind of purity of spirit. He was never concerned about how he looked to others, and he was without interest in ornament. He was preoccupied only with the essence of things, whether it was opera or theatre or his private life. I found this a very attractive quality, and it is not unlike certain traits I remember from Klemperer. I grew to not only admire him, but to feel very close to him, and in many ways he became one of my closest friends in Berlin. Our relationship was made easier because we also shared a love for Cuban cigars, and liked to spend long evenings chatting into the night!

When a new production of *Die Meistersinger* was first discussed for Bayreuth in 1996, I had already conducted two productions of *Tristan und Isolde*, a *Ring*, and *Parsifal* there. It was clear that I wanted to do *Meistersinger* as well, and I already had it in mind for Berlin later on. I decided to conduct *Meistersinger* in Bayreuth because, just as with *Tristan und Isolde* and the *Ring*, I had a chance to find either a new generation of singers or a group of singers who had not sung this repertoire before. Wolfgang Wagner wanted to stage the production himself, having done the two previous Bayreuth productions, and I told him that it was absolutely essential to find a new cast. Otherwise there would have been no justification for staging it again. He agreed, and we put together a cast of singers most of whom were new to their roles, and some of whom were even singing Wagner for the first time.

Robert Holl, who already had a wonderful reputation as a recital singer, was my choice for Hans Sachs. I thought that the combination of his intelligence, his voice, and his capacity to play with words – to bring out all the colours in the text – was a great advantage for the role. I also liked the idea of having an experienced singer of songs as Sachs, since Sachs is half poet and half shoemaker in the opera. Andreas Schmidt, who is also very experienced with songs, was chosen for Beckmesser, which was a completely new line for him as well. Peter Seiffert was our Stolzing, and Renée Fleming, who was singing Wagner for the first time, was Eva. This combination of new blood with Wolfgang Wagner's intimate knowledge of the work brought a very positive aspect to the whole production. I doubt that there is anyone else in the world who knows *Meistersinger* as well as Wolfgang Wagner, because the piece is like the story of his own life and family.

Over the years, I have become more and more convinced that Wagner's compositions are absolutely essential for any conductor. Every expressive element is taken to its extreme in Wagner's music. Therefore, a conductor who occupies himself with Wagner in a thorough way – not just learning the score but really trying to observe every expressive element – learns the essentials that he needs for nearly every other musical style. One can then arrive at the necessary conclusions – about style, about phrasing, about articulation, about the building up of whole acts – in Mozart, for example. Wagner, along with Mozart, remains essential for the development of any musician, especially a conductor.

The *Ring* was at the centre of my activities and thoughts in the late 1980s. I spent four and a half months in Bayreuth in 1988, rehearsing the première cycle, and in the following years I spent about three months of each season there, preparing and conducting the *Ring* until it finished in 1992. It was not only the amount of time, but also the intensity of it, that made it a central event in my life. Many critics thought that the *Ring* improved enormously in the years following its première. From the production side, basically nothing changed. But what did change is that nearly all the members of what was essentially a no-name cast — or a cast of first-timers — have maintained a dominating status in the Wagner repertoire ever since.

I never made a conscious decision to leave Bayreuth. It was a process of evolution. In 1997, I decided that I wanted to return to Argentina in the summer of 2000, because I had played my first piano recital in Buenos Aires on 19 August 1950. The desire to return and play a concert in Buenos Aires on 19 August 2000 ran in a slightly sentimental vein. I would have preferred to appear in the same hall, which was very small, but it does not exist any more. Therefore, the concert was to take place at the Teatro Colón instead. I shared my thoughts with Wolfgang Wagner, who understood perfectly well, and I told him jokingly that, like a true criminal, I had to return to the scene of the crime. Ideally, he would have liked to have someone conduct *Meistersinger* in my absence. However, as we pondered the options, it became clear rather quickly that it would have been very impractical to have someone else conduct it for one year, and have me come back the year after. It made more sense to have the same conductor in 2000 and also in 2001. So the decision to leave was simply the result of reason and timing.

12

musical activity, which suggests that the new profile of the conductor is a result of social and not artistic necessity.

We are all blinded by statistics. There are many more concerts now, orchestras have to play all year round: the public wants to go to concerts in the summer as well as in the winter. This was not the case before, and therefore more people are now needed to provide these social occasions called concerts, although the repertoire has not grown accordingly. With a few exceptions, the music written during the last fifty years has unfortunately not become part of the regular repertoire. More and more we see only the same works being performed that were played fifty years ago. I am not sure that we play them very much better – although technically the orchestras are more advanced, there is greater flexibility, and perhaps they can do things more quickly. But the need for a longer season is not a musical need. It has arisen as more people can go to concerts. The public is constantly fed on music, and not always at the highest level. This means also that there are more people playing and singing and there is a need for a far greater number of soloists, instrumentalists and singers.

We have tried to solve this problem by the creation of competitions. There used to be at least four or five major piano competitions every year in Europe. With very few exceptions they all gave first, second and third prizes. That means that in one decade, for instance between 1950 and 1960, fifty pianistic talents must have appeared on the scene. Where are those people today? Some of them had very short, but successful careers, and others had no careers at all because the principle of competition goes against the very nature of music and against the nature of the musical and human development that an artist needs. Very often, when young and undoubtedly talented musicians win competitions, there is one or more recording company waiting in the wings with offers of contracts. This is the root of the problem. The young musician who has just won a competition does not have the repertoire to keep producing one record after another, but he must do so if he is to keep his name alive, even though he may not have the experience or the stamina required to go on producing. And then the point comes when the financial interests are so strong (and they have become stronger daily), when so much effort and money have been invested in an artist, just as they are invested in products like cosmetics or food, that the sense of values and the real importance of the artist are dominated by the promotional effort behind him.

Very often, while watching television, I have seen an advertisement for some sort of food and I have felt the saliva in my mouth and wanted to taste what was being advertised. Similarly, if you keep seeing on record covers and on television the faces and the names of certain artists you assume that they must inevitably be very good. However, some artists have the ability to project themselves, particularly on television; they can dazzle the eyes while at the same time charming the ears of the public. With immediate access to every private home and every public place, the media can build up or tear down people, not because of artistic value but because they have very attractive personalities. Unfortunately these people often come to believe that they are what the media has projected them as being.

I think that many young artists believe that they have discovered the way to become famous and popular quickly without realizing that over-dependence on any help, managerial or otherwise, always has a detrimental influence on the quality of their work. It is particularly dangerous for young musicians at the start of their careers. It is very confusing for them, when they are only just becoming well known, to be offered great contracts, not only with a lot of money, but also with the possibility of recording a lot of repertoire which will be decided, at best, in agreement with the record companies and, at worst, with the artist being told what he can and cannot do. This young artist will very quickly forget that his greatest privilege as an artist is not to be well known and not to make a lot of money, but to achieve total independence. The more you grow as an artist, the more independent you can become, and the less you have to try to adjust to public taste. Indeed, you are able, in your independence, and with your knowledge and talent, to influence public taste.

One of the paradoxes in the artist's life is that he wants to please, to be loved and admired, but in order to do so he must control this instinct and in his music be totally oblivious of it. A young conductor will want to please the orchestra. He will feel that a certain section – wind or brass, for instance – is more comfortable playing part of a piece at a slightly slower or faster tempo or in a louder or softer dynamic, but he must have the courage and the independence and clarity of thought first of all to establish if this corresponds to what the music says, or if it is a question of physical convenience for the players. If what the players suggest answers a musical need, he must be able to accept it as a constructive suggestion. If, however, he is convinced that not only does it not add anything, but that it is just a matter of personal convenience, he must have the courage to refuse and risk at that moment being less well liked.

The relationship between a musician and his audience or critics is something that requires a bit of thought. You may play your heart out in a concert, yet a critic may write a very negative review – it is only natural and human to be upset about it. The next day you may well play a concert with which you yourself are dissatisfied because you were unable to do what you set out to do, and you get wonderful reviews! This has happened to me many times. If I allow myself to be upset by a negative review, I should also feel uplifted by a positive one. Yet no positive criticism has ever helped me overcome my feelings after concerts with which I was dissatisfied.

The perception of the relationship between composition and performance has changed over time. First, prime importance was accorded to composition. Then the emphasis was put on the performer, and now we idolize the reproduction of the performance. What a comedown! Liszt was the first composer regularly to play music by other composers in public. In fact, he practically invented the piano recital. 'Recital' comes from the word 'recite', which means in this case to recite music by other composers. With Liszt's arrival, the mere interpretation and public performance of music became of paramount importance. Now this has further given way to a fascination with the reproduction of performances. It is inevitable that, in the course of these events, music changed from being part of the cultural world to becoming part of the world of entertainment. I am not saying that Mozart's concerts were not entertaining and I do not wish concerts to become limited to painful, intellectual exercises. But the main quality that interests us today in the music of Bach, Mozart and Schubert, although they are two or three hundred years away, is a transcendental quality, a quality which requires intimacy or solitude, and which cannot easily coexist with the popularization and the commercialization of music.

We are now in the age of television, and we have seen its influence on music and also in politics. We have seen how public opinion can be influenced by the appearance or the charisma of a presidential candidate. Ours is an age of image more than of ideology. Milan Kundera makes this point in his book *Immortality*, where he says that the ideological differences between political systems have become less important than the image of their leaders – imageology versus ideology! The presentation of the subject has become more important than the subject itself.

An excessive preoccupation with tradition can only be a sign of a weak culture. A constructive and spiritually rich civilization is one that is very aware of what has become tradition but adapts it to the future, to new ways, and I see very little of that today. Oscar Wilde claimed that art ceases to exist when it becomes archaeology, when it becomes interested only in civilizations of the past. This reminds me of what Boulez says today, that it is a sign of weakness in a civilization that it cannot destroy things. This mania for keeping everything shows a lack of courage, courage which is needed in order to use the experiences of the past as stepping stones to the vision of the future.

19

LIFE AND MUSIC

~

I would not claim that Spinoza is the only philosopher who can help maintain equilibrium, but whenever I have been in a difficult situation, professional or personal, it has been Spinoza's emphasis on our ability to reason in everyday life that has come to my rescue. We must understand the possibility, even the necessity of negative aspects of our lives, such as depression, lack of energy or unhappiness. Reason can show us the difference between what is temporary, and what is permanent. In a desperate situation, unless you are able to apply reason, the logical conclusion can only be suicide or, at the very least, anguish. Similarly, the significance of a musical statement lies not only in what it expresses but also in its temporary function within the structure. A phrase is the result of what went before, and the precursor of what is to follow. Therefore it cannot be expressed as something isolated: it must be put in relation to the whole. If one phrase represented the totality of a composition, it would not require the compromise which is the basis of any relationship. How often, when you experience a moment of extreme happiness, or extreme clarity of vision, do you wish you could preserve that moment – yet know that you cannot do so. The moment can only exist within the fluidity of life. The same thing applies to a musical composition.

Since we are committed to this totality, our statement of a particular phrase must express its own character, as well as its sub-jugation to the whole. It has its place in the musical composition in the same way that each human being has his place in the universe. (Spinoza felt that knowledge of one's place in the universe was essential for human happiness.) We exist in relation to time, and we exist in relation to the rest of the universe. When we realize that each composition has but one climax, and that the other high points are used as steps towards it or leading away from it, the concept of expressive denial becomes clear. Expressive denial means that over-indulgence in one particular phrase is detrimental to the concept of the whole, although it may, at that moment, have a very obvious and attractive expressive quality. One needs to apply a certain amount of expressive denial in order to put a phrase in the context of the whole.

Routine is the arch-enemy of musical expression. We must con-stantly be aware of the dangers of artificial comfort, of falling back on familiar territory. It is the interpreter's duty to find not only new ideas, but also a new vocabulary for old ideas. And it is important to remember that a musical masterpiece is not a communication to the world – it is the result of the composer's communication with himself. An objective reproduction of this communication is impossible because the very writing down of the composer's thoughts is in itself a transcription, a compromise between his independent thoughts and the limitation represented by the transmission of musical notation to paper.

One danger for the performing musician is the search for easy technical solutions, inevitably at the expense of musical expression. I am sure that the line of least resistance inevitably leads to least expression. Having done something in a certain way, repeating it brings tranquillity, the comfort of the familiar. However, real tran-quillity can only come from understanding what was done and how it was achieved, and then trying to better it. The only real assurance – having absorbed past experiences – is to start again from scratch. To look for the easy, physical, mechanical, or technical solution is an indulgence.

Another important counterweight to all the conscious aspects of music, and to our rational capacity, is the use of illusion. It is essential to express what one might call the inexplicable side of music – this I call illusion. Expertise in the use of illusion is as important as a musician's ability to reason. We know that music is an imitation of nature, and therefore, by definition, the creation of an illusion. A piano is not able to sustain sound like a string or a wind instrument, yet, by intelligent use of his hands and the pedal, a pianist can create the illusion of continuous sound. He must first hear the sound in his head, and then use his hands to realize his recollection of it. By balancing the different notes he strikes at the same time, the pianist creates the equivalent of perspective in painting.

Reason and illusion are not necessarily opposites. Guided by reason, illusion can be put to use as a means of expression or communication. There are many technical ways of creating illusion with the piano: it is possible to create the illusion of a portamento, going from one note to the other without a break. You can do this by the careful use of volume, by going from a note that is lower to a much higher note, and slightly delaying the higher note, playing it a little more softly, with the help of the harmonies.

I have learned a lot about music by reading books that have nothing to do with it – books by Spinoza and Aristotle, for instance. Books about music always seem to tell you rather subjective things about the people who wrote them! Philosophical concepts can sometimes be applied to what one feels about music. In his *De Anima*, Aristotle tells us about the faculties of the soul – sensation first, then the internal sense of imagination and memory, and then reason. To me, this represents the right path to absorbing a musical composition. It is a never-ending process of adaptation to the work, of absorbing it until it becomes part of ourselves. Only when we reach this stage, can we recreate the work. In the actual performance, the Aristotelian order is reversed: we reason before we start, and then, through our senses, recollect our first sensation. The sensory impression of a musical composition can be experienced either through reading or through playing it. Every musician possesses a certain capacity for *hearing* a work simply by reading it. His first sensory contact is extremely subjective – he perceives the work through the effect it produces on him and this perception is not always reliable or necessarily compatible with knowledge of the work itself.

There is an interesting and amusing story which illustrates what I mean. When Brahms was asked what performance of his Second Symphony he considered the best – there had been several performances of the symphony within a short time – he replied that he heard the best performance of the symphony when he read the score.

Your language is also of great importance in interpretation. It is impossible for a child who has been hearing French from the day he or she was born not to be influenced by its sounds when playing music. The same applies to Germans, Russians, and any other nationality. The fact that in French a heavy accent is often placed at the end of words produces difficulties when trying to work out musical phrasing. There is nothing more unnatural in music than an accent at the end of a passage or a sentence. The German language, however, due to its heavy consonants, possesses a certain weight which is reflected in German music. In several ways German music is the opposite of French music. The main difficulty with German music, from the dynamic point of view, is the slowness of the build-up, of the *Steigerung* and the idea of *allmählich steigern* which one often sees in German music scores. It is difficult to translate this: it means approximately 'increase' or 'gradually increasing'. One could describe this particular difficulty in German as an almost structural one. In French music, in Debussy and Ravel, we have exactly the opposite – there it is the swiftness of the dynamics that is so difficult. It is like a sudden spark that flashes up; there is a crescendo or diminuendo in a single note, and you have to execute the dynamics as swiftly as possible. The French use a very descriptive word for this: *étincelle*, meaning spark. These are basic characteristics of language which are audible in the way musicians of different nationalities play. French musicians have a basic difficulty with solid rhythm, solid sound, but a fantastic capacity for very imaginative sound colours and swiftness. The German musician tends to possess a better sense of rhythm but probably less imagination for sound.

There are certain things in music that need to be underlined, emphasized – things that are not connected with a sudden slowing down, or interruption, of the flow of music, but with the *placing* of a certain note or a certain chord. It is very difficult for a musician who does not understand German to achieve this in a natural way. When Wagner builds up his rhymes or monologues, whether for Wotan or Isolde, he frequently employs a sequence of words commencing with the same consonant, and this creates an accumulative effect, an alliteration known in German as *Stabreim*. It is the same thing when you have four or eight bars where each bar has one emphasized point of forte piano. At the end of the introduction to Beethoven's Second Symphony, for instance, you get this before going into the Allegro – there is a forte piano in every bar. There is a certain way of *placing* the first beat in the bar to produce its natural weight. To me this corresponds to the sound of the language, and when you try to explain this to a musician who does not speak German, he will of course be able to carry out your directions but there may be something unnatural and contrived about the way it is done. I consider that differences in language really do have an influence on musical performances. It has to do with the question of tempo, and the question of colour. In Latin orchestras the strings often display an ability to play thinly, lightly, which is very appropriate for a lot of music. And some German musicians, with a natural tendency towards a weightier sound, have greater difficulty with this kind of music.

The element of flair and colour, and an ability to attach as much importance to the least significant detail as to the most important, is a very French characteristic. One cannot begin to read a Debussy score unless one knows this, and has a feeling for it. You see this characteristic in other areas of French life – the importance the French attach not only to food but also to its presentation, for instance. They have a capacity for devoting an incredible amount of time and energy to what would seem to other people to be unimportant details, and this emerges very clearly in their music. They can do something quite out of the ordinary from sheer enthusiasm, which, at its best, is exceedingly attractive. Because of this I have many happy memories of my years in France. On the other hand, with good German musicians you feel the foundation of the music in the way they play. One of their most impressive qualities is their ability to play loudly and intensely, yet never harshly.

The French brass players have serious problems with their language when they play non-French music – they have to come to terms with the fact that they are used to French 'ü' sounds and do not really have the 'a, o, and u'. Therefore the sound has a tendency not to be well supported.

I remember an experience I had when I was conducting Bruckner's Fourth Symphony at the Teatro alla Scala in Milan many years ago. At that time there was a talented horn player in the orchestra who had never before played the piece. There was no way he would play the short note in the second bar of his solo with the necessary weight – it was just not broad enough. That really has something to do with language. Musically speaking, the little notes always belong either to the note before, or they lead into the next one. As soon as you have a rhythm with a pointed note, and then a short note, the short note will be played later and faster in all Latin countries, because the Latin languages have a tendency to go forward, and the little notes always tend to be late, and to go into the next note. Whereas a German musician would play that same little note as if it belonged to the previous note.

From early on in my life I have had a close relationship with the Israel Philharmonic Orchestra – due to a certain kind of warmth in their playing which comes very naturally to Jewish musicians and a generosity of spirit, which was linked to the personal attachment I felt for so many of the musicians. I have felt a kind of fanaticism – I mean this in the positive sense of the word – when standing in front of the Israel Philharmonic Orchestra. At such a time nothing else in the world matters for them, nothing else exists.

One thing the best Jewish musicians and the best German musicians have in common is that unusual ability to detach themselves from everyday life and their non-musical activities as soon as they start to play. I would call this an almost metaphysical or transcendental ability – with the Jews it could be explained as stemming directly from their respect for learning. At Jewish religious schools nothing else in the world matters as soon as you start to study the Torah and the Talmud. This is why, during the pogroms, so many Jews were killed while they were lost in the world of their studies. At such times they would not even stand up to defend themselves.

If we wanted to over-characterize and say that the Latin musician is elegant and the German musician intense, then we could describe the Jewish musician as having particular warmth – some people speak of a 'Jewish tone' on the violin.

20

On Interpretation

Every masterpiece is open to any number of interpretations, as long as they do not falsify it. However, it is not possible to combine all interpretations in one performance, just as it is impossible to live more than one life. The interpreter or the performer can never perceive all the many details of the many possible interpretations. In any one performance he can only glimpse them.

We often become obsessed with one particular viewpoint or idea, and thus become blind to its opposite. But to me, dualism, the paradoxical nature of things, is the very essence of music. It is no coincidence that the sonata form, which is based on this dualism, is one of the most perfect forms of expression. The structure of a classical sonata or symphony by Beethoven is based on this principle of dualism. It brings out the dramatic essence of music, which does not consist merely of loud or soft, of fast or slow, for music in itself is dramatic, even in its more epic forms such as the compositions of Bach. The first subject may be more heroic, and the second subject more lyrical in character; it is the juxtaposition of these opposing elements that lends the music a feeling of tension and excitement.

I have, rightly or wrongly, not occupied myself actively with period instruments. I have always toyed with the idea of playing Bach and Scarlatti on the harpsichord, but it has never happened. I have never had the inclination, and certainly no strong urge, to conduct Mozart with an orchestra playing so-called authentic instruments. But I think that a lot of the work done by the best musicians who have dedicated themselves to this has provided all of us with much food for thought, especially on the need to articulate eighteenth-century music as clearly as possible. Somewhere around the middle of the twentieth century, immediately after the Second World War, there was a reaction against the nineteenth-century tradition of play-ing Haydn and Mozart, in the form of the so-called objective school of performance, which wanted to do away with the excesses of the Romantic school and with all the elements which were stylistically unsuited to the performance of eighteenth-century music. In some of these older performances, there was a tendency for the actual articulation or the phrasing in Haydn and Mozart to be sacrificed for beauty or fullness of tone and a generally freer attitude to tempo.

Good musicians who have concerned themselves with authentic instruments have not limited themselves solely to the use of such instruments, but have tried to enquire and experiment with the expressive use which the instruments had in the eighteenth century. I obviously think it is perfectly possible not to perform Haydn and Mozart on authentic instruments. But one should be able to play Mozart and Beethoven as if Wagner had never existed, and I do not mean this only in relation to the orchestration. What I mean goes further than this. Wagner invented or at least developed expressive elements that were previously unknown. Sometimes it is tempting and attractive to use those means in other music, and to play a Mozart or a Beethoven movement with the kind of legato, with the kind of unlimited dynamic range of Wagner. Of course this goes against the nature of the music. At the same time, it would be childish not to adopt certain uses of expressive means we have become aware of through Wagner. It is very important to know which can be used for all music, and which can only be used in his music or in music which came after him. To play Mozart and Beethoven with the freedom of tempo, with the huge dynamic range that one needs for Wagner, would be a kind of 'retrospective anachronism'.

Goethe said that he did not know how much he had derived from Spinoza's *Ethics* or how much he had put into them. The moment you absorb something, it becomes part of you, but then you must adapt it to your needs.

In music in general, and in performance in particular, it is quite important to understand the nature of what Spinoza calls 'the attributes'. Different attributes are not necessarily different aspects of the same thing. Different performances are not just different inter-pretations but often different aspects of the same interpretation. This is why performances are rarely as different as we think they are: the essence of the interpretation is the same. Nor are performances always as similar as we imagine them to be. As long as the relation of the parts to the whole is correct, the parts differ without changing the organic whole. As long as one has an understanding and a feeling for the structure and the nature of a phrase, there are many ways of expressing it. This is another example of how philosophical thinking can come to one's aid in clarifying certain aspects of musical interpretation.

There is no such thing as a perfect interpretation. You can only progress by permanent observation of the different means of expression in every single performance or rehearsal. I have often found that as long as there is a clear conception of what has to be underlined in a performance, the actual contrasting can vary from performance to performance. You can create tension in any act of a Wagner opera by using opposite means of expression. There have been performances, even in Bayreuth, where the constant change between yielding to a phrase, and then maintaining a certain strictness of tempo, have created tremendous tension. And paradoxically, the same kind of tension has often been created through relentless, unyielding insistence on strict tempo. I have sometimes heard performances where the most atrocious crimes were committed against the written text, as far as articulation, dynamics, and balance were concerned, but nothing of this was remarked upon by the critics. They very often limit their remarks to observing the tempo of the performance.

It is very important for performers, listeners and critics alike to remember that tempo is only part of a whole. It is relative to the whole, not an independent, objective force. Some music not only tolerates but requires greater freedom and more flexibility of tempo than other music. To use rubato in the 'Danse sacrale' in the *Rite of Spring* would be as wrong as not using it in the Chopin nocturnes or a Wagner opera.

The problem of interpretation becomes more complicated when you play somebody else's work. Nobody would dream of arguing with the liberties Boulez takes when he conducts one of his own pieces, but people would be up in arms at the slightest liberty he might take in conducting Stravinsky or Ravel.

I think that there is something physical in one's feeling about tempo. You should feel uneasy when a tempo is not correct. This may apply to a particular moment, in a particular place, with a particular acoustic, tension and volume. In an over-resonant church you are forced to take a slightly slower tempo than in a building with a dry acoustic, because the sound needs more time to come into being. If you were to play the whole *Figaro* overture or the last movement of Beethoven's 'Appassionata' Sonata pianissimo, you could play it even faster than a fine instrumentalist or orchestra would normally perform it, and the ear would still be able to take it in. As soon as there are great dynamic contrasts, as actually prescribed in the music, this will influence the tempo. If it exceeds a certain tempo, the ear cannot fully grasp all the material that is being produced.

The other extreme is that of slowness. If there is not enough intensity in the vibrato of the strings, or in the harmonic tensions of the music, even a relatively fast-moving tempo will sound too slow. When the tempo is right, all the different ingredients can correlate with each other in perfect harmony. Most composers who use metronomes tend to write down metronome marks which are too fast – we know this not only from some of Beethoven's exaggeratedly fast metronome marks, but also from Bartók's. When you work at an opera house and rehearse with a singer at a piano, when the weight of the sound is considerably less than that of a full orchestra, you naturally take the music at a slightly faster speed. When the sound has weight, it needs time to move. The weight of the sound is a determining factor for the correct tempo. If you have an orchestra able to produce the necessary weight, you can take a certain tempo more slowly. With an orchestra lacking this weight the same piece has to be taken imperceptibly faster.

The metronome is the equivalent of a watch. The watch ticks unyieldingly as long as its mechanism works. This corresponds to the objective time shown by the metronome. The subjective time has to do with the way it is filled. During a period of time when we are enjoying ourselves, or when we are particularly absorbed in something, we do not notice the passing of time, although the clock is ticking away at the same speed. And at the other extreme, during a time of great boredom or annoyance, five minutes can seem interminable. The metronome represents objective time, and rubato subjective time. And the feeling of tension is created by the way you fill the sixty seconds of each minute.

As soon as a composer completes a composition, that composition enters our cosmos, our universe. It becomes independent of the composer, and subject to the laws of the cosmos, to the acoustic laws, the weight of the sound, the ability of the ear to grasp a certain minimum or maximum of notes at a given moment. As interpreters, our relationship to a composition resembles that of the composer to the cosmos. Before the composer has put it on paper, before it has been realized, the composition is dependent only on the composer's brain. It is encompassed within his imagination. The moment it is on paper, it is dependent on the reader's imagination, and the moment the piece is played, it becomes subject to the laws of the universe. The composer is not automatically his own best interpreter. As long as the piece of music is in his imagination he is the sole and perfect judge of the different elements in the composition. As soon as it assumes physical reality, however, there is no guarantee that he will perceive all the elements that have gone to make up his creation.

There is an obvious but vital distinction between musicians who create and those who interpret. The performer lacks the originality, the creativity of the composer. He is original in his re-creation, but he is using material which already exists. He realizes the music physically, but it is the composer who has had the vision.

~

To my mind one of the most important qualities which distinguish the human being is his capacity to strive for freedom – not just political freedom but freedom of thought and action. But man is very often enslaved by nature – he is the slave of his emotions – what he loves, what he hates, family, society, the church. To be free of one thing very often means being enslaved by something else. To become the master, having been the slave, frequently means becoming the slave in a different way – in the sense of dependence, of physical, material or emotional needs. This is, to my mind, very often a result of the close relationship which exists between freedom and fear. This was very apparent to me, in a political sense, in the society which existed in the Soviet Union and in Eastern Europe before the wave of liberal thinking and the first steps towards democracy took place. It was always maintained that one of the most cruel aspects of the Soviet system was that people didn't have freedom to travel and to do many things which were readily available to people in the West. This I found less offensive than the fact that the Soviet system produced a human being whose whole existence was dominated by fear. I don't think it is absolutely essential for every inhabitant of Riga or Leningrad to travel to Naples for their holidays. It can be very pleasant of course, but by no means essential. To me it is much more offensive to make people live in a society where the main emotion has become fear, where every individual fears his friends, his family, and fears for his life because of his opinions. For me, this relationship between freedom and fear is extremely important.

One result of being enslaved is emotional or mental anxiety. This is a subject on which Spinoza writes very well, and he has helped me in forming my conceptions about music and my personal life. This mental anxiety, this emotional anguish which we feel at times is the element that prevents us from being as creative as we could or should be. As we know that the things that give us pleasure in life are temporary, we constantly try to secure them for ourselves. We may collect insurance policies in a literal and a metaphorical sense – but we cannot overcome our fears of losing the object of our affections. We must therefore find ways of relieving or diminishing our anxiety.

In music it is as important to see the details in relation to the whole as it is for human beings to see themselves in relation to nature or the universe. A musical performance that displays no awareness of this is no more than a collection of beautiful moments. It is equivalent to a life spent enjoying only the sensual aspects of life, regardless of true values, and of our place in the universe.

If you decide to spend your life with music, you are dealing with a different sphere. There is no insurance for correct musical thinking, and certainly no insurance for musical performance. There is always maximum risk. It is easy to fall into the habit of looking for 'safety first'. Woodwind and brass players in particular might tend to say: 'If a note is difficult to control, don't play it too softly.' Therefore, safety first – play a little louder, and you can be sure that the note will be there. But this is not really what music is about. Music demands total commitment from the performing musician, utter devotion and discipline – not superstition. We know how easy it is to succumb to superstition, and to believe in some magical superhuman power to whom we can appeal in the last resort. I sometimes think the difference between an optimist and a pessimist is that the former believes that his God will help him when all rational means fail, whereas the pessimist believes in advance that God will not help him!

And sometimes God does seem to help. With problems of memory for instance: you have thought about something, analysed it, and worked it out, and then comes a moment when your concentration fails – which is inevitable sometimes. Your memory goes, yet somehow the motoric memory works – in your fingers playing the piano, for example. And nobody else is aware that, for a short moment, you suffered a slight memory loss.

As to methods of work on a piece of music: you must try out every possible form of expression, and the realization of that expression, before deciding on a particular one. There are so many different ways of phrasing something, and balancing it. There is more than one way, and the correct way – the one you want – cannot always be found immediately. It is almost like a kaleidoscope – we have different options for building each phrase of our performance, in fact there are more than we can use. We must therefore eliminate some and opt for one. Celibidache says rightly that rehearsing means saying a thousand times, No! Unless we have tried and rejected the others, we cannot be convinced that we have chosen the best. This even applies to matters which seem purely technical, such as fingering, or bowings for a string instrument. But it does always have to be the most expressive fingering – sometimes a repeated note needs different fingering, so as not to become mechanical repetition. We must constantly endeavour to distil the essence of the piece of music we are working on.

We also have to work from the complex to the simple. Complexity – until methodically analysed – is chaos. After analysis, it is revealed as an accumulation of orderly details. Beethoven's sketchbooks show that his method of composing went from the complex to the simple. The final version, as we know it, is often considerably simpler than his first version. A composer's initial inspiration, like the initial reaction of an interpreter, is often disorderly, and therefore unnecessarily complex. If one wanted to oversimplify it, one could say that the distinction between a great composition and a lesser one is that the great compositions have all been worked out from the complex to the simple – not in a primitive sense, but from the point of view of greater clarity. If you take the *Notations* by Boulez for instance, they look indecipherably complex at first sight. But when you start to analyse them, you see that they are very transparent and very clear – not only from the point of view of orchestration but also with regard to the musical discourse.

Spinoza has written of knowledge as not just an amalgamation of information; there is indeed a difference between experience and knowledge. Many problems, like nervousness before starting to play, have to do with too great a reliance on purely intuitive feelings, or empirical knowledge. Once you know how something is constructed, how it reacts to the laws governing sound and phrasing, then there is less reason for nervousness. This does not mean that one can always control one's nerves, but there is a nervousness that springs from a fear of not being able to realize everything one wants to, and of course there is a nervousness which comes from insufficient knowledge. Mechanical repetition is a musical equivalent of superstition. You repeat something mechanically and feel more secure because you have done it three or four times. This is a fallacy, and illogical thinking.

The contact with the audience inevitably brings a new element which can be inspiring or destabilizing because it removes the solitude in which the performer has worked and gained increasing confidence. What is important for a musician in the process of recreation is that he should be able to 're-compose' a composition, to take it apart and put it together again. This is always a creative process, a process that can help him penetrate the world of the composer. The composer has an idea, a melodic fragment, a harmonic pattern, and he elaborates on it, simplifies it, complicates it, develops it. He may put it in juxtaposition with some other musical idea he has. And then, after great inspiration or hard work, or both, he arrives at the final form. He progresses from the detail to the whole.

The interpreter can only perceive the finished unity. He must therefore find his way back from the whole to the details. Even if a composer has written a piece in a flash of momentary inspiration, relying on subconscious creative instinct, the interpreter must employ reason, understanding and observation, to consciously recreate the subconscious element. If the interpreter works only, or primarily, by intuition, he may arrive at something entirely different. If he can verify his subconscious instinct towards a piece of music through conscious observation, he will be dealing with associations and patterns deriving solely from the composer's creation. This does not, of course, guarantee that he will grasp the composer's intention exactly, but it does remove the danger of subjective misinterpretation.

The composer has what might be described as a dual authorship – one expressed in the conventional system of written music, and the other in unuttered musical thoughts. It is the equivalent to the relationship between the letter and the spirit of a text. The written notes can lead us to the imagination of the composer – to his unexpressed musical thoughts. But, paradoxically, only through the imagination can we understand the full significance of the written notes. In music there can be no separation between thought and emotion, between rationality and intuition – all these elements add up to one unity. Thorough observation helps us to understand the construction of a piece of music, and to memorize it. Einstein said that the most inexplicable thing about the universe is that it is explicable. One could almost paraphrase him and say that the most explicable thing about music is its inexplicability. After every observation and analysis, there is always an element that remains incomprehensible. This to me is music's transcendental quality.

~

What I have learned from Spinoza's philosophy on the capacity of reason to deal with emotional anxiety has helped me in my attitude towards music and everything surrounding the world of music – the media, the adulation, the criticism, and the envy. We musicians are constantly confronted by people who live on the periphery of music – agents, managers, administrators, members of the general public, and critics. Music is one of the subjects on which everybody feels they have a right to express an opinion. I have often met people who were either very enthusiastic, or greatly disturbed by a certain tempo, and who talked about it without any understanding of the decisions behind that tempo. I know no other profession where so many people feel called upon to express opinions about anything and everything concerning it.

But no musical performance represents the end of the road: it is always the beginning of a new one. It is a culmination of what has been up to that performance, and the prelude to the next. No performance should be allowed to pass without the performer having gained some degree of further understanding. It is very important for performing musicians to learn a composition not only instinctively or subconsciously but also to observe and digest the different ingredients used by the composer in creating it. No composition has sprung fully grown from the brain of the composer. It has, on the contrary, developed stage by stage with the composer leaving aside what was superfluous for his purpose and retaining only the indispensable – as in Beethoven's sketchbooks – another example of expressive denial. We can only express our own selves by acquiring an intimate knowledge of the composer's text, and by finding our own way of 'de-composing' it.

I think it is important to understand how a composer came to write what he wrote – in other words, what means did he use? What were the harmonic relations, the melodic course, the rhythmical patterns, and the interrelation between the three? What are the *instructions* he gave us for performance? The composer has written down conventional symbols, notes – this is explicit. What *we* must look for is the means of grasping their full significance. I have often arrived at a particular phrasing or fingering while working on another part. The obviously simple often becomes unnecessarily complex, but on the other hand a complicated passage may not only become simple but also more expressive.

If the score says allegro, and you play adagio, then you have gone too far; similarly if the score says crescendo, and you play diminuendo. Freedom of rhythm should occur neither wilfully nor capriciously. All these elements must in some way relate to the organic whole. There are, of course, stylistic differences between composers: some things, especially as regards volume and flexibility of tempo, are possible for Puccini but certainly wrong for Bach, or vice versa. But the concept of freedom is the same for Bach, Stravinsky, Puccini or Wagner. I do not attempt to change the composer's instructions, but I try to find a relationship between the different instructions. This relationship also applies to the quantity: when it says accelerando – how much? And when it says diminuendo – how much? And when it says nothing … ? From a particular point in the finale of Bruckner's Seventh Symphony, there is a momentum that builds up to the final climax and cannot, to my mind, be interrupted or held back. From that particular moment the music has a forward drive that goes on to the end.

As a musician, on the one hand I constantly learn new works, yet, on the other, I keep coming back to and studying again some of the works I have known and performed since childhood. As I continue my life in music, the distinction becomes clearer between the works that have an occasional interest and those that have become lifelong companions.

21

MUSICAL AFTERTHOUGHTS

Early in my career, when I lived and worked in London in the 1960s, I was very closely associated with two very great conductors of Mahler, Sir John Barbirolli and Otto Klemperer. And yet, I still have to confess that at that time I disliked Mahler's music profoundly. As a result, I am something of a late convert to the composer, as well as a selective one.

Klemperer always used to poke fun at me about my difficulties with Mahler. I remember going to hear him conduct Mahler's Seventh Symphony in London's Festival Hall one Yom Kippur eve in the late 1960s. The hall was half empty, but it was a fantastic performance, quite unlike any other. Afterwards Klemperer was very surprised to see me. He said: 'You are such a rascal. You hate Mahler but you hate going to the synagogue even more. That's the only reason you are here tonight.'

When I say I disliked Mahler profoundly, this is perhaps an exaggeration. A more accurate way of putting it would be to say that I disliked some of the symphonies. I always loved the Mahler songs, including *Das Lied von der Erde*. I felt that Mahler seemed to need text to work best. But I didn't like the bombast of some of the symphonic last movements, and I still have great problems with the Eighth Symphony.

One of the aspects that I most disliked at that time was Mahler's use of artificial folk tunes in several of the symphonies. This folk quality always struck me as false, in contrast to the folk mood in the music of Brahms, Schubert or Bruckner. With Mahler it always seemed to be in quotation marks. The other difficulty I had – and still have – with Mahler is the fact that his music has so often been talked about in non-musical terms. He was stereotyped as the first post-Freudian composer. Or he was the culturally conflicted Jewish composer. His music was constantly described in terms of personal hysteria or the social disintegration of pre-1914 Europe.

I have never liked the idea that you cannot understand the 'real' message of music unless you understand it in non-musical terms. It is a problem that dogs Mahler, and more recently Shostakovich. Every composer's music is partly autobiographical, of course. But music that is primarily or exclusively autobiographical would be of no interest. The interest is because the music transcends these factors. I simply do not think that Mahler performances stand or fall according to their Jewishness.

The thing that fascinated me when I began studying Mahler was the way that he writes. Mahler was really the first composer to write individual dynamics for different groups of instruments. Composers such as Beethoven, Brahms, and Wagner mostly wrote their dynamics for the whole orchestra, and in only a very few cases would they write opposite dynamics for different groups of players. Mahler was different. In Mahler there are unison passages between clarinets and violas in which the clarinets are marked mezzo forte crescendo to fortissimo and the violas are marked fortissimo diminuendo to mezzo forte – all on the same note. In other words the texture remains the same but the colour changes radically.

That tells you two things. First, it tells you what a highly professional conductor Mahler was. A few years ago in Vienna, I had the good fortune to be shown Mahler's own score of *Tristan und Isolde*. It was very heavily marked, but always in the same way. Whenever there was a crescendo, it was taken away from the horns, say, or the trumpets and trombones, and placed two, three or four bars later. The point was to improve the audibility of the passage so that details did not get lost. What I draw from this is an acute awareness on Mahler's part of dynamics, and of why he wrote this way in his own music. Second, it tells you that his sense of colour is extraordinarily delicate and subtle. There are very few composers who demand that degree of detail, and it is something I find lacking in very many performances of Mahler's music. It was an aspect that Klemperer took great care over. He too was very fastidious about dynamics and balance. This was a pivotal insight in my understanding of Mahler.

I think that a lot of the vulgarity and the bombastic aspects that disturb me in Mahler came because conductors did not always really understand the sense of the music as music. It sounds very pre-sumptuous to say I wish to purify Mahler, but I do think, in a sense, that Mahler now has to be purified of all these non-musical precon-ceptions that have become attached to him. I think that audiences perhaps need to think about him afresh. Certain composers need this more than others. I think of Mozart or Chopin here, as well as Mahler.

As someone who has made the journey to Mahler in a hard way, overcoming quite a lot of obstacles, I think it is very important to bring forward the harmonic construction of the Mahler symphonies. This is an aspect that sometimes I miss in Mahler performances and it matters greatly, because Mahler's music is sometimes tonally anchored and sometimes tonally disorientated. It is one of the things that makes him a post-Wagnerian revolutionary.

Compare the beginnings of two symphonies that I have conducted in recent years. In the First Symphony, there is a very clear harmonic orientation in the first two movements. Everything is related. You know where your home key is. And then suddenly the last movement starts with a crash and we are in F minor, a totally foreign key, and there is this feeling of tonal disorientation. You have entered a new world of new music. It is no coincidence that Wilhelm Furtwängler, who was not a great Mahler enthusiast, found the last movement too problematic.

Now take the opening of the Seventh Symphony. From the word go there is a sense of disorientation. Mahler takes us immediately into the unknown. There is an iron rhythm, but harmonically it is all over the place. The process is the exact opposite of the First Symphony. In the First we go from certainty to dissolution. In the Seventh we go from uncertainty to harmonic solidity. The problem of the Seventh Symphony is often seen as an architectural problem, of how to build it up. Yet in many ways, I think this is a mistaken approach. Conducting the Seventh is like carrying out an archaeological dig. When the first movement starts, you feel you are digging down through the layers, looking into dark places and examining them in the light.

These contrasts show why it is so difficult to speak about Mahler in just one breath. You feel with Mahler that there is always a search for a new idiom for each symphony. Look at the difference between the Second and the Third, or between the Seventh and the Eighth. In that respect he is very similar to Beethoven. Mahler always poses the question: which Mahler?

Different conductors will always find different qualities in the music of any composer. Barbirolli, for instance, used to make Mahler sound quite like Elgar, and he would talk about the two composers in similar terms. Rafael Kubelík, on the other hand, felt the affinities with Mahler's Bohemian origins. He could conduct the First almost as if it were by Dvořák. I often thought I was missing something in Mahler until I listened to Kubelík. There is a lot more to be discovered in these pieces than just a generalized form of extroverted excitement. This is what Kubelík showed. And it is also what I seek to do.

~

Over these last years, I have become more actively involved in non-European music. This began in Argentina, quite by chance, when I met two wonderful tango musicians, Rodolfo Mederos and Hector Console. As often happens in my life, one person, in this case José Carli, brought seemingly unrelated events and people together. He used to be a violinist with the Teatro Colón and has become an absolute master orchestrator of Argentinian music. He put together many of the arrangements on my tango recording, *Mi Buenos Aires querido*, and is also responsible for several orchestral arrangements of tangos for the Chicago Symphony and the Berlin Philharmonic.

~

For the celebration of the fiftieth anniversary of my first perform-ance on stage, an entire series of concerts was planned at Carnegie Hall, where I was given the chance to be active as a pianist, as a conductor, as a recital accompanist, in chamber music concerts, and as a teacher. Teaching is becoming more important to me now, because I feel a responsibility to give to the next generation what I myself was fortunate enough to receive in my life. I was very lucky to start so early, which enabled me to experience many different styles of performance. I have seen so many fashions come and go that I feel it is my duty and my privilege to pass this on. The most extraordinary element in teaching for me is what one learns from students. I learn something just from the way a question is put to me. Through teaching I am forced to look at what I think, or maybe instinctively feel, and try to articulate it. Therefore, teaching is not an altruistic activity. It is a necessity for me, because through teaching I am learning.

~

There has been a neglect of the matter of harmony in music education and composition for the last ten years. Even in my relatively young years, I was aware of a change that started in the 1950s. I began studying harmony with Nadia Boulanger in Paris, in a very thorough, even dogmatic way, and I later continued with Ben-Haim in Israel. It is not the scholastic functions of harmony which are the most important, but rather the realization that when you establish a home tonality, you automatically give yourself the option to travel in strange harmonic worlds, a process we call modulation. Until you establish a home key, nothing seems foreign in comparison. How to do it is another matter, but what is often missing in today's music making is an understanding of the function of harmony.

The mere fact that harmony can move more slowly than rhythm and melody makes it even more powerful. When the decision about a tempo is made too early, one will never be able to develop the details and tensions that arise through the interdependence of these different elements in music. It's as if you decide before you have a conversation with someone you find amusing or likable that you are only going to talk for a certain length of time. It is much more interesting to start a conversation and see how it develops and where it leads before you decide whether you give it five minutes, an hour, or five hours, isn't it?

The other misconception about tempo today has to do with the necessity some musicians feel to adhere to the metronome marks, which reveals a complete misconception about the role of the metronome. The metronome is there only to give an idea, not to dictate a speed. I once asked Pierre Boulez why it is that when he conducts his own works he sometimes takes a different speed from the metronome marking. And he answered with his typical Boulezian sharpness and charm, 'When I compose I cook with water, and when

I conduct I cook with fire!'The weight of the sound and the acoustic conditions determine the speed.

Today, there is a kind of forced morality to observing the tempo and sticking with it no matter what, as if this was a sign of strength of character, loyalty, and creativity. Mahler once said that a tempo is right only when it can already be changed in the second bar. That most certainly does not apply to all styles – where it may be right for Mahler's or for Wagner's music, it most certainly might not be right for Stravinsky's. For me, though, the necessity of imperceptible changes in tempo is a fundamental principle of music making.

~

We live in an age where we expect political correctness, which in this context means awaiting directions, even though we strive for freedom of thought and action at the same time. These two aspects – the need for more freedom and the need for direction – are very interdependent. I see that in many aspects of today's society. To transfer this to a musical context: in every movement in the history of music, there have always been people with a higher level than others. For example, our preoccupation with original instruments and original performance practice has no doubt given us some very talented musicians. The problem does not arise with the talented ones, but with the less talented ones, however, because they have an ideology to follow.

I very often feel that they have nothing to say about the music, but must follow directions anyway. They know a half-truth about how things were played in the past, but they don't feel the need to make any kind of adaptation. That leads to absolutely senseless conclusions, such as a general belief that Bach, Haydn and Mozart should be played with a small number of strings. They are forgetting or ignoring that Mozart himself wrote to his father, after the first performance of his Symphony No. 34, how incredibly happy he was about having twenty-four violins!

Today, you sometimes hear performances – for example those of Bach at the Berlin Philharmonie or comparable large halls – where four or five first violins are used, without taking into account that the acoustic and size of the hall require something else. If one believes that this music can only be played with four or five violins, one should go back to the places for which these pieces were written and first performed. Questions often arise regarding different versions of works – new 'authentic' editions, etc. I cannot help feeling that musicians very often sit in front of a score – not unlike a student who is confronted with an exam for which he is not prepared – and go absolutely blank. The score is only a notation of what was in the composer's imagination. It is a result of his whole being – of his thoughts, his feelings, his temperament – and it is simply not enough to play with the knowledge of the printed page. To do that is not difficult, nor is it something to be particularly proud of. Neither is it sufficient only to play with temperament or with feeling, which in itself is also not hard for someone who is relatively talented and well trained. It becomes difficult when you put all the elements together – but that is also when it becomes music.

Sound is not music. You can have a collection of beautifully played sounds, but you won't have music until all the ingredients are combined in an interdependent context. That brings us to the question of why music is related to religion. What is religion – regardless of which one – all about? Monotheistic religion is about a concept of something which you cannot divide, where everything is one. This is also the principle of music: when you cannot divide feeling from thinking, thinking from sensing, and temperament from scholarship. The further we move away from the time when the music was written, the less courageous we become. In other words, when you hear a performance of a world première or a recently written work, you may encounter sheer difficulty, a lack of familiarity, an intensity, and a feeling that your whole body and soul is involved. But when it is music that has existed for many years and for which we only have the famous 'black spots on white paper', you have a much weaker feeling about the total involvement of the human being.

~

I have been very fortunate to come in contact with composers who have given us very interesting and beautiful music. My friendship with Pierre Boulez continues over the years without any decrease in intensity and pleasure, but I have also got to know and grown to admire Elliott Carter and Harrison Birtwistle. Both wrote operas of which I conducted the world premières in Berlin (I also took

Carter's work to Chicago and New York). Carter and Birtwistle are two very different composers who give the lie to the argument that all of today's music is either very light and popular or very complex and difficult.

The development of Elliott Carter's music during the last fifty years has been extraordinary. I consider Carter's first opera, *What Next?*, a work of great virtuoso writing for an orchestra; there is something very exciting and pleasurable about the brilliance of his music. *What Next?* starts with the aftermath of a catastrophe – in the Berlin production it is a car accident – of which four percussionists simply reproduce the noise. These same instruments are then transformed, so that they not only give rhythm and make noise, but show the mood of the situation and the music – a transformation from something purely descriptive to something highly expressive. I am fascinated with Carter's writing for the orchestra, especially his poetic feeling for the percussion instruments, which gives so much to the atmosphere of the piece. In some ways it is the perfect companion to Liszt's inventive use of the solo triangle in his First Piano Concerto, which is also totally unprecedented.

Harrison Birtwistle, a completely different kind of composer, has written many important works over the last few years – a wonderful 'piano concerto', *Antiphonies*, masterful orchestral works such as *Exody*, which he composed for the Chicago Symphony, and opera, such as *The Last Supper*, which we have done at the Staatsoper. I don't know if these two composers know each other and what they think of each other. But it would not surprise me to find either that they have mutual respect for each other, or very little interest in each other. They are alike only in that they both belie the idea that today's music can be put in one drawer because it is all the same.

Very often I hear either 'Oh, I love contemporary music' or 'No, I do not like contemporary music at all.' Both statements are without justification, because there is such a variety in style and quality. Whenever I hear musicians say one or the other as a generalization, I know that they are only paying lip service. You cannot love it all or hate it all – you may be interested in some parts more than in others, just as you feel about music of the past.

In Chicago I have the reputation of doing too much contemporary music, and in Berlin I am accused of doing too little – so I guess my level of involvement has to be about right! During the last ten years I have found tremendous excitement, interest, and pleasure in several contemporary compositions. In 1999, Pierre Boulez delivered another of his *Notations* for orchestra, VII, and I consider it a master-piece. It is longer and larger than his older ones, and it further develops his concept of transforming music. He explores new territory in it, and I am eager to have the next instalments in this series. I have not yet given up the hope that he will write an opera, which I believe would be a very important contribution to the form. Twice before he has begun to plan an opera, first with Jean Genet and then with Heiner Müller, who both died, unfortunately, before any headway could be made.

~

Quite understandably, the debate over Wagner resurfaces in Israel at regular intervals. No consensus can yet be expected on this topic. Thus it seems necessary to take some time to consider the historical background. Bronislaw Huberman founded the Israel Philharmonic Orchestra in 1936, at a time when no taboo existed against Wagner's works. At that same time, conductor Arturo Toscanini, a well-known anti-fascist, decided to stop performing at the Bayreuth Festival, because of Hitler's presence at a performance of Wagner's music at the second inaugural concert of the Israel Philharmonic Orchestra. The Israel Philharmonic was independently managed and did not decide until after Kristallnacht in 1938 to stop performing Wagner. The associations connected to Wagner's music because of its misuse by the Nazis were deemed too strong.

After several failed attempts, the Israel Festival invited me to conduct a concert on 7 July 2001, during the Israel tour of the Berlin Staatskapelle. The programme included, among other works, music by Wagner. I have the greatest understanding and compassion for all Holocaust survivors and their terrible associations with Wagner's music. Therefore, Wagner's works should not be played during concerts for regular season-ticket holders, when faithful subscribers would be confronted with music that raises painful memories.

However, the question must be asked whether any person has the right to deprive any other person who does not have these same associations of the possibility of hearing Wagner's music. This would indirectly serve the misuse of Wagner's music by the Nazis. After all, the Israel Philharmonic's decision to cease performing Wagner's music was not based on Wagner's anti-Semitism, which had been well established since the nineteenth century, but on the terrible associations created by the Nazis. Certain decisions are absolutely correct and understandable at the time. However, new developments sometimes change situations, making a revision of past decisions necessary.

An example of this is the position taken by the Israel Philharmonic, after the Second World War and the Holocaust, not to engage soloists and conductors such as Bruno Walter and Otto Klemperer, who had converted from Judaism before or during the war. Given the circumstances at that time, this decision was understandable. However, over time this policy was cancelled, as conversion was no longer considered to be a sign of weakness or as an attempt to improve one's personal fate through assimilation. Nowadays, there would be no problem in inviting a converted Jew to perform music with the orchestra.

The present debate about Wagner is very similar. In 1938, the decision against his music was understandable, as its terrible associations were too strong. I also understand that some people cannot forget these associations, and one should not ever force them to listen to Wagner's music in a concert. However, Israel should also act as a totally democratic state. This entails not preventing people who are free of these associations from listening to Wagner's music. It is not my intention to wage a missionary's war in favour of Wagner in Israel. I do feel, however, that this is a case where Israel can, and should, define itself as a democracy.

The concert with the Staatskapelle took place in Jerusalem on 7 July, with a programme of music by Schumann and Stravinsky, and an encore by Tchaikovsky. Afterwards, I turned to the audience and proposed the Prelude and Liebestod from Wagner's *Tristan und Isolde* as a further encore. Of course I did not want to play Wagner for an audience that was unprepared for it, and therefore I engaged in a long dialogue with the audience that lasted some forty minutes, indicating that those who wanted to leave should do so, but that if others wanted to hear it, we were ready to play. Some twenty or thirty people left. And the rest stayed and gave us a standing ovation at the end, which gave me the feeling that we had done something positive. It was only the next day that the scandal really erupted, which means that it was organized by people who were not there but who had some political agenda, which greatly saddens me.

In a democratic society like Israel there should be no room for taboos. The boycott on Wagner is very capricious – the Israel Philharmonic is not allowed to play Wagner, but you can buy Wagner records in Israel, you can hear Wagner on Israeli radio, you can see Wagner videos on Israeli television, and you can go around Israel with cellular phones that play 'The Ride of the Valkyries'. I do not believe that someone who sits at home in Tel Aviv or Jerusalem suffers because he knows that in another city someone is playing Wagner.

Unfortunately, the whole debate about Wagner is linked to the fact that we have not yet made the transition into being Israeli Jews, and that we cling to all sorts of associations with the past – which of course were valid and understandable at the time – as a way of reminding ourselves of our own Judaism. The fact that we say that Wagner will not be played in Israel gives us a further link to the Judaism of the 1930s and 1940s. Of course we need to have a sense of history, but we also need to know who we are today as Israeli Jews. And until we are able to do that, we will not be able to establish a fruitful dialogue with non-Jews. This is why there is a connection between the Wagner issue and the relationship with the Palestinians.

~

As Naguib Mahfouz has written, 'The cruelty of memory manifests itself in remembering what is dispelled in forgetfulness.' This statement expresses something that I believe is very important for the relationship between Germans and Jews, since, with respect to each other, both are dealing with the problem of the past. Certain matters require the generosity of forgetfulness, and others demand the honesty of remembrance. From my point of view, this is the difficulty with postwar German generations, although I have never had any personal experience of xenophobia or anti-Semitism in Germany. A recent statement by a well-known Berlin politician about 'the Jew Barenboim' was made in a context that had nothing to do with Judaism, and I interpret it as a sign of his misunderstanding of Judaism.

It is true that Judaism is not easily explained: it is part religion, part tradition, part nation, and partly an immensely various people. It is hard to deal with, as much for the Jews themselves as for everyone else, and especially for a country like Germany, which has such a horrible common history with the Jews. Sadly, after spending years in Germany, I have a deeper and deeper impression that this part of German history has not been assimilated or understood by many Germans. Such ignorance could lead to a new anti-Semitism, or to philo-Semitism, which would be as wrong as anti-Semitism.

I don't believe in collective guilt, especially not after so many generations have passed, and therefore I have no problem living and working in Germany. But at the same time I expect every German not to forget this part of his country's history, and to be especially careful in considering it. Each German will be able to do this, however, only if he has an understanding of his own self and the past that helped to form it; for if you suppress an important element of yourself, you are constrained in your dealings with others.

Such thoughts lead to the question of German identity and to the general question of what an identity consists of. Is there really only one identity for a person or for a people? The Jewish tradition has two distinct tendencies: the more fundamental one, represented by the philosophers and poets and scholars who were interested only in Jewish issues and in the Jewish *Weltanschauung*; and the other tendency associated with great figures such as Spinoza or Einstein, and to a certain extent also Heinrich Heine, which applied the traditions of Jewish thinking to other cultures, including German culture, and to other issues. It is not difficult to see how a double identity developed among Jews.

In my opinion it is impossible for anyone at the beginning of the twenty-first century believably to claim a single identity. One difficulty of our times is that people restrict their concerns to ever smaller details, and that they often have little sense of how things are intermingled with one another, and together form part of a whole. The Germans have given the world so much by way of spiritual enlightenment – we have only to think of Bach, Beethoven, Wagner, Heine, Goethe, to name just a few – but perhaps the horrific experiences of the Nazi era, and shortly after, have made it particularly difficult for a German today to confront his own history as a whole.

I look at the question of identity both as a musician and from the perspective of my own history. I was born in Argentina, my grandparents were Russian Jews, I grew up in Israel, and I have lived most of my adult life in Europe. I think in the language that I happen to speak at a particular moment. I feel German when I conduct Beethoven, and Italian when I conduct Verdi. This does not give me a feeling of being untrue to myself; quite the contrary. The experience of playing very different styles of music can be remarkably illuminating. When you have learned and played a Debussy pianissimo, and when you then return to a Beethoven pianissimo, you know even better what the differences are, and you realize you are dealing with two entirely different sounds. With Debussy the pianissimo has to be bodiless, and with Beethoven it has to have a physical core of expression and sound.

It is only natural to find excursions into different cultures valuable, but of course German culture is something extraordinary, and there should be no false modesty about it. If you understand Beethoven as somebody who was at the same time German and universal, it also becomes apparent that Germans, much more than those of many other nations, have occupied themselves with past cultures – for example with Greek mythology, literature, and philosophy. All of Beethoven's work is based to some degree on the Greek principle of catharsis, which reflects a typical German attitude: one should not fear to enter the dark and re-emerge into the light. The first movement of the Fourth Symphony, for example, starts from the depths of chaos and finds an extraordinary way to order and jubilation.

I found a speech the President of Germany, Johannes Rau, gave in 2000 especially apt when he spoke about the differences between nationalism and patriotism. He said: 'Patriotism can flourish only where racism and nationalism are given no quarter. We should never mistake patriotism for nationalism. A patriot is one who loves his homeland. A nationalist is one who scorns the homelands of others.' These seem to me very important points. I believe that many Germans lost their sense of patriotism, their affection for their country, during the second half of the twentieth century and did so partly out of fear of nationalism. This is unfortunate. The change took place during a time of large-scale immigration, when more foreigners wanted to come to Germany, or felt compelled to come, than ever before. Germany opened its gates and made use of the immigrants without having acquired the tolerance of a state based on immigration, such as, for example, Argentina or the United States. The attitudes of many Germans who are hostile to foreigners seem to me to derive from the fact that the last two or three generations of Germans have not adequately learned what immigration means. They fail to understand that it is possible to have more than one identity at the same time and to accept that people of foreign origin, with foreign customs and a foreign culture, can become part of one's own land without threatening one's identity as a German.

The best example of this specific German problem is the current situation in Berlin, in which some people fear that their capital is becoming multicultural, or multidimensional. This fear surely stems from a past that has not been entirely assimilated. Berlin was the only divided city in Germany, and the two parts of the city had unusual external support; both the Federal Republic of Germany and the German Democratic Republic considered Berlin a city with a special status. My hope is that Berlin will not lose its special status because of reunification – on the contrary. Because of the forty-year-long division and the existence of the East and the West side by side, Berlin, in my view, has a unique potential for encompassing differences, a potential that should now be made use of. Instead of complaining about the division caused by history, one should treat it as a positive force, for Berlin and also for the city's relations with the rest of Germany and with other countries. After all, Berlin is the only city where neither a delegation from Moscow nor a delegation from Washington will feel wholly foreign.

If we are to understand the phenomena of nature, or the qualities of human beings, or the relationship to a God or to some different, spiritual experience, we can learn much through music. Music is so very important and interesting to me because it is at the same time everything and nothing. If you wish to learn how to live in a democratic society, then you would do well to play in an orchestra. For when you do so, you know when to lead and when to follow. You leave space for others and at the same time you have no inhibitions about claiming a place for yourself. And despite this, or maybe precisely because of it, music is the best means of escape from the problems of human existence.

233

For me Busoni's definition of music as 'sonorous air' is the only one. Everything else that is said about music refers to the different reactions that it evokes in people: it is felt to be poetic, or sensual, or spiritual, or emotional, or formally fascinating – the possibilities are countless. Since music is everything and nothing at the same time, it can therefore be easily abused, as it was by the Nazis. At the workshop in Weimar, musicians from Israel and the Arab countries have worked together and shown that rapprochements and friendships previously thought impossible may be achieved through music; but this does not mean that music will solve the problems of the Middle East. Music can be the best school for life, and at the same time the most effective way to escape from it.

APPENDIX

Remarks by Daniel Barenboim at a ceremony held in conjunction with a concert of the Israel Philharmonic Orchestra in Tel Aviv, during which he was presented with an honorary Doctor of Philosophy degree by the Hebrew University of Jerusalem, 25 December 1996.

It is with feelings of great emotion that I stand here before you to receive the honorary Doctor of Philosophy degree from the Hebrew University of Jerusalem. My emotions are stirred for various reasons, but mainly because of the great honour of being included within a long list of distinguished and important people who have preceded me in receiving this degree. The second reason is that the degree is in philosophy, an area which enables one to distinguish between merely putting together notes and making music, an area which helps one to understand music and to see in it not just a collection of notes but a general cosmic expression. The third, no less important, reason is my feeling upon receiving this degree from this prestigious and important institution, the Hebrew University of Jerusalem, with the emphasis on Jerusalem.

Although I was raised in Tel Aviv and went to elementary school as well as high school there, Jerusalem to me was always the symbol of the ties between the tradition which comes from yesterday and the future which begins tomorrow. The source of all European culture is in fact Jerusalem. The cultures of Rome, Greece, Eastern and Western Europe were nurtured from the sources to be found in Jerusalem. Every person who has any connection whatsoever with culture – whether one is speaking of music, literature, or science – returns, upon his coming to Jerusalem, something that he has received there, directly or indirectly, and therefore I see in Jerusalem the spiritual centre for all nations.

In this time, which is not an easy one in terms of political tension between various factions among our people and difficult conflicts between the Orthodox and the secular, I believe that first of all we must try and define who is a Jew. The definition of an Orthodox Jew is understood; however, the definition of a secular Jew is complex, and until we can make this definition, until we are able to explain what brings a person to be and to feel himself a Jew, we will not be able to explain to ourselves the foundation of our existence; we will also not be able to conduct a dialogue between ourselves, and between ourselves and our Palestinian neighbours.

This is our fundamental problem. And until we understand this problem and are intelligent enough to define it, the State of Israel is likely to reach the situation of a theocratic state, as the Arab states are likely to develop along fundamentalist lines. A person who is unable to achieve self-definition and self-satisfaction will not be able to conduct a dialogue with others, and so we also will not be able to develop normal, reasonable relations with our Palestinian neighbours. Then, to my sorrow, the vision of the State of Israel and Zionism would become a passing, historic episode.

The greatest struggle of every mortal being is to try and halt the passing of time, and this of course we cannot do. Therefore, in my opinion, the concept of Zionism also must develop and find the golden mean that will lead to harmonious internal and external relations. This harmony, as in music, can be achieved even if it is made up of conflicting elements, albeit of the strongest and most radical nature, as long as each element can develop itself to its fullest.

It is my dream that all of the problems I have raised, of Jewish self-definition, of relations between religious and secular, and of the need to reach a situation of proper and fair relations with our Palestinian neighbours, will be solved soon. I believe that this is the only way and I believe that if this will be so, Israel will become a cultural centre of great importance in the Middle East, and will become, and not just figuratively, a light unto the nations.

I am pleased that the Hebrew University of Jerusalem chose this house in which we now find ourselves worthy as a place for presentation of this degree. This house is close to my heart and especially so because it is in this hall and with this Philharmonic Orchestra that

I have appeared so many times for over forty years; the ties between us are strong, sturdy ties built upon mutual appreciation and professional and friendly relations. Therefore I see this degree as being given not only to me but also to the members of the orchestra who are sitting here tonight on this stage and also those who have shared with me important musical experiences in the past.

I hope that I will justify the trust that you have placed in me by presenting this important degree to me on behalf of the Hebrew University of Jerusalem, and that I will be able to continue to contribute with all of my ability to the state as a whole and to Jerusalem in particular.

I thank the Hebrew University of Jerusalem and its leaders for presenting to me this degree of which I am so proud.

EDITOR'S NOTE

The 1991 edition

Over the last ten or fifteen years there has been something of a boom in books by musicians. Most of these have been biographical in form, although some have included considerations on music itself and – particularly where conductors are concerned – on the professional skills of music-making. In many cases one could justifiably question the need for such books and in many instances too great artists, who are constantly in the limelight, have allowed their names to be used without having written a single word of their own, in the hope that a book will bring them even more publicity.

None of this applies to *A Life in Music*. For at least ten years Daniel Barenboim has intended to write a book on music, on its nature and its outward forms. However, throughout the 1980s his formidable timetable of engagements both as conductor and pianist made it impossible for him to find the lengthy period of quiet concentration, which is essential for an undertaking of this nature. An opportunity arose, however, after the Bastille project fell through. Barenboim felt that, despite the numerous concert engagements scheduled to take place before he was to take up his duties as chief conductor of the Chicago Symphony Orchestra, he would none-theless have enough time at his disposal to embark upon the project at last.

I was introduced to Daniel Barenboim in Bayreuth by Harry Kupfer. I had been invited to write about what has since become a legend – *Der Ring des Nibelungen* under Barenboim and Harry Kupfer – so we worked together for the first time. In the course of our collaboration Barenboim asked me whether I would be interested in helping him, for it was clear that, once he took up his post in Chicago in the autumn of 1991, he would have no further opportunity to work on his book for a long time. I agreed immediately, for I had already recognized that Barenboim was by no means in search of a ghost writer or co-author. He had already amassed a great deal of written material on the subject and we discussed the form in which the book was to be put together and details of the way in which further work was to proceed.

In spite of any assistance I was able to give him, the book which resulted is exclusively the work of Daniel Barenboim who, throughout the comparatively short period in which it took shape, put himself at my disposal whenever necessary. *A Life in Music* was written between Bayreuth and Chicago, Paris and Dresden, London and Salzburg, Gstaad and Vienna. My task was to collate and organize the text for our next meeting, so that Barenboim could complete the project within the time available.

Nonetheless, the book could never have become reality without the spontaneous enthusiasm and creative support of Lord Weidenfeld, who offered constant encouragement from beginning to end.

I should also like to say thank you, on behalf of Daniel Barenboim and myself, to the splendid people who worked with us, without whose contribution it would have been impossible to finish the typescript in such a short space of time. We thank Lesley Fuchs-Robetin who had the extremely difficult assignment of transferring many of our taped discussions and corrections to paper in readable form, and Gitta Deutsch-Holroyd-Reece who helped me to prepare the first draft version of the book. I also wish to convey my thanks to my colleague, Irmelin Hoffer, who played an important part in setting up the actual form and layout of the material.

Last not least my very special thanks to Hilary Laurie, editor at Weidenfeld & Nicolson, who not only watched over the book at all stages but dealt with all the multilingual problems which cropped up during its development with great patience and profound knowledge, and who cooperated with Daniel Barenboim in preparing the final version for publication.

Vienna, July 1991   Michael Lewin

~

The 2002 edition

When the idea of re-evaluating Daniel Barenboim's thoughts about music came up in spring 2000, it was clear that a new edition – ten years after the first – could not simply be a new version with some corrections. The past decade had been too full of new challenges for Daniel Barenboim, as well as new developments in his views.

The greater part of the new material was produced in his Berlin home in September 2000 in the same way that the original book had been written. But over the following year my own business concerns, together with Daniel Barenboim's worldwide travels, made it almost impossible to finish the work which we had begun. I was therefore very grateful to Phillip Huscher, who was able to complete the work with Daniel Barenboim in Chicago.

Berlin, May 2002   Michael Lewin

Inevitably, the passage of a decade has added significant chapters to Daniel Barenboim's life as a musician, including major new posts in Chicago and Berlin. Most noticeably, his work over the past ten years has demonstrated, even more profoundly than before, the interdependence of his life and his art. That is reflected again and again in this revised edition of *A Life in Music*, which both updates the original material and adds six new chapters. Daniel Barenboim managed to work on the revision of *A Life in Music*, first with Michael Lewin in Berlin and later with me in Chicago, without interrupting a very busy performing schedule, providing daily evidence of the natural and seamless connection between music-making and thought that characterizes his career.

I wish to thank Benjamin Buchan, the patient editor at Weidenfeld & Nicolson, who saw this book through to its completion, and the many others who helped provide information, correct errors, and supply photographs. Nevertheless, the essence of this book belongs entirely to Daniel Barenboim and his steady vision of music as an inseparable part of living.

Chicago, May 2002   Phillip Huscher

INDEX